PotemkinPress

Kazimir Malevich

THE WHITE RECTANGLE

WRITINGS ON FILM

EDITED BY OKSANA BULGAKOWA

POTEMKINPRESS

BERLIN • SAN FRANCISCO

First published 1997 in German.

Malevich, Kazimir
THE WHITE RECTANGLE. WRITINGS ON FILM
In English and Russian, with distinct notes

Edited, and with an Introduction, by Oksana Bulgakowa

Annotated by Oksana Bulgakowa and Anna Muza
Translations: Oksana Bulgakowa, Elif Batuman, Amelia Glaser, Lyubov Golburt, Lilya Kaganovsky, Anna Muza
Translations edited by Anna Muza
Graphic design by Gregor Hochmuth, impulsio.com

Library of Congress Cataloging-in-Publication Data
Malevich, Kazimir Severinovich, 1878-1935.
  The white rectangle : writings on film / Kazimir Malevich ; edited by Oksana Bulgakowa.
      p. cm.
English and Russian.
First published 1997 in German.
Includes bibliographical references and indexes.
  ISBN 3-9804989-7-2 (pbk)
1. Art and motion pictures. 2. Motion pictures--Philosophy. I. Bulgakowa, Oksana. II. Title.
  N72.M6 M35 2003
  791.43'01'5--dc21   2002013985

PRINTED IN THE UNITED STATES OF AMERICA
www.PotemkinPress.com

A NOTE ON TRANSLATION AND TRANSLITERATION

The translators of Malevich's texts into English have generally tended to subjugate the roughness and obscurity of the original to the "interest of accessibility." In the present edition, we have attempted to preserve and convey the spirit, if not the letter, of his idiosyncratic diction with its radical 'shift' of the anticipated and conventional. The articles in this volume have been translated by graduate students of Stanford University and the University of California at Berkeley, whose inspiration and commitment the editors gratefully acknowledge.

In our rendition of Russian names, we have relied on the transliteration system of the Library of Congress, except in a few cases when the familiar Western spelling has been retained (Babel, Benois, Eisenstein, Kandinsky, and Lissitzky).

THE EDITOR WISHES TO EXPRESS HER GRATITUDE TO
—Troels Andersen, Silkeborg, Denmark, for kindly providing the original text of the article "Cinema, Gramophone, Radio, and Artistic Culture";
—the Czwiklitzer family, Baden-Baden/Paris, for the permission to publish the script "Art and the Problems of Architecture";
—the Stedelijk Museum, Amsterdam, for the permission to publish Malevich's letter to László Moholy-Nagy;
—Mary Petrusewicz and Susana Sosa, as well as Gabriela Muller and Ellen Handler Spitz for their editorial contribution.

TABLE OF CONTENTS

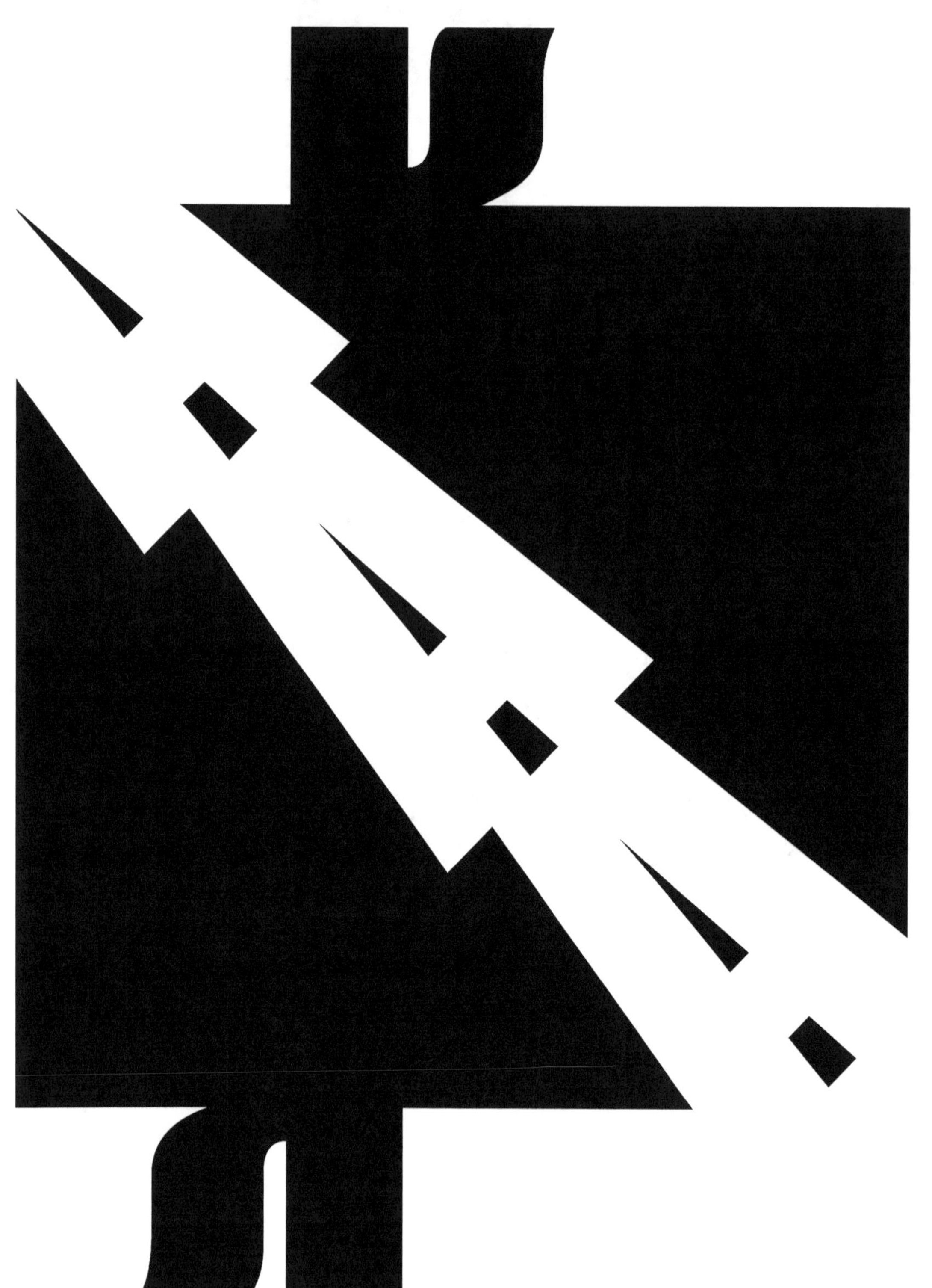

OKSANA BULGAKOWA
MALEVICH IN THE MOVIES: RUBBERY KISSES AND DYNAMIC SENSATIONS

What could possibly draw Kazimir Malevich (1878–1935)—prophet of abstraction, liberator of Nothingness—to film, that mechanical preserver of "everyday tripe" and life's "marketplace hubbub"?[1] As early as 1924, Malevich described film, citing Lenin, as a system that "fixes reality outside artistic invention,"[2] because, like science and religion, film relies upon concreteness and lacks vision: that is, film is powerless to show us the authentic whereas art is abstract.[3] Nevertheless, between 1925 and 1929 Malevich was to publish four articles on film, which became, however paradoxically, the final statements[4] of the artist deemed by the Soviet press a reactionary and a mystic.[5] His essay "Cinema, Gramophone, Radio, and Artistic Culture" (1928) was rejected for publication, as was a short text on the relationship between photography and painting in the form of a letter to László Moholy-Nagy. These manuscripts were rescued from the archives and published by Troels Andersen only in 1978.[6] They are missing from both the French editions of his work[7] and the Russian edition begun in 1995; also absent is Malevich's script for an "artistic scientific film," which survived the bombings of World War II in a Berlin basement. Although exhibited several times, the script had been reproduced in the catalogues as a purely visual artifact[8]—without a textual reconstruction.[9]

These seven texts might not exhaust Malevich's writings on film; however, because his archive has not yet been consolidated, our small volume is at the time of its publication the most comprehensive of its kind.

Malevich's views on film are rich in paradox, questioning not only the usefulness of film's mimetic abilities—an unsurprising snub, coming from the originator of abstract art—but also its capacities to represent dynamics and to renew perception. Malevich challenges the very qualities of film that made this "mechanical art of movement" an epitome of modernity for the avant-garde artists, Futurists and Constructivists.

We may safely say that this mistrust of cinema did not stem from ignorance: Malevich was well acquainted with Sergei Eisenstein and Hans Richter, directors who were radically reforming the language of film. Furthermore, judging from his texts, Malevich often went to the movies as an 'ordinary viewer' to see not only 'artistic' films but also such popular hits as Mary Pickford melodramas, the comedies with Monty Banks, Igor Il'inskii, or Pat and Patachon. In their use of contemporary idioms and catch-phrases, Malevich's writings also testify to an awareness of the cinematic debates in the Soviet press, which sometimes served as an impetus for his own work. Even his texts on painting frequently incorporate the metaphors of film and photography.[10]

The texts on film address problems in the analysis of pictorial art, which engaged Malevich in Vitebsk and later in Petrograd, where he served as director of the Institute of Artistic Culture (GINKhUK) and as head of one of its five sections. Malevich used film as a new field of application for his earlier hypotheses: the theory of the additional element, and the evolutionary model of modernism.

Malevich delineated the theory of the additional element between 1923 and 1926. The term itself appears to be borrowed from Marx,[11] but draws from the Freudian realm: the additional element—usually dynamics—alters the established order in the connection between "the conscious and the unconscious" during artistic activity, restructuring the perception, reflexes of motion, artistic world of the painter, and destroying the norm of representation.[12] Malevich's lecture series on contemporary art, delivered in 1928–1930 at the pedagogical department of the Kiev Art Institute,[13] was intended to lay the foundation for a new science, "izology,"[14] the study of the evolution of visual culture through the history of pictorial arts, from Impressionism to Suprematism. Malevich's texts on cinema embrace new forms—posters, photography, film—in this evolutionary model. The continuity of terminology and imagery in Malevich's theoretical works on visual arts and film attests to the link; for example, the camel, which in academic painting carries "odalisques, Egyptian and Persian kings, Solomons and Salomés,"[15] is used in cinema to transport "everyday tripe."

Textual history

Malevich's first articles on film were written in May and June of 1925, precisely the time of his first encounter with Sergei Eisenstein. In the early 1920s, Malevich shared a dacha in Nemchinovka with an old friend, the professional revolutionary Kirill Shutko, whom he met during 1904–05 in Moscow. Shutko, who attended Aleksandr Adashev's private acting studio, studied directing with Meyerhold and worked in the underground social democratic party. After the revolution, Shutko held several important film-related positions in the party hierarchy: he worked in Agitprop, was director of the publishing house Teakinopechat' (Theater-Cinema-Press), and sat on the editorial boards of various film magazines. In 1927, he served as the cinema and arts advisor in the propaganda division of the Party's Central Committee; subsequently he headed the arts division of Gosplan (the State Planning Committee).

In the early twenties, Shutko was married to Nina Agadzhanova, fellow professional revolutionary and screenwriter of *The Year 1905*, a film commemorating the twentieth anniversary of the first Russian revolution. *The Year 1905* was to be directed by a young protégé of Shutko: Sergei Eisenstein (who called Shutko a "gray cardinal"; Shutko and Malevich were members of the special commission that entrusted Eisenstein with this important state task). In Nemchinovka, Eisenstein and Nina began to outline the anniversary film, which would later evolve into *The Battleship Potemkin*; Eisenstein simultaneously collaborated with the writer Isaac Babel on a script based on his Odessa stories, entitled *Benia Krik*.

Of great interest for Eisenstein, as for Malevich, were the mechanisms of art's impact on the beholder. Eisenstein developed his own theory, "the montage of attractions," incorporating psychoanalysis, reflexology, and Marxism. Prior to his career in film, Eisenstein had an incomplete education in civil engineering, as well as some theater experience: although obviously influenced by Cubism, he studied with Liubov' Popova, Russia's first Constructivist set designer.

Eisenstein's brief memoir of his acquaintance with Malevich, dated 1939, omits any mention of Suprematist theories, or of Malevich's work on the Futurist opera *Victory over the Sun*;[16] instead, Eisenstein conveys his vivid impression of the painter's physical strength and capacity for violence, relaying the artist's anecdotes about the sexual prowess of donkeys, or about the village youths who had once beaten him up: in a gory act of vengeance, the creator of Black Square had broken their arms and knocked out their teeth.[17]

It is possible that Eisenstein, who had signed the declaration of the Association of Revolutionary Cinematography (ARK), prompted Malevich to participate in one of the association's weekly debates, which addressed both individual films and general cinematic questions; one debate dealt directly with a clash between Eisenstein and Vertov. Between 1925 and 1926, three of Malevich's texts appeared in the ARK newsletter, *Kinozhurnal* (Film Journal) *ARK*.

The screenplay and the text on photography and painting were written in Germany. Having lost his job at GINKhUK, which was closed in November 1926, Malevich requested some time abroad. He left for Warsaw on 8 March 1927, and on March 29 arrived in Berlin. Subsequently he traveled to the Bauhaus in Dessau, looking for work. At Walter Gropius's house, he met László Moholy-Nagy, at that time the film and photography editor of the journal of the European Constructivists *i 10*. The journal, published in Amsterdam, initiated a discussion of the relationship between the new and old visual arts—painting and photography—inspired by an article by Ernst Kallai. Contributors included Adolf Behne, Vasily

Kandinsky, and Piet Mondrian. Moholy-Nagy invited Malevich, too, to present some opinions—but did not publish them. Malevich's *The World as Non-Objectivity*, however, was printed by the Bauhaus book series supervised by Gropius and Moholy-Nagy.

In Berlin, Malevich saw German abstract films for the first time, and met the director Hans Richter, whose works inspired him to write his own script for an abstract film. "He felt that we had to realize this dream of his together," Hans Richter wrote in 1966:

We must have met often to work on the project—the odd thing is that, though I do remember a lot of trivia about past years, I have completely forgotten about my film work with Malevich. Two years ago Dr. Haftmann, who was involved in publishing Malevich's texts from the von Riesen collection,[18] asked me whatever became of the film project I had planned with this Russian. At first I could not even remember such a project. My astonishment was all the greater when I saw, in the published book, color illustrations of film apparatuses with the dedication: 'film for Hans Richter.' Our collaboration must have taken place in 1926 or 1927. With what pleasure I could have worked on this script over the past forty years![19]

Upon his return from Germany, Malevich, like a number of former GINKhUK employees, found refuge at the State Institute of Art History. In August 1928, Eisenstein approached him to request some written comments on the relationship between theater, film, and painting. Eisenstein was engaged with this problem in connection with the advent of sound in cinema, a transformation troubling to some critics and directors, who feared that film, having started to talk, was becoming a "photographic speaking theater."

In June 1928 Eisenstein co-authored, with Aleksandrov and Pudovkin, "A Statement on Sound," in which he radically rejected the archaizing of film's visual culture. In August of the same year, after a recent tour of a Kabuki company in Moscow, he wrote an essay analyzing an alternative approach to the acoustic and visual stimuli in the practice of the Japanese theater ("An Unexpected Juncture").[20] At this time, Eisenstein entertained the idea of taking over one of the film journals, and proposed to Malevich a subsequent collaboration; Malevich refused. In a letter of 13 August 1928, preserved in Eisenstein's archive,[21] Malevich writes that, because he disapproves of the line taken by Eisenstein and "Maiakovskii's Left Front of AKhR," he cannot contribute to "their" journal—notwithstanding the article he had already written that April on a relevant topic, "Cinema, Gramophone, Radio, and Artistic Culture."

This article was subsequently rejected by *Kino-Front*, a successor to the *Kino-zhurnal ARK*. It took a year before an article by Malevich would appear in print: his "Pictorial Laws in Cinematic Problems" was published by the newly formed *Kino i kul'tura* (Cinema and Culture), which had supplanted *Soviet Cinema* and *Kino-Front*. The editor-in-chief was Petr Bliakhin, and Kirill Shutko sat on the editorial board. Their journal, which included a digest of articles in German, was concerned primarily with the technological rather than the cultural aspect of cinema: that is, developments in film stock, lighting, and sound. Malevich's article in *Kino i kul'tura* had escaped the notice of scholars for almost sixty years, because it was signed "*W*. Malevich"—evidently a misprint. This was the artist's last Russian publication in his lifetime.[22]

In 1929 Malevich was fired from the State Institute of Art History, and in the autumn of 1930 he was arrested and held for interrogation. His release that December is ascribed to Kirill Shutko's intervention: two dramatic letters from their 1930 correspondence have recently been published.[23] Malevich died in 1935 from liver cancer. Shutko was arrested in 1937 and executed the following year.

Film discussions and film discourse

Malevich's texts, occasioned by contemporary debates in the press, refer the reader to two poles: a momentary (and no-longer-remembered) concern, and aspects of modern visual culture at large. Malevich considers its dynamic development in the framework of his own theory of the genesis of modernism as projected onto three problems: mimesis versus abstraction, statics versus dynamics, and visual perception in the age of optical instruments.

Malevich approached cinema through his reflections on movie posters: artistic works that represent film in the landscape of the modern city. Notably, Malevich himself did not produce a single poster. An oil painting in the Tret'iakov Gallery, advertising Fritz Lang's *Doctor Mabuzo* [sic], though often attributed to him, is most likely the work of his disciple Il'ia Chashnik.

Malevich's text represents a specialist's reaction to the first exhibition of film posters and its anachronisms. New art forms, advertisements, and posters, are treated in terms of the old easel paintings, and hang around the city as in a museum hall. Malevich discusses the data obtained in his section at the GINKhUK on the importance of typography, the structure of the brand icon, the combination of straight and curved lines, the contrast of colored planes, and the principles of the posters' placement. Posters will stand out within the cityscape only if they adhere to the laws of contrast.

These comments went unheard. The second exhibition of film posters, organized the following year in the foyer of the Moscow Kamernyi (Chamber) Theater, followed the same principles of display as the first.

Mimesis, abstraction, and film

Malevich's second essay, "And Visages Arc Victorious On The Screen," addresses the unconsummated rapprochement between art and film—unconsummated, because film, for Malevich, is a continuation of modern painting, based on dynamism and abstraction, while contemporary moving pictures merely resuscitate a dead mimetic tradition.

In this article, Malevich enters into the polemics between Sergei Eisenstein and Dziga Vertov, sparked by Eisenstein's screen debut, *The Strike*, and Vertov's first full-length film *The Cine-Eye*. Eisenstein and Vertov belonged to the Left Front of the Arts, and their manifestoes were printed in the third issue of the journal *LEF* in 1923—which included, notably, an excerpt from Malevich's "The Suprematist Mirror"!

The debate began when Vertov accused Eisenstein of plagiarism—the final scene of *The Strike* contained documentary footage of a slaughterhouse, which was the subject of Vertov's *Cine-Eye*—and opportunism: by imitating the innovations of *The Cine-Eye*, Vertov claimed, Eisenstein, 'a 'Cine-Menshevik', assisted the establishment of artistic surrogates, "film dramas" that would "shroud the eyes and brain in a sick fog" and "intoxicate the proletariat with kino-vodka."[24]

Eisenstein, in turn, declared Vertov a bourgeois Impressionist aesthete and practitioner of "art for art's sake," indifferent to art's agitational utility: as for their "effectiveness," Vertov's works were "impotent."[25] This political vocabulary, borrowed from the rhetoric used against the Party opposition, could be instrumental in deciding which director held artistic supremacy, but the real verdict came from Paris: in 1925 at the Exhibition of Art and Industry, Eisenstein's film received a gold medal, Vertov's a silver.

Boris Arvatov, one of the leading theoreticians of the Left Front and Eisenstein's collaborator in Proletkult, tried to reconcile the directors, opining that their films and ideologies were not really so dissimilar.[26] In his article, Malevich—who had, three years earlier, received harsh criticism from Arvatov[27]—disagrees, maintaining that Vertov's and Eisenstein's methods differ significantly: while Vertov works with the texture of the object, freeing it from "objectness" through optical deformations ("shifts" implemented by the camera), Eisenstein, in his composition of the frame, is traditional, tending toward the realist aesthetic of the Itinerant painters.[28] However, Eisenstein perceives more acutely than Vertov the "law of contrasts." The "shift" defining Vertov's aesthetic comprises, according to Malevich, the essence of Futurist artistic practice; the law of contrasts—the analytical collision of planes and trajectories—is the formative principle of Cubism. Malevich uses the latter term to describe Eisenstein's montage, which the director himself called "attraction," alluding to the stimulation in Pavlov's reflex (and similar to Walter Benjamin's notion of the flow of film frames as a "shock"[29]). Malevich is concerned not with the neurotic effect of the attraction but with the law of its formal organization, which he inscribes in his own theoretical frame.

Vertov did not respond to Malevich's article; Eisenstein responded four years later, in "The Fourth Dimension of Cinema." "It is simply naïve to pass judgment on the pictorialism of a cinematic shot," he wrote:

This may be expected from people who are familiar with painting, but who absolutely lack the qualifications to talk about film. Kazimir Malevich's statements on film could serve as an example of this kind of judgment. Today, not even a novice in film would try to analyze a frame in terms of easel painting.[30]

According to Eisenstein, Malevich does not understand the fundamental principle of film: namely, that a shot does not exist as a unit of perception, but is realized only through the dynamics of montage. Malevich, for all his devotion to kinetics, remains a prisoner of immobility. His concept of dynamics is marked by the perspective of a painter—of an artist without access to the fourth dimension.

Eisenstein treats Malevich with even more acerbity in another text, "The Dramaturgy of Film Form," written in German, which addresses not the Russian audience but the European avant-garde.[31] Here, Eisenstein applies to Malevich his own "theory of the additional element"—from the opposite end. According to Malevich, the additional element distorts static forms of representation—but once it is subtracted, Malevich himself turns into a German neo-classicist academician: "The hypertrophy of teleological initiative—of the principle of rational logic—leaves art frozen in mathematical technicality. A landscape becomes a topographical map; a

'St. Sebastian'—an atlas of anatomy. The hypertrophy of organic naturalness, of organic logic, diffuses art into formlessness: Malevich turns into Kaulbach."[32]

However, the attack of Malevich forced Eisenstein to formulate his thoughts on mimesis in film—thoughts, which he did not attempt to publish in Russian, presenting them instead, in German, at the Congress of Independent Film in La Sarraz, Switzerland (1929). Taking up Malevich's theme, Eisenstein structured his paper as a self-defense: "Imitation as Mastery."[33]

At home, Eisenstein dismissed the abstract films of the European avant-garde as children's playthings, "enfantillages."[34] He felt obliged to justify his own mimetic preferences when he found himself in the company of the abstract filmmakers, Walter Ruttmann and Hans Richter, to whom he admitted that the art of film was, for him, too primitive.[35] Eisenstein built his self-vindication on his rejection of film's mimetic representation of motion—that is, the *illusory* motion of static photograms projected in rapid succession; what he created was a *concept* of motion, conveyed by the collision of static images (often those of statues).[36] But the discussion regarding the illusory and the conceptual cinematic movement—hinging upon the distinction between the external and internal dynamics of the object so crucial for Malevich—is not taken up by Malevich and Eisenstein. In his last article, Malevich responds indirectly to "The Fourth Dimension in Cinema" by disparaging Eisenstein's "village film" that shows "how pigs are fed on the state farm, or how the 'golden crops' are harvested."[37] Annette Michelson, the first scholar of Malevich's writing on film, refers to these aborted polemics as a "dialogue des sourdes" (dialogue of the deaf).[38]

However, Malevich's texts should not be dismissed as instances of mere in-house bickering among film people; rather, they belong to the discourse on film in the context of the other arts that dates back to the beginning of the twentieth century. Cinematography was initially understood as a continuation of photography, supplementing static reproduction of nature with recorded motion. The early no-

menclature of this new technology—*moving* picture, photographie *animée*—
pointed to this "additional element," while cinema was associated with existent
forms of spectacle: photo*play*, *théâtre* muet, *tableau vivant*. Traditional aesthetics
placed film in the context of the proposed crisis of representation and referred it
to the school of naturalism: film imprints an ugly, chaotic, vulgar, and banal version of nature, rather than sublime and ideal, that is, aesthetic. Malevich's articles
lexically partake in this discourse.

But this is only one perspective, and any conclusion we might draw about the
'non-encounter' between the abstractionist and the medium of film would be
oversimplified. Further refinement of the illusion was, from Malevich's point of
view, inessential. Art, in his neo-platonic conception, is not a recording or dou-
bling of reality, but an instrument of 'super-vision': a product of culture and history, not a feat of optical technology. Only in this sense film—kinetic painting
with light—can be integrated into the evolution of the arts. Malevich places Eisenstein and Vertov inside his evolutionary model of modernism—from figuration to
abstraction, from Cézanne, via Cubism and Futurism, to Suprematism. For Malevich, the ultimate meaning of this process is not abandoning the imitation of nature but liberating thought from the bonds of developed categories and existing
forms, including the mimetic dogma.

Describing the art of the new epoch as "materialistic," Malevich means that, because it is not religious and does not serve a cult, it does not require an image.[39]
This art will be able to convey the metaphysical experience of the Suprematist
world. Malevich has no naïve illusions about equating cinematic image with nature. This image has been shaped by the technique of vision and representation of
space, which had been developed by artists working since the Renaissance, and
from which the masters of film cannot free themselves. Modern "metallic" culture—gramophone, radio, and film—alienates us from organic life: we deal only

with imprints, which transform nature into an "abstract matter," revealing pre-fabricated essence of our perception.

Historicity of vision

If a film-director-turned-painter and a painter-turned-film-theorist misunderstand one another so profoundly, how are we to understand the painter's role in film? For Malevich, the painter is the only professional who can consciously employ and manipulate the categories of historical vision. "The Artist and the Cinema," published in early 1926, is most likely a reaction to the discussion of set design in film, which went on during that year in *Sovetskii ekran* (The Soviet Screen). European films that pursued elaborate decorativeness, such as *The Cabinet of Doctor Caligari*, *Raskolnikow*, *Nibelungen*, and *L'Inhumaine*, were contrasted with *The Strike*, a film with practically no studio-built sets at all.[40] Also published was the essay "Architecture, Painting, and Film Sets" by the German set designer Ernö Metzner, a collaborator of Ernst Lubitsch and G. W. Pabst.[41] German Expressionist films, the first foreign pictures to appear in Russia after the economic blockade, were first and foremost art films. In Russia they were perceived as a "decorative Cubism" in the vein of Aleksandr Tairov's Kamernyi Theater, where sets were often designed by the Cubo-Futurists Georgii Iakulov and Aleksandra Ekster.[42]

In 1924–1925, an international discussion of "the artist in film" emerged in French, German, and Russian journals, as increasing numbers of painters and architects were invited to work in movie studios.[43] Fernand Léger and the modernist architect Robert Mallet-Stevens designed the sets of Marcel L'Herbier's *L'Inhumaine*; in Russia, Isaak Rabinovich, who had worked with Evgenii Vakhtangov, collaborated with Aleksandra Ekster to transplant Tairov's multi-leveled stage onto the set of *Aelita*, and to dress the actors in Cubo-Futurist costumes.

The Russian leftist film avant-garde, on the other hand, could dispense with the artist in favor of original factory interiors and city exterior whose bridges, train stations, and staircases were interpreted as sets. Only "conformers" like Iakov Protazanov, Vladimir Gardin, or Czesław Sabinski, whose films Malevich cited, worked in a tradition of high-budget movies, following the compositional principles of naturalist paintings and the two-dimensionality of the theater set design, with no sense of specifically cinematographic space and style. Directors, according to Malevich, are taught to see crudely; therefore, they reproduce in their pictures a mixture of different spatial systems and transform time into a spatial category:

One shot of the landscape belongs to the year 1840; another, to the 1880s; a third, to the year 1925. It turns out that the protagonist of *Tailor* runs through all time periods of an entire century.[44]

It is in this text that Malevich demystifies the Constructivist approach to film and Vertov's cine-eye, which purports a new world vision enabled by new optical instruments. Malevich considers such a claim naïve because the vision of the mechanical camera's eye is similarly informed by historical perception:

The cine-eye does not see anything new in nature; it looks at nature through the artistic eye of a painter (a painter-luminographer) and everywhere sees nature either through Polenov's eye or through Perov's, through Monet's, through Shishkin's, Rubens's, etc. For now, cinema can see only that representation of phenomena that was seen by the painter.[45]

The task of inventing a new system of vision cannot originate in the new apparatus, which is merely a technological means of recording; it has to be refined in visual culture, whose aim lies in the transmission of a special vision, different from that of the eye. In this work art plays an auxiliary role. Like other new apparatuses, such as the gramophone, the camera, and the radio, film is still bound to the old art and its models of perception: painting and theater. Vision is formed by their standards and is a product of ideology, to the same extent as the technology of representation itself: "And for a survey of objectness, my eyes can be taken into a waxwork museum like attributes of the Middle Ages."[46]

Such is the theme of Malevich's unpublished article of 1928, which responds to one recent technical innovation—sound—and anticipates two future innovations: color and stereoscopic film. But for Malevich, technology is not the real issue; Moholy-Nagy's invitation to take part in the discussion on photography and painting had, by that point, already offered him ample opportunity to voice his views on the subject.

In Moholy-Nagy's framework, the divisions are clear: Painting is a matter of color, which is absent in photography and cinema. Photography is a matter of light; cinema, a matter of light and motion. Photography, unlike painting, lacks textural materiality. Where Ernst Kallai finds photography culpable for its lack of texture, Moholy-Nagy, with his system of sharp demarcations, exonerates it, on grounds of the new paths opened by the medium of light. Malevich's own view— that texture is a mere psychosis of contemporary artists, a secondary issue[47]—does not help him in this polemic.[48] Moholy-Nagy does not publish the response of the Russian painter because, for Malevich, painting, photography, and film are phenomena of the same order, subject to the same laws. Minor issues, such as texture (or the lack thereof), are just distractions from genuine vision, and from the understanding of (technical) media.

Malevich's meditations on optical perception as stemming from culture, and not physiology, recall Pavel Florenskii's analysis of perspective as a cultural phenomenon,[49] as well as Walter Benjamin's historical investigation of models of perception.[50] A new society striving to free itself from old symbols—a society developing a new body language, a new design of clothing and living spaces—needs new standards of perception as well.

Cinema as a continuation of Suprematist painting by other means

Malevich's script—an experiment with a scientific tendency—had both to popularize his theory of the evolution of visual culture, and to test the capabilities of film. It deals with the transformations of three basic forms—the square, the cross, and the circle—first on a plane, and then in three-dimensional space.

The motion of geometrical figures as a new form of 'narrative' was pioneered by Malevich's colleagues in other media: the typographical, as El Lissitzky's *Tale of Two Squares*,[51] and the performative, as the Suprematist ballet staged by Malevich's pupil, Nina Kogan, in Vitebsk.[52] In the latter performance—which Aleksandra Shatskikh proposes as a possible source of inspiration for Malevich's script[53]—actors were concealed by geometrical figures painted on cardboard,[54] which assumed various configurations (arcs, crosses, etc.) with their movements across the stage. These tableaux vivants, intended to illustrate the principles of Suprematism, were based on the 'narrative' of the figures' emergence from the black square, their movement in space, and their subsequent transformation and return to the square.

Film for Malevich is not painterly or mimetic, because filmic space—unlike two-dimensional stage space with its façade—is three-dimensional. In spatial terms, film is closer to Cubist or sculptural art, where light creates volume; like Suprematism, film is essentially architectonic.

Within the Bauhaus, Ludwig Hirschfeld-Mack, Werner Graeff, and László Moholy-Nagy experimented with light reflections, using mobile plates, tinted by colored rays in various installations. Such "kinetic light-painting" was conceived as a precursor to abstract film. But Malevich was unconcerned with such experiments. His selection of Hans Richter—whose experiments in abstract film had already been publicized in the first issue of Aleksei Gan's journal *Kino-Fot*[55]—hardly seems accidental: in his *Rhythm 21* and *Rhythm 23*, Richter worked exclusively with black and white squares, in contrast with Viking Eggeling's diagonal 'combs,' or Ruttmann's round, organic shapes; that is, with the basic forms that Malevich saw as the expression of "Intuitive Reason."[56]

For the modern viewer, the square has become empty and incomprehensible "as the language of a Chinese man declaring his love to a Russian girl";[57] for Malevich, this painterly surface is "more alive than any face, with a pair of eyes and a smile bulging out,"[58] and the transformations of such forms are intrinsically dramatic.[59] "The three Suprematist squares establish a world-view and world-structure: black as a sign of economy, red for revolution, white for pure action."[60] For Malevich, the three squares corresponded to the three stages in the development of Suprematism, which he had already presented in the exhibits of 1915–16, as well as in his publication *Suprematism: 34 Drawings* (1920).

Richter's film is constructed upon rhythmical compression of square forms and their disappearances in the illusory depth of the (screen) space. Richter, unlike Ruttmann, does not draw his film; he manipulates cut-out squares of different sizes on a black plane, which turns white when the film switches to negative. Ignoring light, Richter works with space and kinetics of surfaces.

Malevich's appeal to Richter, however, can be seen as a misunderstanding. As Norbert Schmitz notes:

Richter's films are similar to the Gestalt psychologists' experiments with the perception of geometric forms, the motion of abstract squares in space and time. For Richter, film is a process of identifying objective functions of human perception, a peculiar mimesis of the functions of the sense-organs; for Malevich, film represents a liberation from such physiologically concrete, experienced functions.[61]

In his script, Malevich privileges the image photographically closest to Suprematist painting. He presupposes an exit from two-dimensionality, not just into three-dimensionality, but also into the space of the real city, presenting Constructivist buildings and their subsequent amelioration by Suprematist architecture. The script breaks off in the sixteenth episode of the first part, which deals with "various sensual experiences of the surface"; the two remaining parts, "architectonics as a problem" and "architecture in life," are not elaborated.

Cinema and kinetics

Malevich's final essay testifies to his ability to identify even in photographic images the face of Non-Objectivity. He is inspired by seeing the film that first realized the new kinetic "painting with light": Vertov's *Man with the Movie Camera*, described by its director as the first experiment in "absolute film language."

But in this text, Malevich again becomes involved in topical newspaper polemics.

In 1926, following the premiere of his *The Sixth Part of the World*—a commission for a commercial reel promoting the export of Soviet furs—Vertov was fired from Sovkino. He found asylum only in Ukraine, where he shot three consecutive films: *The Eleventh Year*, *The Man with the Movie Camera*, and *The Donbass Symphony (Enthusiasm)*. At this time Vertov was being attacked both by the Left Front, which associated his films with the theory of "factography," and by his superiors, who demanded that film be "understandable for millions" as per the slogan of the 1929 campaign, which presupposed compliance from Soviet filmmakers.[62] The editors may have accepted Malevich's text after Konstantin Feldman, a former sailor on *Potemkin* turned movie critic, spoke in Vertov's defense in his article "Debating Vertov," published in the journal's previous issue (5–6). Earlier, Kirill Shutko, a member of the editorial board, had defended Vertov both in *Pravda* (23 March 1929) and in *Sovetskii ekran*, urging a wider distribution of *The Man with the Movie Camera*.[63]

In the Vertov debate, Malevich assumes an unorthodox position: at a time when Vertov's films were evaluated for their compliance with the principles of documentary, Constructivist, socially engaged art, and production art, Malevich defends the director as "the only cine-Futurist." Malevich contrasts two films, compared by critics since their debuts on the big screen: Ruttmann's *Symphony of a Big City*, received as a work of *Neue Sachlichkeit* (the New Objectivity), and *The Man with the Movie Camera*, representing Vertov's shift from political to absolute film. Osip Brik, a theoretician close to the Russian Formalist school, had censured Vertov's 'noncomprehension' of cinematic language—namely, his reliance on the word to broaden the frame's semantics, without deploying its purely visual information.[64] By contrast, Malevich sees Vertov as the first director to fulfill the principles of contemporary painting—indeed, of visual culture as a whole—in film: from the Cubist pulverization of the object, to Futurist dynamics and the shift.

Malevich does not subscribe to the prevalent conception of film as the latest stage in representation of motion: from Baroque painting to Impressionism, Futurism, and Constructivism, with its kinetic sculptures and installations; nor does he greet cinema, "a new technique of conveying dynamic sensations," as an *a priori* dynamic art. "The Futurists," he writes, "despite the fact that motion is the content of their work, did not use cinema, nor did cinema call upon Futurism for its rejuvenation or liberation from romantic woes and passionate kisses."[65]

Dynamics can be understood in different ways. For Lev Kuleshov, the first Russian experimenter in film, dynamics and acceleration belong to the sphere of modernist machines: cars, airplanes, locomotives, steamboats, factories. In this conception, the human body can approach dynamism only by subjecting its movement to an artificial rhythm, inscribed in a geometrical scheme—in short, by becoming a machine—through sports, chases, and acrobatic leaps.

Malevich excludes the human body from the catalogue of dynamic objects. In fact, he draws all his negative examples of misunderstood film dynamics from slapstick comedy (Monty Banks, or the Russian comic Igor Il'inskii); that is, from the very sphere which theoreticians like Benjamin have regarded as an arena for the development of these dynamics: through the collision of the body's movement and the camera's kinetics.[66] For Malevich, these two types of kinetics, mechanical and human, are too objectified to match the new dynamism, which is a "dynamic power" existing independently from objects, a movement "which our eye cannot catch, but which can be sensed."[67] Malevich has an abstract notion of dynamics, built on the contrast with motion. In the text on film posters, he defines cinema as a "running" motionlessness; thus far, in his view, only painting had successfully conveyed real dynamics, the sensation of speed detached from corporeality.

The formulation of "dynamic dynamism outside of movement"—dynamism as an invisible energy existing outside the body—clashed with rational analyses of perception and film techniques. In Russia, the discourse on the representation of motion in film was influenced by Henri Bergson as he was perceived by the Formalist circle, critics whose new analytical models drew from the literary practices of the Russian Futurists. Bergson uses film as a metaphor of human consciousness, which creates a model of the metaphysical sensation of movement that does not correspond to reality, and thus indicates the limitations of the concrete perceptive mechanism. For this reason, the Formalists consider cinema as an "art of conceptual motion."[68] "Film is not a material reproduction of movement; it transmits an idea of movement."[69] Malevich supports this view, and believes that motion is as illusory in film as in painting.[70] Its image appears in the viewer's consciousness.

The Russian film avant-garde treated motion analytically; it was concerned not with the synthesis of motion, but with the realization of a gap, an interval, a moment of stasis between the photograms, which was effected both by Eisenstein, in his montage of statues and static objects, and by Vertov, who treated the interval as the organizing moment of film montage.

Malevich, who outlines a rather metaphysical theory of motion as an optically imperceptible phenomenon, has noticed this strategy only in Vertov's case—and perhaps only because the frames recall the abstract paintings of the Futurist Balla, which transmit not an illusion of movement, but a phantasmagorical sensation of speed. Not by chance does Malevich illustrate his article on Vertov with a still from *The Man with the Movie Camera* and a reproduction of Balla's *Abstract Speed*, which he renames *Abstract Motion*. (This particular painting by Balla was reproduced in the anthology *The Isms of Art* (1924), in which Malevich represented Suprematism, and Hans Richter, absolute film.) This is the dynamics invisible to the eye, which explodes the body and transcends mimesis.

Vertov and Ruttmann are juxtaposed precisely on the basis of this principle. In Ruttmann's case, modernist objects are inscribed in a narrative scheme, proceeding from initial immobility to acceleration. For Vertov, motion is the quintessence of modernity: an equation of the motion of the object, the motion of film through the camera or projector, and the motion of the city. Film techniques themselves become, to use Malevich's terminology, an "additional element." The camera disintegrates motion, which is then recomposed as a cinematographic entity: compressed, extended, stopped, fragmented, multiplied in numerous exposures, in the superimposition of multidirectional motion; the fragmented frame sets objects in motion differently than nature. Unsurprisingly, the term Malevich uses to describe this phenomenon is the Futurist shift.

Malevich's views will seem radical even to present-day readers. He opposes cinema, a "running motionlessness," to contemporary painting—the art of dynamics, invisible to the eye. The artist suggests a sensation of speed—but this sensation, like eyesight itself, is detached from the body. Vision is not determined physiologically or psychologically; it is a product of culture, above all of painting. Suprematism creates new models of 'super'-vision, for abstract essences. Film is a continuation of Suprematist painting, in another medium. Malevich demands film's subjection to the principles of painting; insofar as he finds affinities between the two forms, he accepts this new technology. Thus, despite his appeals to reject easel

painting, addressed to directors and filmmakers, Malevich remains in his understanding of cinema first and foremost a painter.

Translated by Elif Batuman and Lyubov Golburt

ВЬ

ЯВЬ

**On Exposers.
Posters**

An exhibition of film posters, or, as I would call them, exposers, was put on by the film section of the State Academy of Artistic Sciences.[71] But these were not posters. These were paintings, exaggerated almost decoratively, created on various principles of easel painting. They diverged considerably from the organic essence of the poster-exposer. The so-called 'impenetrable surface' does not exist either in painting or in Constructivist art, but without it the exposer will never achieve its goals.[72]

All posters, even those produced by Constructivists, are made with no regard for the 'impenetrable plane,' though many of them do combine the actual element of the surface 'as such' and photography, which distinguishes them from the so-called 'academic realism.' But these and other posters unquestionably depend on easel painting and rely, in their true essence, on the same rutty surface of the picture's 'painterly field,' that is, the surface pulverizing vision.[73] This is why the pictorial field of an easel painting will be perceived at a small viewing distance.

This technical feature allows one to distinguish the decorative element as opposed to the painterly element. True, decorative posters often lack the impenetrable surface, that is, they contain no planes isolated from light, linear and aerial perspectives. All this increases the number of airy crevices in the poster, which destroy its 'resistant surface,' and that in turn makes it impossible to set the exposer on a single temporal plane.

The debate arranged by the film section was, I suppose, meant to resolve the problem of the Soviet film-exposer. But of course, like most debates, it could not yield the desired result. The problem should have been approached differently, by means of a laboratory-based scientific analysis, and the exhibit, also completely different, should have been a display of the results of that investigation. Only along this path is it possible to define one or another form of exposer, and in particular—film exposer, for film posters should, of course, have generic differences from all easel painting that depicts milieu, history, and so forth.

At present, work on 'exposers' relies on individual gimmicks, lying outside any scientific system. Nevertheless, it is necessary that this art form also be embraced by scientific research. No one has touched this topic in the debate. Obviously, the question has never even been raised in the film section: otherwise, an exhibition of posters would not have been set up like an exhibition of easel painting. The task of the State Academy of Artistic Sciences and its film section is to arrange exhibitions not for the sake of aesthetic perception of works of art but for their scientific analysis. That, it seems to me, should have been the film section's first step toward the organization of a new film exposer. Any other approach to the creation of the 'Soviet exposer' is unthinkable, since that alone will ensure the correct way for the film poster to find its form.

As yet, the poster-exposer does not exist. In particular, there is no specific 'exposer' for film. But perhaps there is no specific film-exposer simply because film itself has not yet come into being? What has come into being is only the film camera that has substituted pencils, brushes, and the variegated palette as a new means of making the same pictures on which the artists of old wasted so much effort. And film, so far, is only a new technical medium serving ever more accurate reproduction of reality in art, while film directors are but new painters whose works resemble static pictures. As a result, what we have is not posters but snippets of the plot moving across the screen, adorned with some static artistic jumble, and the particular type of jumble makes it possible to distinguish among all the dramas, tragedies, and characters competing for the viewer's attention.

The story-maker—the script writer—picks from life certain moments, from which the artist in his turn selects a picture for the 'exposer,' that is, for the field where he must expose the given moment. The field of the exposer may be red, white, green, or black. This is the impenetrable surface on which the picture is to be exposed. Here happens what I described above. The painting annihilates the impenetrable surface, that 'distinctive element of the field of vision.'

Who should reign supreme over the making of exposers? The script writer? The film director? The artist? None of the above. All three always design their work according to the principle of local effectiveness, that is only within the field of vision demanded by the work itself. Elements multiplied by elements equal fragments. Fragments multiplied by fragments equal whole productions. In their essence, the latter are easel paintings—works that have not been multiplied by time. The decorator partly differs from the easel painter in that his elements are always multiplied by distance: he works, above all, with space, and has to take into account the so-called 'active exposers' in the street. Apart from that, he can regard his 'field of exposure' as a space for the artistic decorative treatment of the thing being advertised, which he always converts into the decorative element. Posters designed in that manner create a 'placard-poster ripple,' in which the rays of vision meet no resistance and disperse over the tiny forms of disparate spatial relationships. Such an 'exposer' will perish. Another method consists in bringing the exposer and the exposed down to a single constructive relation, which creates an integrity crucial for the artist and properly organized for his studio, yet utterly pointless on the street, where the 'exposer' fades into many other similarly designed posters, and also 'perishes.' These examples show that a master of poster-making is nowhere to be found. This domain is dangling, so to speak, among different movements and trends in visual arts, and cannot go off on its own. A master of 'exposers' must have a sharp sensitivity to the planar orientation of spatial relationships; he must be able to estimate the size of a plane, the length of the exposers' trajectories in the acting fields of the streets, as well as the distance between the exposers; he also has to determine the profile of the exposer curve. Only these estimates will allow him to determine the point closest to the viewer, and target, with extreme precision, the entire field of the exposer's action.

One must place the exposer in the nearest point of the profile, while the exposed may be positioned on any plane: in an exposer of one hundred square feet the exposed can occupy one square inch.

Spatial relationships in that case will be different, but still the result is bound to be better than when the exposed is made on the scale of, say, a ten-story building. (From the experiments run by the section of photography of the Institute of Artistic Culture.) All exposers, in form and in color, should take into account the character of other exposers acting in the street. Otherwise, the very best posters—that is, in the artistic sense—can nevertheless perish, get lost in the layout of the street poster-field. (That is why every master of exposers must produce active exposers.) Not long ago, two exposers for the film *The Strike* were pasted into poster-fields acting in the street. One was issued by the Goskino, the other by the movie theater Coliseum. Let everyone judge for himself which of them was based on a more rigorous estimate of the demands of the poster-field. I believe that the first poster is more successful in terms of fixing the film in memory, and ought to be followed.

The placement of exposers has to be calculated as well. A person posting exposers must be knowledgeable: he must be trained at a 'technical school of exposer-making,' he must know where and beside what to place a new exposer. Offices sell spaces for hanging posters, but any such spot is turned into a dumpsite where any poster will be buried. Offices, however, are not really to blame, since they sell the most visible places, which become 'dark' as soon as they are filled up with a dozen or so exposers. This is a fairly important issue for the commercial firms that need to set up a 'technical school of exposer-making.'

Many firms, desiring to expose their product, imagine that if their offer is placed on the front page, it will necessarily be noticed. The experiments at the Institute of Artistic Culture have proved that, depending on the form of the exposer, things advertised on the last page are remembered no less vividly, even when the advertisement is significantly smaller in size than an exposer occupying a whole page.

No movement or trend in art can serve as a model for the exposer, for none of them had the same generic origins. One can borrow from them only the elements that are identical to the elements of the exposer.

To borrow from essential, systematic properties of a movement, such as the overall form or composition of elements, would be yet another mistake. Exposers cannot be patterned on Cézanne, nor on Cubism, Futurism, or Constructivism. Nor can they imitate the manner of the Itinerants.[74] Only some elements and some principles can be borrowed.

It is possible to imprint the form of the exposer on the viewer's memory without suppressing adjacent exposers. Quite the contrary—calculated posting will make it possible to use the forms of all the exposers reciprocally, whereas in their current condition they are for the most part obscured and therefore fail to reach their goal. Experiments have proved that when the exposers advertising a wide variety of objects are positioned in strict accordance with the newly discovered Cubist law of contrast, none of them will be lost.[75]

It has to be recognized that enterprises in general, and film enterprises in particular, for the most part approach advertising without any method. Moreover, they are afflicted by a number of prejudices, as a result of which many posters properly correlated by the artists with the already active exposers are rejected. Institutions see the exposer as a painting, measuring its quality by the yardstick of easel painting and digging out analytical, astronomical, and botanical references. One gramophone firm wanted to advertise the record 'Stella' (star) on the backdrop of the starry heavens and commissioned a poster to an artist, who duly depicted 'Stella' among the stars. The firm's administration posed a profound question to the artist: "Are the stars drawn correctly—and is the number of the stars around 'Stella' accurate?" In another instance, the artist submitted an exposer that displayed two intersecting lines, conceived in contrast to other exposers already present in the street. In the patron's mind, however, the poster conjured an association with the cross, which scared him to death; eventually, he settled on an exposer that depicted Pegasus with a rider holding a torch, and some palm leaves and a broken heart at the bottom. A poster was once made that depicted three burning candles. The poster was done in such a way that not a soul could overlook it. But the firm rejected it out of superstition: "Three candles spell death!" The firm ordered a safer poster, with forget-me-nots, as well as a church service, just in case.

The patron thinks that the exposer should correspond to his product, while the exposer may have another goal, too: its task is to expose the product by whatever means, be it all saints if necessary.

Not everyone remembers titles, surnames, names, and patronymics, etc., but all remember faces, form, color, and number. In order for the viewer to remember the external image, it is very important that the image actually become an exposer. Often housewives, asking someone to buy a product, give the instruction, "Get the one with the Negro on it" (the label),[76] or, "Look for the triangle"[77] (that is, the shape).

Once I demonstrated two covers: everyone read 'sindetikon,' 'sindetikon,' while in fact it read 'koldetikon.'[78] When they changed the color of the cover, leaving the original inscription, viewers noticed that the first cover read not 'sin' but 'kol.' Another example: shop windows of two stores bore the following signs: one had the brand name "Skorokhod,"[79] the other said "Footwear." Despite that, it turned out that many went into the store marked "Footwear," imagining that they were going into "Skorokhod." What was the reason for this? Simply that the word 'Footwear' was given in the form of the other exposer: a familiar flourish. The viewer did not notice the letters but the familiar font of "Skorokhod" compelled him to enter the store marked "Footwear." Thus, it is possible to reach the goal with a single flourish.

Translated by Amelia Glaser and Anna Muza

Arvatov claims that in Eisenstein's and Vertov's profound view, it is ultimately necessary to destroy all art, including production art, leaving behind nothing but "bare production, that is, technique."[81] If such is the case, and if Vertov imagines that what he is making now is not art,[82] then we must conclude that the same mistake has stolen into kinetic art as into painting. By the words "down with art," we must understand an art which, instead of objectless art 'as such,' exposes life's snout. We are talking about an art that wants to make a primrose out of a pig's nose. [A rose, but not art itself. The new art differs from the old art precisely in that it exposes its own nature; new artists are non-objectivists.[83]]

If every era in every human order has striven to mount the carriage-box of art and have its face exhibited through artistic images, then our contemporary critics are likewise steering contemporary artists in the same direction. The bourgeois class had itself painted, with all of its everyday tripe, through the painter's art on a canvas, or in sculpture, theater, music, or poetry; for this reason, critics argue, today's victorious working class must also have its own tripe painted. If the bourgeois class had established itself in art, then we too must smear ourselves on canvas and establish ourselves there in the image and likeness of the bourgeoisie.

Many of these switchmen are interested in directing art, through the artists, along the old figurative path of transforming mugs into images.

[This idea, even from my point of view, is purely bourgeois.

Art for the proletariat has to have a different purpose. Above all, the proletariat must not fabricate its own images, or symbols, for in its very essence it is without an image, it is objectless.[84]

Its art has to be art as such, and the artist in a proletarian society is not an image-maker, not a painter of its sacred images or its daily tripe.]

Let the switchman-critic forget his habit of seeing in the camel an animal specially designed by nature for carrying the Kirghiz, and of seeing in the artist a master granted from above the power to 'animate,' to reincarnate the disfigured as the figurative.[85]

According to Arvatov, "However much the individual members of the intelligentsia may blab about the overthrow of all art (excepting production art), the working class must take into practical consideration the fact that it has not yet reached a state of complete organization and societal consensus. The working class still needs to persuade concretely—that is, by means of art" (agit-painting and agit-cinema).

For Arvatov, art is, in the first place, a means of agitation—almost a tool designed for just this purpose, as it was for the early Itinerants.[86] Thus, as soon as the need passes for a concrete persuasion of society, agitational art will become redundant. Art, in his opinion, will cross over into production. This view still leaves some hope that figurative easel painting will disappear provided that the proletarian society promptly achieves a complete uniformity of thought. Others maintain that the proletariat must assert itself in art exactly as its enemies used to do. In this scenario, the demise of figurative easel painting is indefinitely postponed, because the painterly function of art is realized along an already trodden path. Indeed, comrade Arvatov himself is not opposed to agitational art, nor to figurative art in general, including that of AKhRR. At the same time, Arvatov wants to direct art, via the artist, along a different route, one leading to production: "art into production." This slogan seems to imply that art issues from technical goals. Art thus goes in tandem with the utility of objects. It refines that which cannot be completed by "bare technique," wherein the forms of objects arise from purely physical necessity, rather than from their forms as such. The "technique" of our organism created fingers of different sizes on our hands—created them, not on the strength of formal artistic considerations, but on the strength of pure utility.

Form for form's sake does not exist. Form as such does not exist either. Thus, neither art, nor the artist—let alone easel painting—is necessary for the development of objects. And, once we transpose the slogan "art into production" as "production in art," we arrive at a completely different point of view, one which will lead to many outcries of "Down with!" in the sphere of "bare technique," and in the social order as a whole.

[Symmetry (composition) is demanded by the latest trends. The new easel painters dynamically unfold life in time, and unfold their picture on thousands of little canvas-frames, and as a result the picture shows some fact or fiction in its integrity in time.]

The bourgeoisie, like all ruling classes before it, daubed its visages, by means of the artist, in a rather primitive way, and in doing so, also drew the entire picture of life. The proletariat is executing, and will continue to execute, its supremacy at the moment of great technical advancements of human organs—ears, eyes, feet, hands. One such advancement in the sphere of art has been cinema, which has engendered new cine-artists, directors of pictures. Any film production bears the name of 'picture,' and any etude of such a picture is dubbed a 'frame.' Thus all directors are, to a great extent, flesh of the flesh of painting's ancient elders. In their hands lies nothing more than a new tool of production, enabling them to unfold a picture in time, to record with light a phenomenon in a film frame, in much the same way that they earlier painted with light an etude.

Every director of pictures has his own peculiarity, determined by the compositional upbringing of his painter-parents. For some it may be old predilections dating to Rembrandt's time. Others may be inclined toward the Barbizon school, the Impressionists or the Itinerants, and they will set up and represent phenomena in accordance with the laws of these artistic trends.

[In the first case, it is the ideology of production that reigns supreme, in the second, the ideology of art, and then easel painting as such fully comes to the fore.]

Herein lies their difference from the old technique, in which a picture frozen on the canvas acts upon the viewer by setting in motion the image reflected in his brain. One begins wondering about the circumstances behind the given episode, and its consequences. Modernity has introduced new technical advances into arts, which in the old times had been exploited by idea-givers and enumerators of societal interrelationships.

As for Eisenstein's plan to liquidate all easel-painting, save for agitational easel painting: such a plan demands that he commit himself to the affirmation of agitational easel painting, to which he is committed at present, for he elaborates the truth of agitational content, conveying it by means of contrast.[87] His frames live off their content; translated into the language of painting, this equals the Itinerants, whose pictures lived off the same source. Painters at that time devoted themselves to characterizing the face in its many psychological states and 'moods'; they expressed happiness and unhappiness, everyday life, varieties of grief, hope, and joy—instead of exposing painting 'as such,' or, in the case that concerns us, 'cinema as such.'

But Eisenstein has one advantage over other directors, and that is a certain understanding and skill as regards the law of contrasts. Further intensification of contrasts will guarantee him eventually a complete victory over content—by way of contrastive structures. [It will lead him to non-objectivity, which means cleansing the screen of concrete-agitational forms, and then whatever our art critics and switchmen can get a hold of will come down upon his head.]

Every director strives to convey in his picture not form 'as such,' not light 'as such,' not painting 'as such,' not art 'as such.' He uses light first and foremost as a technical tool for showing how people behave in different circumstances [that make them anxious or upset. Heroism, magnanimity, fairness, sufferings, and so on. Literature that is made up not of letters but of people. How similar this is to the old painters.]

For example, let us take, in *ARK* No. 8, the frame *The Black Heart*—not, by the way, a bad title, utterly medieval and mystical, suggesting that realism is yet far away. This etude-frame itself is constructed after the manner of the German painters of the 1860s.[88] The relative placement of heads and figures annuls the reality of their spatial-volumetric relationship. This positioning of present-day faces in a long-past time, outside of space as we know it now, can by no means be modern; the element of light is used as previously by the Itinerants. Consider also *Cross and Mauser*, a mysterious sign discovered one beautiful morning in Boston or Cleveland.[89] The treatment of this frame belongs, historically, in Repin's period, and psychologically, it is identical to Kasatkin's painting *Who is it?* or Repin's *He Returned* (Tret'iakov Gallery).[90]

Let us take also *1905*, a strike in a mortuary:[91] an intense contrast which, through its unexpectedness, should be set in opposition to the picture unfolded as a shift.[92] The utterly impressionistic texture of the frame recalls the time of Renoir, Manet, Toulouse-Lautrec.[93] Likewise, consider the peasant type, on page ten of *ARK* No. 8, a study entirely à la Itinerants or AKhRR: before, *The Cranes Are Flying*; now—*Listening to the Agitator*.[94]

In its application of the theory of painting, cinema lags behind in a distant past, while the essence of art has attained a new form, as expressed in architecture, poster, and stage design. New art is neither painterly nor figurative. New art is above all architectural, and has not been understood in its proper sense even by the artists of the 'left.' These artists have arrived at an individual aesthetic, an intuitive mood. Out of garbage, they have created the eclecticism of photomontage and thereby have erected a barricade to the formal progress of new art 'as such.'

But even this eclectic photomontage is not, as Arvatov would have it, an alternative to easel painting.

Eisenstein and Vertov are indeed first-rate artists, with a leftward leaning; the first relies on contrast, the second, on the "display of the object" as such. However, both still have a long way to go to reach Cézanne, to reach Cubism, Futurism, or Abstract Suprematism, and the trajectory of their further artistic development can proceed solely from an understanding of the principles of these schools.

I salute the proposal of comrade Arvatov regarding experimental cinema, for this is the most essential task in the cinematic arts.[95] Only through such experimental section can we create 'kinology' and a special 'pharmacy,' without which the cinematic organism would surely come down with a catarrh.[96] About Vertov's "pure display," I will say that the object indeed may be shown 'as such,' isolated from various ideological and agitational contents.[97] I do not know whether this is how Vertov understands the "pure display of objects"; if so, it is a correct leftist positioning of the question in art.

Earlier artists maintained that there was no art outside ideological content, and that there was no content that would not contain art. Consequently, art for them depended on some aristocratic snout, without the snout, art seemed to the artist groundless, shapeless, meaningless, purposeless. New artists understood that the main thing was not the snout, but painting, and that painting 'as such' has no less value than all other phenomena.

In the "display of objects" Vertov already half-liberates the viewer from objects and material phenomena under a make-up of ideas. Showing the object 'as such,' he forces society to see objects without the make up: real, authentic, independent of the ideological order, thereby presenting a picture far stronger and more interesting than visages and their 'contents.'

In Cubism, art has freed itself from ideological content and has begun to build its form. For many centuries, it served its ideological mistress, cleaned her, powdered and daubed her cheeks and lips, and penciled her eyebrows. Today it refuses to do so, in the name of its own culture. The same holds true for cinema, another such maid, who needs to liberate herself and understand, as did the Cubists, that art can exist without the image, without everyday life, and without the idea's visage. Only then will cinema contemplate its own culture 'as such.'

Eisenstein has perceived the law of contrast, which makes his film production interesting, but he must also recognize the fact that his contrasts can create an environment advantageous for an idea but not the contrasts themselves, which will, in this case, lose their inherent force, and will not expose contrast 'as such.' If he grasps the law of contrast, and it can be grasped exclusively through Cubism as the only school of the laws of contrast, then he will rise to the level of the new art of the future.

It was until recently believed that new art in general, and Cubism in particular, were falsifications of art. This outstanding analysis suggested by our experts on Western art was analogous to the analytical thinking of the monkey in Krylov's fable, who, unable to deduce that glasses should be worn on the eyes and not on the tail, found them completely useless and smashed them to bits.[98]
Contemporary critics have likewise decided to prove the worthlessness of new art, and to warn the proletariat against the emergence of an incomprehensible, futile artistic phenomenon, called Cubism, Futurism, Suprematism.

This monkey's skill of judging the purpose of every idea in relation to his own image has from the earliest times forced art to align itself with the priest or the pharaoh as a utilitarian visage, or a container of great ideas. The artist was raised on this method, and thinks that the human mug is indeed the goal in which the artistic image exists in an idea; that this mug and all the tripe of his everyday life, and marketplace hubbub, are the crux of his life.

Moreover, he has become increasingly convinced that he is born out of this hubbub, and that all the interrelationships of these mugs comprise the society of which he is a member and consequently, must resemble it himself. His art has to be composed precisely of images of this hubbub. That is his understanding; that is why he either stands in the ante-room of life's vice-bosses in order to engrave their 'idea-containing' visages, or travels around the globe to smear onto his canvas all of this sprawling, sacred, everyday life.

Nor have film directors escaped this grip of tradition; and visages are victorious on the screen.

Translated by Elif Batuman and Lyubov Golburt

In issue 10 of the *Kinozhurnal ARK*, in my article "And Visages are Victorious on the Screen," I pointed to a similarity in the treatment of 'visages' on the screen and whole pictures produced in the pre-cinematographic era, that is, before that moment when technology found a way of painting living faces on the cinematic canvas. I also pointed out that the painter had invariably tried, with the greatest difficulty, using bristle and paint, to make nature and visage appear alive and natural in all of their movements, and that making those movements expressive constituted one of his foremost efforts. But as a result of all his efforts, the painter would manage to capture on the static canvas only a single impression of this movement and only in a single frame. And the artist remained in this hopeless and doomed position until, on the one hand, technology invented cinema and achieved the reproduction not of an impression but of actual movement; and, on the other, a number of painters resolved for themselves the question, "What is painting and what is art?" From this moment on, art split into two basic divisions: some artists became objectivists (concretists), easel-painters and reproducers of the everyday, never having understood the essence of art; the others, non-objectivists (abstractionists), who understood the essence of art and rejected the portrait and the representation of everyday life.

In that same article, I pointed out that the painter had significantly influenced the compositional nature of the structuring of film frames, as well as the work of directors and cameramen. He subjugated the film-artist to his own school, and as a result, the film, which is a moving picture painted with light, is structured by the compositional laws of easel painting. I pointed out that with time (and we do not have to wait much longer) film technology will acquire the means of coloring frames, that is, not only the chromatic illumination of forms, [99] but also the possibility of obtaining, with the help of the painter, the texture and special underlining of visages by a ray of colored light, of such a quality as to arouse the viewer's emotions, similar to those aroused in him by paintings, for instance, in museums.

The artist, primarily the painter, has had, and continues to have, an enormous influence on directors and cameramen purely in their treatment of frame composition and lighting. In *Dorothy Vernon*, nearly half of the frames (moments) of the picture are structured in such a way that in the end you cannot tell—is it a photograph taken in the Louvre of a painting dating back to Gainsborough, or is it a film shot presently, with living people?[100] In *The Tailor from Torzhok,* there are a number of scenes (frames) done entirely in the manner of Perov or Polenov. Watching the succession of frames in this picture, you lose a sense of time, for it turns out that the film, because of its temporal attributes, either falls through or is shifted in time over several spatial-temporal distances. One shot of the landscape belongs to the year 1840; another, to the 1880s; a third, to the year 1925. It turns out that the protagonist of *Tailor* runs through all time periods of an entire century; of course, this is not evident to the masses, or maybe even to the director. The Americans, who carry out their production in one time-plane, do not have such temporal displacements of frames, not to mention their classical selection of all faces and objects soldered together by time, which is extremely important when one wishes to achieve good quality and unity of all the objects.

If all film productions were examined, with the aim of clarifying the role of the artist, it would be possible to assemble a vast number of documents proving that the painter has exerted an enormous influence on the filmmakers of our time. What is more, not a single director has yet emerged that would be able to see the cinematic material in a different light from the painter. The cine-eye[101] does not see anything new in nature; it looks at nature through the artistic eye of a painter (a painter-luminographer) and everywhere sees nature either through Polenov's eye or through Perov's, through Monet's, through Shishkin's, Rubens's, etc.[102] For now, cinema can see only that representation of phenomena that was seen by the painter. Both of them—the cinematic luminographer and the easel painter—are going after truth, and in that, they converge.

"We represent only the truth," they say, "our art lies only in this capacity for truthfulness." The latter conviction unites the cinematic luminographer with the easel painter and ensures that cinema as such remains unchanged. So there they will remain, stuck forever with their truth, which neither of them knows, and the visages will triumph victoriously on the screen in the image and likeness of painters, for cinematic luminographers are flesh of the flesh of painters, only with new technological implements.

Cinema, it seems, should have overturned the entire visual culture, and it will, of course, be overthrown once the abstractionists bring to it a mind made of new flesh; if not, we will continue to see the same Itinerant pictures[103] being painted with light, the cinematic organism still lacking a sensitivity to color. Cinema retains the essence of an easel painter who has developed to perfection his apparatus for perceiving and reflecting nature's light-and-color on the screen. But he has not been able to grant his visages the mobility that he wanted to convey; in reality, his visages move only in the imagination of the spectator, and what he manages to capture in a picture is only a ghostly intention of movement. Thus, it seems to me that cinema, by its very nature, carries on a continuous painterly line, organically linked to the painter.

But what nonsense this has turned out to be! The painter is invited to the cinema in order to play there the role of a lowly janitor—a scenery painter and furniture arranger, instead of assuming control over this powerful instrument of expression! In it, he has lost the right to link each detail with a face or figure on the canvas, which he had before, when his canvas was not yet the screen. It is true, however, that he himself is still suspicious of cinema and is sure that this 'dead lens' will never be able to capture what he captures with what is, in fact, a 'dead brush.'[104] But as soon as he sees colored rays of light streaming through this dead lens, and discovers that with them he can paint a truly painterly picture with all of its texture, then, most likely, he will take charge, unless cinema itself has not entered by then onto its own path.

In reality, the camera has found for itself new painters-dynamicists, *reformers* in new technologies but *conformers* in their treatment of, and attitude toward, light and subject matter. It may be that the dynamicists have no need for color, because dynamism is most clearly conveyed in white and cold steel-like coloring, and not in the flush of movement; dynamic movement is not illuminated by hot currents. The dynamic of cinema, in its pure form, should have its own spectrum; and this spectrum will demand its own form. But how to achieve this, if Dorothy Vernon's face is pink, and the Tailor's hair red? And yet, the Tailor and Dorothy are singular 'concrete expressions' of life, without which cinema would perish! Therefore, it follows that so long as, through Dorothy and the Tailor, cinema is wholly linked to life, a real cinematic dynamic production, stemming as well from the essence of cinema, will have to wait, because it might turn out not to be 'concrete' ("what one needs," we are told, "is the face of life, but not facelessness").

That is the charmed circle of concreteness in which painters have been turning around and around for a thousand years; and in which cinema too has begun to spin, having thoroughly convinced itself that the concrete can only be manifested in rubbery, pneumatic cine-kisses.[105] And should someone dare to show a screen without kisses, society would label him a crazy utopian, an abstract-minded degenerate offspring of a concrete-minded society. The way out of this circle of concrete kisses lies through new art as a whole. Cinema will only reach a new dynamic-kinetic structure of film through new art forms, through pure abstraction, similar to that already reached by the painter.

Thus, the person whose law cinema now follows plays in it an insignificant role and, moreover, the future of this role is currently put into question. True, it was not the artist himself who raised the question of his fate in cinema; it happened because the director, the cameraman, and the entire crew simply began to regard his work with bristle brushes, palettes, paints, and canvases as some kind of subsidiary element in the business of producing a motion picture; the artist is no more than a trifling detail in the director's power, like the floor polisher who needs to polish the studio floor. It became clear in cinema that neither the artist nor the floor polisher would be making pictures. Into this arena a different kind of artist has entered—the film artist, the dynamicist who, having assimilated the entire art of the painter, is perhaps waiting impatiently for a palette of colored rays, in order to weave with them painterly planes of textures in the likeness of Renoir, Degas, Millet, and others. From this we can see that film, along with all the directors, is in his power; on the other hand—inside the cinema itself, the artist is in the power of the director: here, he has no rights, he is overcome by the director when diverging over the compositional or constructive arrangement of the place of action. In modern cinema, the artist and the director can disagree only for two reasons: one is to be found in technical means; the other, in artistic composition. Disagreement for the second reason comes about as a result of one of them forgetting the order of painterly composition of a major painter or trend in painting (Perov's, Polenov's, Gainsborough's, etc.) It is true, however, that the director, particularly ours, is unaware of all this; and I am sure that it did not occur to Protazanov that many frames in *Torzhok* were painted with light and shadow after the composition of Perov's *Bird Catchers*. But it is likely that in *Dorothy Vernon* many frames were consciously tailored to obtain perfect similarity to the composition of Gainsborough's paintings. And so, if cinema directors consciously or unconsciously follow the path of painters, then the best cinematic luminographer and producer is the one that understands all the painterly ways and their laws. Such a director and cameraman will paint a better picture because, having studied the compositions of a major painter, he will be able to select in a classical manner all the elements of the picture, of the faces, and of the entire setting, will be able to bring out every trifle, and to show each detail of the whole, if necessary. This is very important for the creation of a picture; in this lies its quality and unity.

In the West, little by little, major painters are beginning to work in cinema;[106] starting from purely abstract elements, they work from the very beginning with our future source of new forms. This entry of the modern painter into cinema should lead both him and us to a new essence and significance of the screen as a new means of showing the masses the new life of art.

It is useless, of course, to expect film artists from the GTK, because from the GTK's point of view the painter should be able to come to cinema not as a decorator, janitor, or costume designer, but as a cinematographic artist, a cine-painter of dynamic pictures; and that he should not be called a director, because today's director is that same painter, who, by means of light-shadow, is painting on the canvas (screen) a moving picture. In the same way, the painter, placing before him live models for his static pictures, has appropriated the title of director by mistake, by assuming that he comes from the theater. And in cinema, we clearly see the failures of decorators from the theater, who transpose in color a picture that has already been created by literary means by the writer.[107]

The GTK ought to become the new Academy of Arts, with new technical means of expression and painting of dynamic pictures; but, of course, it must also contain a new special system and methods for the soldering of the historical joint between painterly art and kinetic art, as the ultimate technical pinnacle of art.

From everything that has been said above, the role of the artist as such, as something whole, is obvious, while his role of a decorator's assistant, of a minor tool with specific functions is incomprehensible. A thesis that seems to me no less obvious is that cinema must involve in its practice the most important masters of painting, whose work could subsequently prove useful to the culture of film.

Translated by Lilya Kaganovsky

ART AND THE PROBLEMS OF ARCHITECTURE.
THE EMERGENCE OF A NEW PLASTIC SYSTEM OF ARCHITECTURE
SCRIPT FOR AN ARTISTIC-SCIENTIFIC FILM

The nineteenth century signifies a great variety in the arts. Impressionism brings about a rapid change of points of view on art in the artistic world, as a result of which the end of the nineteenth and the beginning of the twentieth century abound in a multitude of 'isms,' that is different movements and trends in painting.[108]

Painting is an art which has marched most resolutely toward the deformation of all established points of view. Between the mid-nineteenth and the early twentieth century, painters had made deep excursions into the matter, and as a result, different artistic movements and schools came into being. At present, we have approximately fifteen 'isms,' among which Cubism must play the most important role in the history of the architectural problem. We can say that Cubism, at a certain stage of its development, reveals a new architectural problem. I define this stage as the fourth: it is that moment when the painter moves on to the construction of his plastic concept in space, in which he positions various materials and ties them into a construction. Of course, these early assemblages of materials were purely abstract in their painterly relationships and sensation, not treated from the point of view of the possibilities later developed by the artists with an architectural sensibility.

Show a relief.

Picasso.

Along this line, we see only the germs of spatial construction of materials, later transferred by the artists onto the utilitarian path. On this path, they grow into the Constructivist art, originally abstract, then concrete, which has set utilitarian work as a goal for itself, arising, accordingly, from the needs of the day.

Show works of the Constructivist school.

Then, a new movement follows which I call Suprematism. Initially, it remains within the limits of painting (color). Then a two-dimensional expression of sensual experiences evolves into a three-dimensional spatial expression of the same experiences. The Suprematist movement appears at this stage as both two- and three-dimensional expression (surface and volume). Reaching the last, spatial, stage of its development, it creates a new element through which a pre-architectural relationship of all elements, that is architectonics, comes into being.

1. Show the development.

Suprematist surfaces of the square.

Various sensual experiences of the surface.

2. Show architectonics as a problem.

3. Architecture in life.

No. 1. Black Suprematist square. Second square, red.

No. 3. White square.

Nr. 2.   Red   Green   White.
The movement of the square yields a circle in different colors.

No. 3. The circle takes its place in the given space. The black circle is shifted away from the center, the green moves toward the edge of the frame, and the white moves forward producing a dynamic sensation.

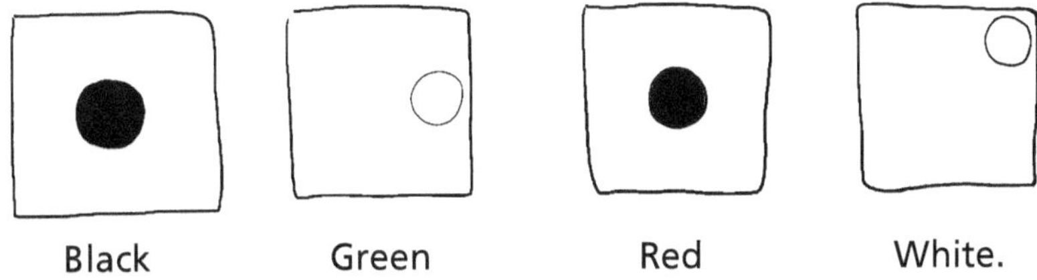

Black   Green   Red   White.

No. 4. The appearance of the circle changes as it is being colored into black-white or red-black.

No. 5. Disintegration of the Suprematist square into two white and two black
cells: two corners of the square get lighter in color till they grow white. The two
black corners remain unchanged and create a new form of the square-relation-
ship.

No. 6. Form No. 5 moves:
The upper black square transforms into a white one, the white one into black;
they form a new Suprematist element, which is colored, in the subsequent transformation, into black-and-red, and in white-and-red.

No.7. Form No. 6 keeps developing and creates a new form, that is, it topples from the vertical position into a horizontal one, upon which the black surface is shifted forward.

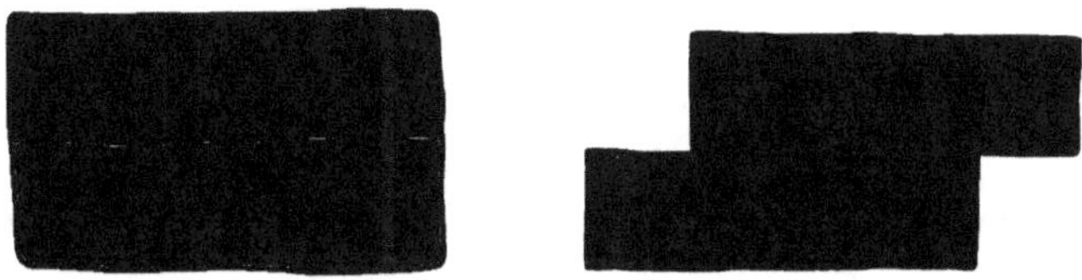

The black surface keeps moving and becomes an independent basic element, which engenders a whole system of new relationships.

Forms of the elements No. 6. Element B forms an independent element.

Element B and the Suprematist straight line start to evolve into a new basic cross-shaped form No. 8.

No. 8.

The cross-shaped forms begin to develop under dynamic conditions.

8 and 9. 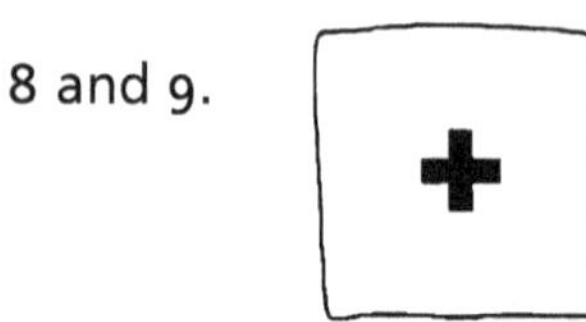

Cf. No. 9.

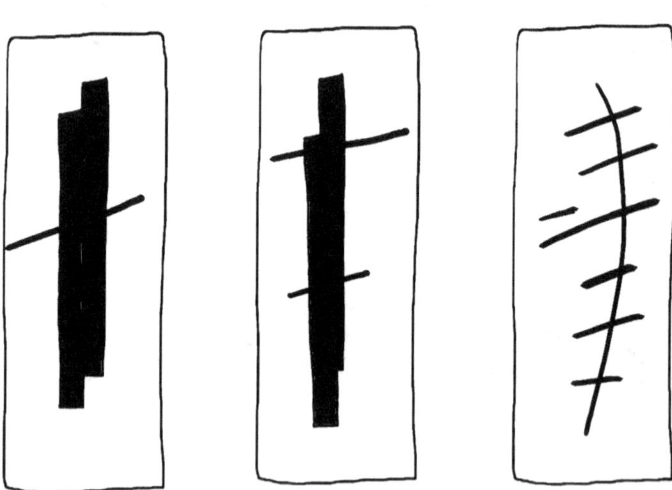

In this particular case of the development of the cross-shaped form, both element B and the red element A are extended downward. The lower ends of the black and red elements have been compressed. The upper end of element A grows in width and disintegrates into single elements; or they remain oblong and in their cross-shaped relation assume a diagonal direction.

No. 10. Form. We see that element A is compressed into a space.
The two subsequent positions yield a cross which, through spinning,
forms a circle and a new figure.

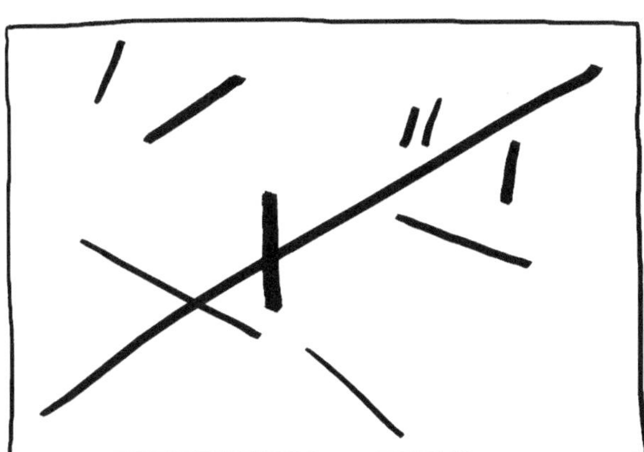

No. 11 forms a colony of Suprematist elements seen from above.

12. We see the development of an element of the Suprematist kind.
A straight line becomes three-dimensional.

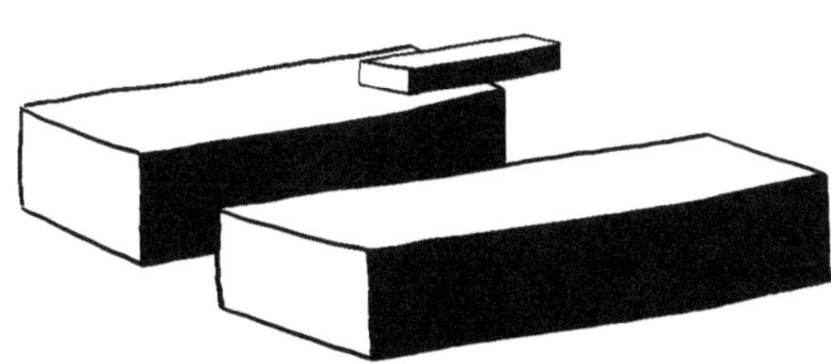

13. Form 12 develops according to the same principle as the surface, that is it produces a disintegration and reassembling of the elements. The reassembling forms produce a cube which involves the adjacent elements into the process of dis-integration and extension through their unsynchronized movement.

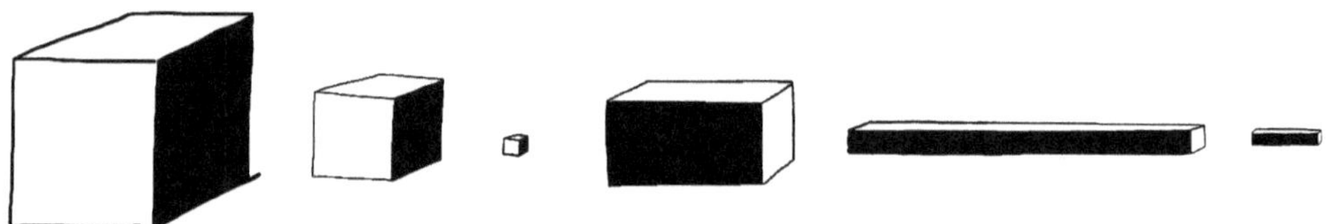

14. Form No. 13 yields an architectonic fragment in its movement.
15. Form No. 13 turns this fragment into an architectonic system.
16. Form No. 15 yields the problem of the new architecture.
Translated by Oksana Bulgakowa and Anna Muza

PAINTING AND PHOTOGRAPHY[1]
A LETTER TO LÁSZLÓ MOHOLY-NAGY

Dear Moholy-Nagy,
I received your invitation to take part in the discussion of the essay in *i 10*, which I have now read. I can see that for the most part it defends painting rather than opposes it to photography. The essay contains an interesting paragraph concerning me, wherein I am accused, as it were, of renouncing painting and therefore art, and of embracing mechanical production of plastic artistic phenomena.[109] This is a misunderstanding which I hasten to set straight. I have never approved of or supported the dead mechanical mirror of the photographic lens, nor have I ever argued in my theory against painting. On the contrary, I have always held that painting is one of the primary arts in terms of the artist's integral experience of the pictorial world, while insisting, of course, on painting as such, that is, abstract painting. If the author finds in my current works an element of painting, in other words, of art, that is a proof that the sensual experiences conveyed by Suprematist elements can only be conveyed through the plasma of art, which the author understands as painting. I have to remark that I do not consider the Suprematist elements to be painting, for I perceive painting as something different from the work of Cézanne or from the early stage of Cubism. The Suprematist plastic elements are a different matter. However, the matter concerns not painting but the method of art as an organic spiritual expression of sensual experiences. If the same sensual experiences could be conveyed photographically, photography would become another technical tool like the brush or the pencil … nothing else.

The problem of photography and painting raised in the essay would be insignificant in another time, but at present the author has undoubtedly noticed a

---

[1] Not originally titled.

tendency that appears to be directed against painting and art. Indeed, there is no smoke without fire. Materialization, mechanization, lithographization, photo-graphization, simplification are being promoted, mostly by the Constructivists. That is truly dangerous, because a machine, unable as it is to express spiritual experiences, cannot be considered a good tool, whereas the brush and the pencil are superior as technical means for they allow the artist to transmit a sensual experience in its full intensity.

For the promoters of photo-mechanization, the printed square Suprematist surface may be sufficient (see the magazine *MERZ* [No. 8–9, April–May 1924, p. 74]), but for me it is a dead element, and whatever collages may be produced out of photographic elements, they will be inherently dead for art, whose content lies in non-objective experiences through which I establish a connection to the universe.

As regards the texture, it is, from my point of view, irrelevant, because the texture does not occur from itself but only as a result of an excitement of the spirit and soul, as the author writes. I would add that the wave of spiritual excitement itself is induced by a particular sensual experience, and thereby that which is being expressed assumes a respective texture.

The author further writes, "Owing to the particular quality of the texture, painterly visions of sublime spirituality enter the sphere of the material perception of reality." I have to take issue with this thesis[110], because such sphere of material reality does not exist for me: what exists for me is pure sensations aside from any awareness of their effects.

The author thus proposes that the creative tension and force of inspiration stem from the discrepancy between the painterly means and the conceptual goal, which differ in their essence and in realization.

The new art makes this point of view obsolete, for this art is non-ideological and non-objective; the art of today exists only as art as such—which does not eliminate the tension that depends on the occurrence of this or that sensual experience.

I very much question the author's view that the more different textures a surface contains the more evident it makes the creative spiritual process of painting. The latter depends not on the quantity of different textures but only on a prudent juxtaposition of contrasting textural elements.

In my view, then, both photography and film are but new technical means, to be used by painters in the same way as pig-bristles, graphite, and paint. They must become transmitters of sensual experiences identical to the pencil, coal, or brush.

If this letter is of interest to you, and if it answers your question, you may publish it in full or in excerpts.

12 April 1927

Translated by Anna Muza

РОКА

Cinema, Gramophone, Radio, and Artistic Culture

According to the most popular point of view, film is by no means a simple ordinary technical tool for conveying scientific thoughts or sensations, sentiments, pictures, ideas, worldviews, and aesthetic impressions. No, film is a peculiar live creature, talented, omnipotent in its creativity, a phenomenon of extraordinary genius. Its vast competence embraces all phenomena and processes of life, and its art is the greatest of all arts.[111] That's about as far as it can get. All other arts are but a misconception of the uncultured past. This genius, however, has a deficiency, namely, its muteness, although muteness and deafness do not diminish its brilliance and do not deprive it of its title of the great Honored artist.

So, film is the 'great mute.'[112] Yet it has one more deficiency: apart from muteness, it suffers from the colorlessness of its visage, and from a lack of volume. Still another flaw is that it is full of philistine tastes and triviality. A creature rather indiscriminate and undiscriminating in such matters. Perhaps the parents who gave life to a deaf and mute creature are to blame. This deficiency needs to be corrected by way of introducing color sensitivity and sound into its organism.

This is necessary in order to make cinema one integral perfect whole. Allegedly, this problem will be solved by scientific means. Sooner or later, science will furnish film with voice and color, and thereby greatly benefit the film audience (as well as the actor and actress). As a result, the viewer will be spared film music, always irrelevant and castigating his ear, for the viewer has come to watch not to listen.

However, even if film is to be granted sound capacity and color perception, the actor and actress will not be able to penetrate the cinematic body in a way that would animate its mechanical silent motion by live speech. Nor can it be colored in live color.

In the meantime, cinema will remain a unique great dead mechanism. The same is true of the radio, another great unique mechanical child of science, grandchild of the gramophone: with its range limited primarily to the sound, it wails unhappily through the loudspeaker.

Such great achievements of technology threaten to invade the live force of humankind; the society of the future (luckily, we will have died by then) will be delighted by the great accomplishments of technology in producing mechanical progeny. But when humankind succeeds in combining the unique mechanical phenomena of film and radio into one whole, it will produce a marvelous supergreat dead infant: mechanical cinema, gratifying the spectator's auditory and visual perception of creative works.

Aged science undoubtedly wished to make a live organism but, because of its senile impotence, created great mechanical apparatuses instead.

It follows, therefore, that the very universal genius of the 'great mute' will prevent cinema from evolving into an independent art. Film, still burdened with everyday junk like a camel, will not be liberated as painting, sculpture, and architecture have been.[113]

So long as the screen remains a site where philistines deposit their everyday junk, film will not become an independent art: it is but a new trash can, invented by the technical power of science, in which the philistine displays his tripe, or a camel burdened with the junk of a Kirghiz nomad. Painting and sculpture should actually rejoice in the fact that the time has finally come for a great genius to take upon himself all the philistine garbage for display in different garbs, and thus painting and sculpture can attend to their own business 'as such' and develop independently.

In order for all that garbage to be expressed by cinematic means, film has to develop a method of its own, as painting and sculpture did a while ago, a method of liberation from the 'philistine cineresques.'[114] But cinema still lacks its own methods of liberation. Cinema is dominated by painting and sculpture, and therefore not considered worthy of its own art, its own composition, system, and material. While painting relies on color, form, and laws of relationships, film is essentially a temporal phenomenon. Art constructs elements and their relationships in space-time; in art, everything is futurized, everything is in motion; phenomena in all their facets are unfolded in time. In painting, this has been brilliantly resolved by Futurism, but film has failed to grasp it and busied itself with garbage. Cinema is a practical, convenient, cheap way of disseminating knowledge, wherein lies its usefulness and, perhaps, its purpose; but as far as it concerns the education of people in the field of artistic culture, film is a destructive phenomenon. If film continues along the path of 'cineresques', it will not be able to develop man any further, or to refine his worldview through the multitude of elements possible in artistically structured cinema. In this respect, film now lags behind all arts because its artistic form is obscured by garbage and kissing. Compared to the works of visual arts, it is not even worthy of criticism. It is a deaf and mute Lovelace, always drifting from one boudoir to the next.[115]

The artistic problem is not to be resolved in film through the object, because the nature of film is motion and objects are not elements of motion; therefore, it is impossible to set up an artistic composition of objects. It is impossible because the relationships among correlated elements cannot change. If a dynamic unit of the whole moves among other, fixed, elements, it will undermine the composition in form; if the composition is originally based on color, it will be tangled up beyond recognition. Therefore, it would be wrong to assume that if cinema developed color sensitivity it would attain the utmost perfection in color reproductions and get on a par with the art of painting.

The design and composition of every work of art, in painting, sculpture, or even architecture, are always based on a complete harmonization of the ensemble, each color spot, and the form. The relationship among them is established once and for all.

We see a multicolored interior of a room. In the room, we see two or three human figures wearing clothes of varying colors, variously situated in time. These figures, in different clothes, have color nuances influenced by numerous reflections of light, which travel in various directions and emanate from all objects in the room. While the figures keep moving, their relationship to everything around them will remain chaotic. Therefore, in order to transform this chaos into an artistic picture, it is necessary to relate all the accessories and figures to a certain palette; that is, to a certain composition of color and painterly relationships.

In order to meet this artistic requirement the painter does not merely reproduce the forms and color properties of objects: he also adapts the intensity of one color tone to the intensity of another, changing and mutually subjugating color intensity. Such adjustment is dictated to the artist by his inner sense of color harmony to which he must respond. The painter's treatment of the form is essentially the same.

Form relationships: the objects also are set up in an artistic composition; they remain correlated and coordinated through the figure's every move around the room. Philistines never notice these relationships; they do not notice how a door's corner or the door itself corresponds to a window frame or a couch, or the tables and chairs, and so on. Preoccupied with a single detail or immersed in the conversation, we fail to take into account the reciprocal artistic correlation of all forms.

Therefore, we hardly ever perceive the ensemble of the everyday aesthetically, being preoccupied with its distinctly non-aesthetic content. An artist, on the contrary, always perceives phenomena aesthetically, correlates objects and figures among themselves, and apologizes frequently for having missed the point of the conversation. When talking to someone, the artist very often responds automatically, concentrating instead on the correlation of the color spots and the form of the person he is talking to. Establishing a correlation, he finds a color tone that will incorporate all other colors and shades. He thus determines one dominant tone, to whose intensity he subjugates, wholly or partially, the intensity of other colors, or, on the contrary, he brings this dominant tone to the fore in much greater intensity than he finds in his model. These principles cannot be followed in a motion picture because this would entail photographing not real people, but figures in a painting painted by an artist. (Such an experiment may actually be of some interest.)

The painter's condition and attitude toward reality allow us to see that he is completely absorbed in the effort of determining the artistic composition, and that his work has no other content. Even when this work does contain figures and objects, we ought not to seek in them any content outside the painterly composition.

There exist other works, however, which express two types of content: painterly, and that of everyday morality. This kind of art is an art-compromise, combining the pleasant and the useful. In this case the artist, even though he finds himself in a bind, still tries to arrange the junk of the comprehensible and useful into an artistic painterly composition, which has not been accomplished in film so far. Once an artistic composition has been imposed on a certain scene, all scenes, forms, and color are determined statically, once and for all. Such is the nature of painting. In a truly artistic set-up, nothing can be moved. There is no motion. Such are the laws of easel painting, and these laws will underlie everything that is represented according to its method.

We shall find a good example in the formal gardens, that is, in the artistic design of plants, which are shaped according to the formula of a certain period in painting. We will see that every year gardeners cut trees, bushes, grass so that their shapes will stay the same. And as spring approaches and the plants get ready to stir, their growth is mercilessly cut back by the very same law of artistic stasis. The cutting occurs and conforms to the palace as a fundamental form of architectural order. The form of the entire garden will depend on the pictorial character and form of the palace.

But, you will say, is there no artistic element in movement? cannot movement itself, as in marches, plastic dances[116], and so on, be artistic? I will allow myself to retort that plastic dances rely on the art of rhythm, and not of painting. Rhythm, from my point of view, is the art of combining repeated movements, and thus an ornamental form of motion. Painting cannot be ornamental because painting is, in its every single moment, a reproduction of this or that occurrence; it is a completed moment. Yet rhythmical movements, which draw an ornament out of themselves, are an incomplete (infinite) whole. Thus, in plastic or ornamental movement we observe a repetition of forms. Therefore, movement as such is missing, even though it is represented through the movement of the human figure or the dynamics of a painting. It follows that even in this non-pictorial rhythmic ornamental art, which resembles rather a colored sculpture in a live environment, we encounter the same law of artistic stasis.

Is it possible to achieve an artistic work in cinema?

In response to this question I can say that from film's earliest beginnings to this day, no artistic picture has come into being. Stories cannot be produced as works of art. The bare content of everyday junk is merely put in a certain order following the logical consequences of a particular function of that junk. These consequences need to be tied into a whole, but as for their artistic composition, it does not matter in the least. Therefore, one can hardly talk of a "picture of outstanding artistic merit." This would mean deceit and abuse of the ignorant philistine, who falls for such a ventriloquist advertisement simply because he wishes to see, at long last, the content of his garbage in an artistic form, forgetting that his garbage, due to its very nature, can never become artistic.

An immaculate artistic film can be made only in a non-objective form, and that can be accomplished only if the production is based on pure aesthetic sensation and perception of the elements of form and color in their non-objective essence.

Since film technology does not have a color palette, the artistic film may follow the path not of painting but of sculpture. This is the only path toward an artistic film with no story to tell. Light, space, and form are the foundations of such a film. Incidentally, even the films with objective content should rely on the same foundations.

Knife-fights, brawls, and other kinds of offense are the technique by which vividly and brightly the philistine expresses his content. We habitually regard this technique as artistic if the philistine succeeds in manifesting his manifestations in film, where he becomes no longer a philistine but a decorator of the everyday and offensive. But this philistine habit of thinking is wrong, for it blocks the manifestation of the truly artistic.

Philistines steadfastly strive to bring into film, as well as into painting, sculpture, and even music, the content of their everyday life, in order to elevate art, raise its quality and value, and make sense of its nonsense. That is their common belief. Philistines or keepers of life's junk, in their naiveté and imbecility, have always regarded art as a set of special trash cans whose advanced design allowed them to put in order the chaos of daily junk. These trash cans, of course, were the artists, who could not possibly imagine themselves without this function. Neither the philistine nor even the artist could conceive of an art disconnected from the philistine's progress. They believed that art was 'historically' linked to the philistine, and that art and artistic culture could live and develop only through telling a 'historical story' of his activities.

By the same token, the 'great mute' exists in order to display the philistine's everyday life and all of his manifestations in their multiple forms.

Cinema has been duped and utilized in the same way as formerly other arts, namely, painting and sculpture, had been used, while the path of art as such had been obscured by every possible means. Art has not yet been seen by anyone in film, nor will it be seen if cinema continues to be used for the same purpose of trash-collecting.

The painter, theater actor, director and composer are astounded by the phenomenon of film. Many move from theater to film, instead of fully developing theater's own artistic culture, which remains inaccessible to cinema even in a single image. Yet this migration is inevitable because in theater, formal innovation does not happen fast enough. Therefore, our stern theaters must either vanish or engender new theaters guided by the principles of artistic culture.

Thus, the method of film remains dual: painterly and decorative-theatrical. It is not clear why the two should coexist—maybe because film does not yet have a method of its own. It lacks a formative element by means of which cinema could form its productions. It is not clear why theatricality is purged from film but not the theatrical-decorative method.[117] The reason for purging the clichés of the stage undoubtedly lies in the nature of film itself, namely, its dynamic, through which the film's content unfolds on different planes, while in the theater the action always unfolds on the two-dimensional spatial plane (the façade).

In addition to the decorative-theatrical method, film borrows only too frequently the method of easel painting in order to express its content. It would seem to me that if one is to dispose of the clichés of the stage, easel painting should also be disposed of, since both of these arts are two-dimensional by nature. There persists an odd misconception which has not yet been clarified. The theatrical manner of acting is being chased off the screen because it lacks that new form of expressiveness which cinema seems to be discovering, or wants to work out in the future. On the other hand, however, the overall method of production imitates easel painting, while theater and its actors have been raised on the artistic method of decorative culture. Theater sticks to this line, which does not yet exist in film. Film's current condition is below any criticism, compared to what has been accomplished by the theater, where the activities of the actor, the artist, and the composer constitute one integral coherent form of artistic culture.

Yet theater is below all criticism as well when it imperturbably rests on the laurels of Briullov's and Benois's forms.[118]

It has been proposed that theater is nearing its decline and will be replaced by the movie-theater. Indeed, having slumbered on the laurels of the venerable methods of the 18th and early 19th centuries, it has nothing to do but pass into eternal slumber.

Cinema is a new form of expression of garbage. It concerns itself only with the new methods of expressing the content of that garbage. Anyone working in art is compelled to turn to film, simply to be able to work in this new medium and try to advance the methods of expression.

However, this is not a solution, because by the time cinema turns from a dead mechanism into an animate live creature, the animate live human being will have turned into a great mute-and-deaf.

Nothing will remain of the artistic culture, or, in other words, its variety will gradually be reduced to a mechanical shadow, and mechanical sound, and mechanical music.

As a result, the philistine gets from science marvelous discoveries, which fully satisfy the demand for economy, cheapness, and also convenience. But eventually the future generation, having been brought up on film, radio, gramophone, will lose any sensitivity to life, for all things living will appear to them incomprehensible and abstract.

Cheapness and convenience at home may cost man dearly outside the home.

Art has been misconstrued as a part of culture whose progress would inevitably lead to film and reduce its creative variety to a shadow, or even bring about its self-destruction.

For the real concern is not art as such but the content of everyday garbage... To display the latter, no particular luxury like artistic culture is at all necessary. Garbage can appear exactly as it is seen by the eye.

The imminent downfall of theater as an institution is inseparable from the downfall of artistic culture at large. As I have said, cinema purges from its screen the clichés of the stage and thereby the decorative method, but it remains based on the pictorial method of easel painting. However, it would be natural for film to pay more attention to the expressive method of sculpture. The two methods and working approaches should be kept strictly apart in film productions. Lighting designers need to study thoroughly the methods of both sculpture and painting in order to provide different lighting for different things in the frame.

Film actors, on the contrary, are created anew, with vision and voice castrated. An actor becomes acceptable for the screen after he has become deaf and mute.

There are some positive shifts in this area but none toward the artist-painter and artist-decorator—perhaps simply because the pictures the painter has always been painting do not talk. This is why his method, albeit reduced to a shadow, is nevertheless akin to film.

I am beginning to wonder whether the treatment of the frame may not benefit from the method of sculpture, which relies on light, form, and space as essential means of expression. This is in case a fully original cinematic method of expression cannot be found.

One more remark: if cinema wants to achieve a 'picture of truly outstanding artistic merit,' its organism has to comprise some artistic elements. In order to articulate the artistic element, it forms its crew after the theatrical model: a writer, a director, a composer, an artist. Perhaps this crew needs to be different, without a pianist, script writer, director or artist, since the problem of art is not raised in the movie-theater.

The roles of the film director and of the artist are enormous. Who is the leader? Analyzing any production, especially an artistic production, it is hard to tell. The entire artistic side depends on the artist, not on the director. The artist will or will not succeed in presenting the content in an artistic form, whether in a historical picture or in a film of everyday life, depending on how well he has studied the artistic style of the period. The artist must know everything, from an entire building down to the smallest button, in terms of form and color. In addition, he must know the laws of composition of different epochs, as well as possess a rich compositional creativity of his own.

The second tendency: every frame in an artistic film follows some trend in painting because every film artist represents a certain school of painting, leaning in one case toward the decorative element, in another, toward easel painting. At present, film productions imitate the composition of the Itinerant school. Every frame has been seen through the eyes of the Itinerants, or occasionally of the World of Art,[119] or of the Impressionists.

All of the above pertains to films that are set in the present. All historical films follow the order of easel painting of their respective epochs.

The third tendency in cinema is to represent things as they are seen by the eye, and to film them directly. This is a naturalistic plane. Yet even when recording what the eye sees, this method inevitably imitates the composition of the Itinerants. It would appear, on the contrary, that showing things as they are seen by the eye presupposes a new method, which tries to avoid any creative artistic realization of this or that view. In this approach, one no longer has to worry about the 'artistic,' because the objects of representation are not transposed into an artistic form. Perhaps this is what film actually needs since it cannot discover its artistic form through painting.

Cinema is currently going through a trivial form of the anecdotal period of Itinerant painting, simply because it has been appropriated by people raised on the pictorial anecdotes of the Itinerants. No offence intended, but the Itinerants were far from any art, for the majority of them perceived the world as philistines' garbage, through either the political or the Orthodox (religious) prism. Artistic perception was, at best, secondary.

Since this view has been carried over to cinema, film productions can hardly be artistic.

Art, or the artistic expression of perception, does not exist in film as it exists in painting, sculpture, or architecture. It is necessary to seek it, as the painter, sculptor, and architect had sought, constantly getting rid of everyday garbage and its views on art. Since there is nothing to seek in the Itinerant painting, let cinema search the new arts, which are now forming and transforming different kinds of non-objective perception.

The artist and director in the cinema are not the same as the director and artist in the theater. The theater artist is a master who ties the plot together in an artistic composition, and unfolds it in a two-dimensional plane, confronting the perceiving audience. The director also has to abide by this two-dimensionality of the stage, where the content is displayed through painterly-decorative means. He, in turn, positions the faces of the acting elements[120] in the same two-dimensional decorative spatial plane.

Theater is a space in which the artist paints or builds a decorative-musical picture, harmonizing all accessories with the form of the moving elements. The artist also predetermines how these elements will move around, and how they may be combined in this or that position.

Thus, if film triumphs over theater, it will defeat or destroy man's aesthetic artistic perception of the world. Film may be called an offspring of the pragmatic and economic view of the world: it does not consider the world a luxury. The pragmatic approach to life is taking its toll: artistic culture is gradually being reduced to nothingness. Architecture as art has already vanished; it has been replaced by economical boxes. In due course, solely out of economic expediency, people will reduce to nothing all of artistic culture. It follows that we are on the threshold of replacing an aesthetic perception of the world by a pragmatic and economic one.

Translated by Anna Muza

RBP RBP

RBP

RBP RBP

RBP

RBP RBP

PICTORIAL LAWS IN CINEMATIC PROBLEMS

An article by this title would, by rights, be a detailed analysis, copiously illustrated, of a vast array of films, documenting the influence of pictorial representation on the structure of motion pictures.

Such a project could only result in a brochure unfit for publication.[121]

For this reason I will limit myself to a short article, touching on the subject specifically in connection with the work of Dziga Vertov.

Pictorial laws in cinematic problems, although exploited by all, have not yet been formally discovered either by directors, or critics, or students of film.

Everyone considers cinema an independent art. Film directors believe themselves to be new luminographers, completely uninfluenced by painting, whose unique pictures could not be expressed through any medium—except for the cinematic art.

True, film people are aware of the bad theatricality which has been creeping into motion pictures, and which it is necessary to oppose.[122] In particular, what one needs to oppose is the application of theatrical method and principles to expressing a given theme in film.

The method of theater is, of course, decorative, with a two-dimensional unfolding of the action on a flat plane. That is theater's lawful domain. In theatrical expression, the theme inevitably develops on a flat front plane. This two-dimensional space wholly determines the actor's performance. The actor is, moreover, not merely an actor, but also a decorative spot. His costume, like his movements, must in every detail fit into the single established direction and rhythm of the picture.

Film develops its theme also in time, or, to be more exact, it strives to develop its theme over a longer span of time than the theater.

Yet current story-oriented productions make it nearly impossible to employ expanded time in its different varieties; the picture is still contained within a three-dimensional illusionistic pictorial plane. Like theatrical art, the pictorial 'display' also must be met with resistance, because it interferes with film and undermines its composition, that is the montage of the shots into a whole.

Kineticity alone is not enough to lead film away from the illusionistic state of a painted picture.

Having watched a great number of motion pictures, my only impression has been of the advances in film's technical capabilities. Of all the films I have seen, not one poses the problem of cinematic form as such, inherently peculiar to film.

Instead, recent innovations in film fall entirely into the more general plane of pictorial problems. Thus, the problems made up in painting have come to be the problems of cinematic art as well.

As a result, cinematic productions develop in conformity with the pictorial materials that already belong in the archives of the history of painting. The newest films of everyday life bear the stamp of the archival historical epoch of the Itinerants.

For example, Eisenstein the innovator is but an old artist of the Itinerant school, who wishes not simply to bring novelty into cinema but rather to give expression to an old Itinerant picture by using all technical means available to film.[123]

One concedes that his Itinerant pictures are not vulgar, but can be placed on a par with the paintings of Makovskii.[124]

The study of the types of pictorial representation is necessary because the influence that painting continues to exercise over the composition of the shot and overall expression of the theme originates in easel painting.

Studying pictorial forms of representation, we shall encounter a great many new devices in the methods of expression, which will open new horizons in the perception of new phenomena previously hidden from sight.

Study of trends in pictorial representation, by enabling us to organize the material systematically, will afford an escape from the confusion plaguing both composition of the shot and the law of contrast[125]—especially in film forms with pretensions to new discoveries.

Study of the latest painterly material will reveal a crucial boundary: the boundary at which the theme collapses and diffuses, and new, unfamiliar phenomena come to light. We would see not an image of the object, but its new content.

The painting of the Itinerants was a Chinese wall impeding any access to the problems of painting. This wall still stands: the cracks made in it by the storm of the latest trends in painting are being mended successfully.

Contemporary cinema has its own Chinese wall, which protects the 'problems of Monty Banks' from the penetration of new problems.

How else to explain that Dziga Vertov should face the Cine-Chinese Wall of non-recognition at a moment when inquiry into new cinematic problems ought to be widely encouraged?[126]

I know nothing of Dziga Vertov's hopes and aspirations; I have not discussed the matter with him. But I have familiarized myself with his two works, *The Eleventh Year* and *The Man with the Movie Camera*. *The Eleventh Year* impressed me with its uncorrupted sincerity, and a whole range of moments that distinctly set it apart from the security of the Itinerants.

In *The Eleventh Year*—which is, after all, still a picture, whose elements (that is shots) are united by a single theme—one cannot fail to notice new, 'additional' elements: they indicate that somewhere deep in the creative core of Dziga Vertov, new perceptions have come into being that call for a new mode of expression.

No other director has so much as begun to surmise the issues that Vertov's new perceptions are now bringing to light.

The Eleventh Year contains a significant number of 'abstract' moments stemming from the new perceptions, of which the director himself is not yet fully conscious. Even so, this will suffice.

In *The Eleventh Year*, we witness the birth of new, 'additional' elements which will ultimately be arranged into a cohesive whole.[127] These elements will give expression to a new form for conveying a new kind of perception: a new, completely unprecedented film.

Such portents can be discerned and appreciated only by a spectator who understands their source, and knows from what sphere they originate and to which system they belong…

I may add that, in order to make sense of *The Eleventh Year*, one must also understand the Futurism of Boccioni and Balla, and indeed the entire system of Futurism in painting. Any critique carried out 'from the point of view of cinema' is not going to be sufficient but may result in gross errors in the appraisal of *The Eleventh Year* and similar films.

Thus, for instance, Paul Cézanne—a first-rate weaver, not of stories but of paintings—was underestimated by the Impressionists. Mauclair,[128] the ideologue of Impressionism, firmly consigned Cézanne to the category of the third-rate.[129] This happened because he measured and evaluated him solely from the Impressionist point of view.

Looking at Cézanne from this particular point, we will surely be unable to appraise his work as one hundred percent Impressionist.

But this means of evaluation is flawed. To be evaluated correctly, Cézanne ought to be considered from the point of view of painting as a whole.

By the same token, if *The Eleventh Year* were judged from the perspective of 'Monty Banks and its problems', Dziga Vertov would be utterly destroyed; but, contemplating *The Eleventh Year* from the perspective of Futurism, we find in it much valuable material for a film to come.

Viewing *The Eleventh Year* from the perspective of Futurism, I was able to find a wide array of Futurist elements. I do not have all the particulars on hand, but I do have enough material to give some idea of the Futurist influence. I attach two frames by Dziga Vertov and the Futurist Balla in order to demonstrate that Vertov has been guided by Futurist perceptions, that the elements of dynamic tensions are present in him, and that his and Balla's frames convey the same sense of power.

If Dziga Vertov now came to know Futurism in depth, he would promptly synthesize Futurist elements from different films into a new, dynamic film of the purest form.

Already his achievement in *The Eleventh Year* distinguishes him as the pioneer of new possibilities in kinetic art.

The Man with the Movie Camera is a step forward.

Of course, this step must be understood properly, that is, in terms of analogous phenomena in other arts, such as Futurism and Cubism. A spectator familiar with these movements will discern marks of similarity.

I have discovered in *The Man with the Movie Camera* a great many frames with precisely Cubo-Futurist qualities. I do not have these elements on hand, but those who have seen *The Man with the Movie Camera* will remember a whole array of moments: a shift[130] in the street's current, the multidirectional motion of trams, with every possible shift in the movement of objects, wherein the structure of the motion develops not only in depth, toward the horizon, but vertically as well.

The man who edited the film has marvelously grasped the idea or task of the new montage, which gives expression to a new, unprecedented shift.[131]

Like *The Eleventh Year*, *The Man with the Movie Camera* contains valuable material for the cinematic problem. But this value needs to be unmasked and displayed in a consistent, new, dynamic work.

By comparison to *The Eleventh Year*, *The Man with the Movie Camera* is a step forward, for it no longer offers a single theme that maintains its integral form throughout the film: what it offers is the fragmentation of a theme, and even a diffusion of objects in time, through dynamical expression. True, there is no clearly defined single trajectory in either film. Both productions are still eclectic. In them, two elements, or two images, are intertwined: garbage and dynamism. Thus, neither film can be viewed as something whole or complete. Both films will, moreover, cause much indignation, which could undermine Vertov's work as a whole. This would amount to a failure of experimental work which in the future would have yielded important innovations. These innovations are contingent upon Vertov's immediately purging his films of the aforementioned dualism. This should be Dziga Vertov's next task.

Of course, if Dziga Vertov is going to advance further, the Monty Bankses will not let him off. Still, let us hope that Vertov will nonetheless be understood and supported.

Thus Dziga Vertov moves inexorably toward a new form for expressing contemporary content. We must not forget that the content of our epoch is not exhausted by showing how pigs are fed on a state farm, or how the 'golden crops' are harvested.[132] Our epoch has yet another content—its pure force and dynamics.

This content provides perhaps the most powerful charge for our new, young organization, which increases the energy of the whole century.

In order to master the dynamics of our re-formative epoch, young cinematic workers would do better to study Balla, Boccioni, Russolo, Braque, etc., rather than the Monty Bankses, the Pats and Patachons.

My suggestions will certainly cause indignation; I will be told that it is necessary first and foremost to study the achievements of film directors.

I agree—on the condition that these directors be masters of a fully independent cinematic art. Since no such thing exists at present, the best teachers are still the masters of painting mentioned above—mostly Cubo-Futurists, since they have more potential than the Itinerants. There is more contemporaneity in the dynamism of Russolo than in how *Monty Banks Gets Married.*

The achievements of Monty Banks are identical to the achievements of a painting à la *Kitten under an Umbrella.*

Let me make clear that my idea is not to turn all film directors into painters. I am proposing only material for study to avoid blind imitation. I also propose to select the elements that are necessary for the cinematic art.

Our architecture used to be a Chinese wall, but modern painting has managed to force a crack in it. Architects have borrowed much from contemporary Constructivist painting to put into the latest architectural form—without having turned into painters.

Dziga Vertov is the first to raise the new problem of dynamics in film. All champions of film's honor must take the risk of producing at least one new, dynamic film, to see for themselves that dynamism is the true nourishment and essence of cinema.

I will agree that a cow can be used to carry water—but I will not agree that carrying water is a cow's proper occupation. I am not arguing that cinema cannot be used to show the achievements of the Monty Bankses—but I will not agree that Monty Banks is cinema's proper nourishment and essence.

Thus: make way for the newest phenomena, so that film does not expire from a chronic catarrh of the stomach, and from the achievements of the Pats, Patachons, and Bankses.

A few words now about *Symphony of a Big City* and *The Man with the Movie Camera.* I have overheard a murmur at the showing that some elements of *Symphony of a Big City* are to be found in *The Man with the Movie Camera.*[133]

Yes, they are, to an extent, but nothing is to be deduced from that: for these two pictures achieve very different things.

It is possible that *Symphony of Berlin* essentially pursued the same task as *The Man with the Movie Camera*: namely, the expression of a dynamic force. For the former film, the dynamics of a city; for the latter, dynamism as such.

Thus, the 'cine-dynamist' director of *Symphony of Berlin* aimed in principle to show the development of dynamics from the moment of stasis—the city asleep—to the moment of highest intensity.

But Ruttmann turned out to be a trash collector. Instead of dynamics, he showed how daily rubbish wakes up and goes to sleep. He, a cinematic trash dealer, with the help of film technology, displayed all the garbage he had collected in Berlin at the flea-market of spectators—in a 'symphonic mode.'

In its essence, *The Man with the Movie Camera* does not share this tendency. Its tendency is, rather, to rid the urban center of its objectness, without relating a single element to one consistent idea. His film is all displacement and surprise. Here, for the first time in any film, the elements are not shackled together in a whole in order to convey the gossip of existence.

Dziga Vertov does not rationalize or justify a machine by the fact that it manufactures cigarettes or milks a cow. He shows the movement itself, the dynamics whose force had been previously overshadowed by the cigarette-holder or by Monty Banks's back. *Symphony*, by contrast, relies entirely on rationalization, spiced, moreover, with an unmistakable moral.

Thus in their essence, the two productions stand miles apart. Dziga Vertov severs film-objects from trash and transports them into the world of dynamics, whereas *Symphony* invariably deals with garbage, however 'symphonic.'

By directing the camera lens toward the unexamined dynamics of the metallic industrial-Socialist life, we may glimpse a new world, as yet completely unexplored.

Translated by Elif Batuman and Lyubov Golburt

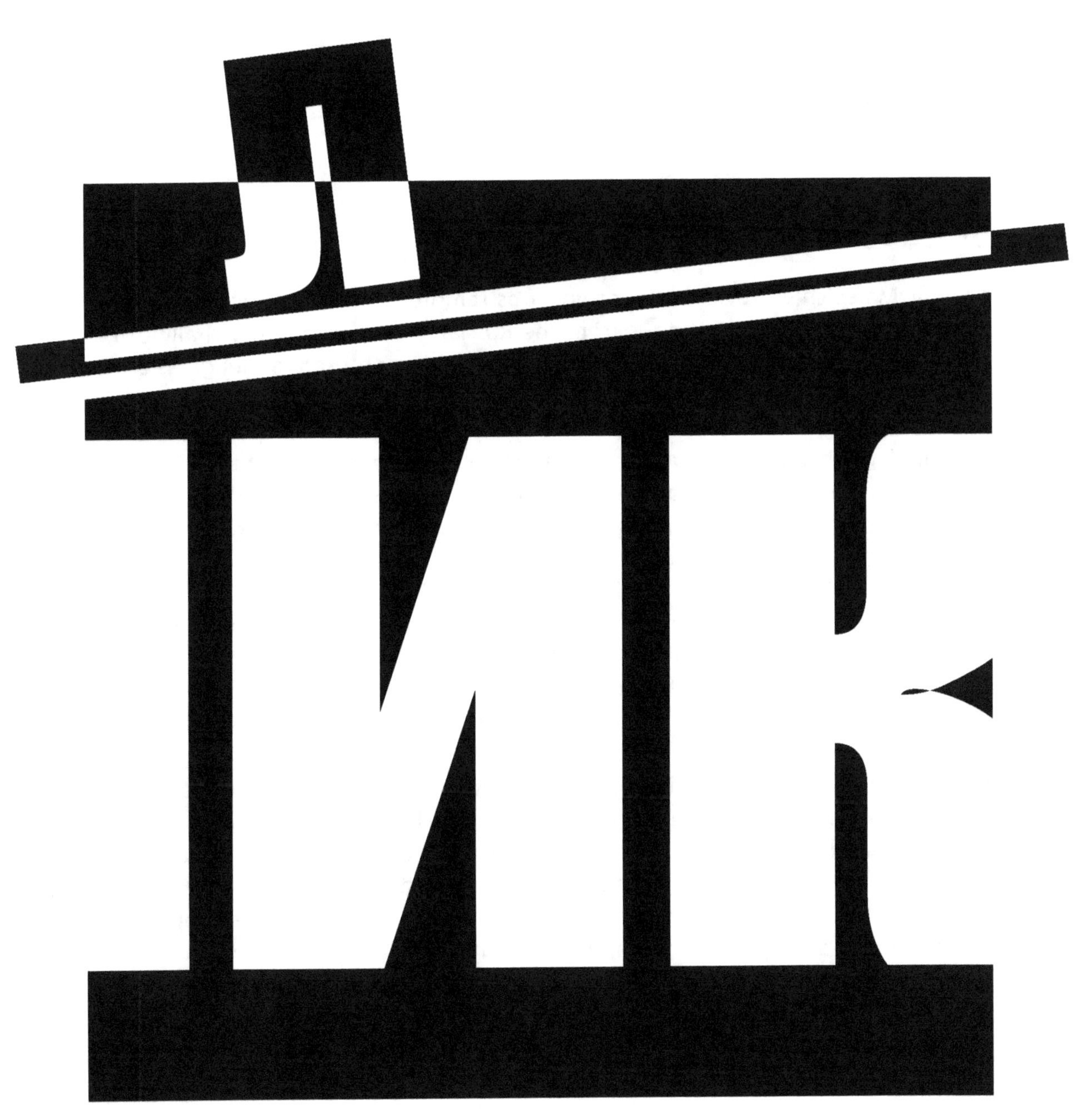

ANNA MUZA
WEAVING TEXTS: A NOTE ON MALEVICH'S USES OF LANGUAGE

Kazimir Malevich's critical prose is almost as remote from conventional norms of Russian writing as his painting is from the Russian realist tradition. An ally of Futurist poets, he shared their disdain for verbal habit, and used language as a raw source rather than as a ready-made tool, coining neologisms, generating puns, giving common words a meaning of his own. More than a playful or provocative gesture, Malevich's linguistic non-conformity is essential to his thought: his texts on film rely on a carefully established network of semantic correspondences, verbal associations and interconnections that signal and refer to each other. Owing to these inner threads, his writings have a specific consistency—not only thematic or intellectual but also textural. In his article "Pictorial Laws in Cinematic Problems," Malevich calls Cézanne "a first-rate weaver, not of stories but of paintings." The 'weaving' metaphor could be applied to Malevich's own work with language, his technique of creating verbal fabric.

While it would be futile to try to gloss all instances of Malevich's linguistic ingenuity that pale or are lost in translation, at least a few deserve a brief commentary by virtue of their conceptual importance. Malevich's very critique of figurative representation, central to his understanding of visual art, proceeds from a verbal source—the inherent semantic origin of the Russian word for 'painting', *zhivopis'*. In Russian, the word is a compound noun whose first root refers to 'life' and the second, to 'painting:' it suggests 'painting of life,' 'nature vivante' (as opposed to *ikonopis'*, painting of holy images). In the context of Malevich's attacks on realist painting in general, and the Russian Itinerants in particular, the no-longer-noticed 'live' component becomes newly prominent and highly sarcastic. It is only appropriate that the art of *zhivopis'* should strive to depict the "garbage of life," life's "mundane tripe." Malevich's repeated animalistic metaphor, comparing art (ab)used for ideological or utilitarian purposes to a camel or a cow, may originate from the same broad allusion to 'life', and the inherent morphological connection between the words 'animal', *zhivotnoe*, and 'painter', *zhivopisets*. (Cf. the Latin root 'anima,' soul, that links 'animal' and, e.g., 'animation.') Life for Malevich has a *morda*—a word specifically designating an animal's face. Offensive or crudely humorous when applied to human beings, *morda* in Malevich is prompted by the animal-painter axis: it reinforces the connection between 'life' and its artist, who tries, "with the greatest difficulty, using bristle and paint, to make nature and visage appear alive and natural in all of their movements..." ("The Artist and the Cinema") *Zhivopis'* in Malevich's understanding of it reconstructs, as it were, its ancient prototype, the Greek zo(o)-graphy in its archaic sense.

All art that mirrors life is epitomized for Malevich by portraiture, which reflects the human image. Scorning figurative representation, Malevich exploits the entire scale of Russian designations of the 'face', from the highly poetic *lik*—which also denotes the image of a saint, an icon—to *morda*, to the equally rude but also funny *rozha*. (The latter noun is particularly suggestive because of its distinct overtone of folk speech and sound interplay with various relevant terms, such as *obraz*, image, and *vyrazhenie*, expression. Its derivative, *rozhitsa*, is commonly used to denote a schematic childish drawing of a face.) However, Malevich introduces lexical diversity merely in order to deny it: he pointedly ignores glaring stylistic and connotative differences among Russian terms, and uses them interchangeably. In his, nearly sacrilegious, vocabulary, *lik* and *rozha* equally signify an outdated method of visual replication of the "snout of life." In a key phrase *I likuiut lIki na ekranakh* / 'And visages are victorious on the screen' (used in the article of the same title, and in "The Artist and the Cinema") Malevich uncovers the connection between the noun *lik* and the verb *likovat'*, to be triumphant, but reinterprets the latter as meaning "to paint or produce facial images," and accuses film directors of perpetuating this practice. The rhythmical sentence, with its poetic opening

'And', suggests an epic process of triumphant multiplication of images. The Russian 'facial' range does not have exact English analogs either at its low or high end, and fails to impress the reader as a cohesive whole. (The 'mug', which resembles *rozha* in its original connection with the painted image, has a much more restricted usage, limited primarily to set expressions and contexts. Unlike *morda*, the 'snout' points to a specific animal. 'Visage,' the closest rendering of *lik*, has a similar lofty quality but lacks the strong religious connotation and, unlike the old native root in Russian, has a foreign 'literary' ring.) Ironically, the regular and stylistically neutral *litso*, the Russian counterpart of 'face' preferred in English in a vast majority of contexts, is not once used by Malevich: this eloquent absence is typical of his aggressive and provocative verbal behavior.

Malevich stirs up the settled matter of language by challenging and replacing some of the common terms whose inherent semantic muteness is beyond repair. Thus, the word he uses for 'film director' (conventionally denoted by the French borrowing *régisseur*) is *svetopisets* (or *svetopisatel'*): 'a painter working with light.' An early calque from the Greek *photo-grapher*, the word did not take root in Russian, perhaps due to its archaic and folkloric overtone, and was abandoned for the sake of its international prototype. Yet it is precisely its obsolete air, and the etymological connection to *zhivo-pisets*, that serves Malevich's point. Cinema remains dominated by outdated conventions of figurative painting, and film artists are but "flesh of the flesh of painters" ("The Artist and the Cinema"). *Sveto-pisets*, being in its sound and meaning flesh of the flesh of the word 'painter,' embodies the conceptual genealogy. Translated back as *photographer, svetopisets* loses its alienating irony. Our invention, *luminographer*, has the advantage of being unorthodox and strange, yet recognizable; but again, the Greco-Latin coinage has a learned and sophisticated connotation, absent from the native and naive Russian coinage. On the whole, Malevich distinctly prefers terms of Slavic origin—unlike, for example, the Russian Constructivists, who, in their pursuit of modernity, chose 'cosmopolitan' western roots over native ones.[134] Russified words of foreign origin, such as *problema*, *element*, or *moment*, stand out in Malevich's texts in their awkward importance, yet, of course, their theoretical and 'scientific' air abandons them in re-translation into any West-European language.

One must also do justice to the semantic tapestry woven in Malevich's texts by the root *iav'*. *Iav'* broadly refers to the real as opposed to the imaginary, the seen as opposed to the unseen; the root has produced numerous literary and everyday words, whose intrinsic affinity is obscured by the remoteness of their applications. While an array of *iav'* derivatives could be expected in any Russian composition, especially one concerning visual art, Malevich uses them in a deliberate manner, creating his own critical terminology. He relies, in particular, on the pair *iavlenie—vyiavlenie*, meaning, respectively, phenomenon (or appearance) and an act of exposing, unmasking, bringing to light. The two nouns, distinguished by the prefix *vy*, designate two diametrically opposed concepts. *Iavlenie* is anything observed in the visible material world; *vyiavlenie* constitutes, or should constitute, the essence of art, it is a practice or an act of creative appropriation and transformation of the *iavlenie* that ultimately leads to non-objectivity. The arts of painting and film have been replicating the images of *iavlenie* instead of revealing and exhibiting the nature of art 'as such.' Malevich distinguishes different arts in terms of those immanent properties that define their methods of *vyiavlenie*, such as light, form, and space in sculpture. Malevich's term for the film poster, *vyiavitel'*, the 'exposer,' is also derived from *vyiavlenie*: instead of reproducing separate frames, "snippets of the film's content," the poster must expose the film's essence in a striking and independent image. Characteristically, Malevich's coinage also offers a Russian alternative to the standard *plakat* and *afisha*, words of foreign (French) origin, 'mute' for the Russian ear.

Despite, or perhaps due to, the lexical richness and variety English affords in the semantic field which Roget's *Thesaurus* designates 'Manifestation,' it is impossible to connect all manifestations of *iav'* in Malevich's texts by derivatives of a single English root. *Iav'* is ubiquitous in his writing, defining all kinds of appearances and expositions. A sentence from "Cinema, Gramophone..." offers an example of particular density: saying that the philistine wishes to exhibit / manifest his various manifestations / characteristic traits in film and that this wrong habit blocks the process of revealing / discovering the truly artistic phenomena, Malevich unfolds a chain of *iav'* derivatives. The shocking pronouncement (in "Pictorial Laws...") that "Eisenstein the innovator is but an old artist of the Itinerant school," relies on the verb *iav*liat'sia, a formal equivalent of 'to be,' which can also mean 'to appear' and, further, 'to present or reveal oneself,' 'to make oneself visible.' The verb is used to describe a holy, royal, or ghostly visitation. The peculiar grammar and syntax of Malevich's phrase enhance the ambivalence and covert irony of *iavliat'sia*: 'Eisenstein is but an old artist' but also 'Eisenstein appears to us / reveals himself through his innovations as an old artist...'

On the whole, Malevich's style conveys a roughness of vocabulary and syntax that John E. Bowlt has described as an "'adolescent' language of mixed metaphor, deliberately misused adjectives, and incomplete figures of speech."[135] This affected linguistic immaturity reflects, to an extent, the properties of the new-born Soviet language, awkward and uncouth, which must have appealed to Malevich precisely by its lack of refinement, its closeness to primitive expression. 'Prettiness' and 'polish' are as unacceptable to him in language as they are in art, reducing both to the state of falsehood:

"For many centuries, art served its ideological mistress, cleaned her, powdered and daubed her cheeks and lips, and penciled her eyebrows." Make-up conceals; art 'as such' exhibits its own essence. Like color and line in painting, words for Malevich are 'exposers' that must overcome convention and habit by revealing the meaning behind the name.

ARK   Assotsiatsia revoliutsionnoi kinematografii—Association of Revolutionary Cinema (1924–1935, since 1929 ARRK—Association of Workers of Revolutionary Cinema), an independent organization of film workers which played a prominent role in decision making in the field of film, exerting pressure on film studios and artists, as well as on the Party and the government. The Association maintained its own publication, the review *Kinozhurnal ARK* (1924–1926, chief editor: Nikolai Lebedev), subsequently renamed *Kino-front* (1926–1928, chief editor: Ippolit Sokolov). Three of Malevich's texts on film appeared in this journal.

AKhRR   Assotsiatsia khudozhnikov revoliutsionnoi Rossii—Association of Artists of Revolutionary Russia (1922–1932, after 1928 AKhR—Association of Revolutionary Artists), a post-revolutionary successor to the Itinerants, formed on a similar aesthetic platform, in political and artistic opposition to the avant-garde.

GAKhN   Gosudarstevennaia akademiia khudozhestvennykh nauk—State Academy of Artistic Sciences, founded in 1921 as the Russian Academy of Artistic Sciences (RAKhN) under the People's Commissariat of Enlightenment; in the summer of 1925 changed its name to GAKhN; in 1930 was merged with the State Academy of the History of Arts and transferred to Leningrad. The sections and departments of the Academy studied visual arts, literature, theater, folklore, sociology and philosophy of art, and brought together prominent artists and theoreticians such as Vasily Kandinsky, Pavel Florenskii, Aleksandr Gabrichevskii, Gustav Shpet, and others.

GINKhUK Gosudarstvennyi institut khudozhestvennoi kul'tury—State Institute of Artistic Culture, founded by Pavel Filonov and Kazimir Malevich in 1923 in Petrograd as INKhUK, Institute of Artistic Culture, with the 'State' designation added in 1925; shut down on 1 January 1927.

Goskino   State Cinema Organization, founded in 1922 and reorganized as Sovkino in 1925, was responsible for film production in the State Studios, and distribution policies within the Russian Federation.

GTK   Gosudarstvennyi tekhnikum kinematografii—State Cinema Polytechnic, created in 1925 on the basis of the First State Film School (Goskinoshkola); in 1930 renamed the State Film Institute (GIK).

Izo   Izobrazitel'nye iskusstva—the section of Visual Arts at the People's Commissariat of Enlightenment.

SS 1   Kazimir Malevich, *Sobranie sochinenii v 5 tomakh: Tom 1, Stat'i, manifesty, teoreticheskie stat'i i drugie raboty, 1913–1929*, ed. Aleksandra Shatskikh (Moscow: Hileia, 1995)

SS 2   Kazimir Malevich, *Sobranie sochinenii v 5 tomakh: Tom 2, Stat'i, teoreticheskie sochineniia, opublikovannye v Germanii, Pol'she i na Ukraine*, ed. Galina Demosfenova (Moscow: Hileia, 1998)

FF   *The Film Factory: Russian and Soviet Cinema in Documents, 1896–1939*, eds. Richard Taylor and Ian Christie (London and New York: Routledge, 1988)

Malevich I   Malevich, *Essays on Art, 1915–1928*, vol. I, ed. Troels Andersen (Copenhagen: Borgen, 1968)

Malevich II   Malevich, *Essays on Art: 1928–1933*, vol. II, ed. Troels Andersen (Copenhagen: Borgen, 1968)

Malevich III   Malevich, *The World as Non-Objectivity: Unpublished Writings, 1922–1925*, vol. III, ed. Troels Andersen (Copenhagen: Borgen, 1976)

Malevich IV   Malevich, *The Artist, Infinity, Suprematism: Unpublished Writings, 1913–1933*, vol. IV, ed. Troels Andersen (Copenhagen: Borgen, 1978)

Eisenstein, Sergei Mikhailovich (1898–1948), Soviet film maker and theoretician, creator of an influential school of montage. Directed seven films, among them *The Strike* (1924), *The Battleship Potemkin* (1925), *Ivan the Terrible* (1946/1958). *10, 11, 12, 13, 15, 16, 17, 18, 19, 27, 37, 40, 42, 43, 78*

Gainsborough, Thomas (1727–1788), English portrait and landscape painter. *46, 49*

Kasatkin, Nikolai Alekseevich (1859–1930), Russian genre painter, member of the Itinerant movement and its post-revolutionary successor, the AKhRR. *41*

Krylov, Ivan Andreevich (1768/69–1844), Russian poet and author of extremely popular fables. *43*

Makovskii, Konstantin Egorovich (1839–1915), Russian naturalist painter. *78*

Makovskii, Vladimir Egorovich (1846–1915), Russian painter, member of the Itinerant movement, brother of Konstantin Makovskii. *78*

Manet, Edouard (1832–1883), French painter and printmaker, associated with the Impressionists. *41*

Mauclair, Camille (1872–1945), French art critic; published several books on Impressionism, one of which, *L'impressionnisme: son histoire, son esthétique, ses maîtres* (1904), was translated into Russian in 1908. *80*

Millet, Jean-François (1814–1875), French painter renowned for his landscapes and peasant subjects. *49*

Moholy-Nagy, Lázsló (1895–1946), American artist of Hungarian origin, worked in Germany as sculptor, photographer, typographer, and filmmaker. Joined the Bauhaus in 1923. Supervised the German edition of Malevich's book *Die gegenstandslose Kunst* (1927). After 1937, led the New Bauhaus in Chicago. *7, 9, 12, 22, 23, 59*

Monet, Claude (1840–1926), French Impressionist painter. *21, 46*

Pat and Patachon: Carl Schenstrøm (1881–1942) and Harald Madsen (1890–1949), Danish comedians who worked together as a duo in 1921–1936. Enjoyed extraordinary success in the days of silent film. Known in Germany, Austria, and Russia as "Pat & Patachon", in Great Britain, as "Long (Pat) & Short (Patachon)". *10, 82, 83*

Perov, Vasilii Grigor'evich (1833–1882), Russian painter, member of the Itinerants, famous for his satirical genre paintings. *21, 46, 49*

Picasso, Pablo (1881–1973), Spanish-born French artist, the principal creator of Cubism. *51, 95*

Polenov, Vasilii Dmitrievich (1844–1927), Russian landscape painter, member of the Itinerants. *21, 46, 49*

Protazanov, Iakov Aleksandrovich (1882–1945), Russian and Soviet film director. His cinematic narratives were influenced by the tradition of Russian realism, psychological acting in the manner of the Moscow Art Theater, and naturalist painting of the Itinerants. Made more than 100 films. *21, 49*

Rembrandt (Rembrandt Harmenszoon van Rijn, 1606–1669), Dutch painter, draftsman, and etcher, particularly famous for his portraits. *39*

Renoir, Pierre-Auguste (1841–1919), French painter, associated with the Impressionist movement. *41, 49*

NOTES

OKSANA BULGAKOWA
MALEVICH IN THE MOVIES: RUBBERY KISSES AND DYNAMIC SENSATIONS

[1] "And Visages are Victorious on the Screen," see this volume, p. 37, p. 44.

[2] *Malevich III*, p. 322.

[3] *Malevich III*, p. 166.

[4] While in 1918–24 Malevich published thirty-nine articles and a few brochures, the years from 1925 to 1935 saw only four of his film articles published in Russian journals, as well as one article in *Modern Architecture* accompanied by an open letter; see *Sovremennaia arkhitektura* 5 (1928): 157–159. His lecture series on the evolution of fine arts could appear only in Ukrainian, in the Kharkov journal *Nova generatsiia* (1928–1930).

[5] Boris Arvatov, who characterized Suprematism as "the most dangerous reaction under the revolutionary flag," advised Malevich to find a place in "the ranks of aestheticism which, having caught up with individualism, has reached a point of full solipsism." See B. Arvatov, *Pechat' i revoliutsiia* 7 (1922): 343–344, as cited in *SS 1*, p. 362. An article on the research work of GINKhUK was entitled "A Monastery on Government Support." See G. Seryi, "Monastyr' na goss-nabzhenii," *Leningradskaia Pravda*, 10 June 1926.

[6] *Malevich IV*, pp. 157–159, pp. 163–176.

[7] Compare Malévich, *De Cézanne au suprématisme; Le miroir suprématiste; La lumière et la couleur; Les Arts de la représentation,* eds. Jean-Claude and Valentine Marcadé (Lausanne: L'Age d'homme 1974, 1977, 1981, 1994); Malévich, *Ecrits*, ed. Andrei Nakov (Paris: Champ libre, 1975; Paris: Lebovici, 1986).

[8] See the catalog of the exhibition *Moskau—Berlin, Berlin—Moskau*, where the script was most recently displayed. *Moskau—Berlin, Berlin—Moskau, 1900–1950*, eds. Irina Antonova, Jörn Merkert (München and New York: Prestel, 1995), p. 306.

[9] First published in German in *Das weiße Rechteck: Schriften zum Film*, ed. Oksana Bulgakowa (Berlin: PotemkinPress, 1997), pp. 58–66.

[10] Compare: "It seems to me that the eye-ball of every human being is a *dead lens* projecting circumstances on the mirror-*negative* of the brain, which is capable of effecting various changes in the reflections in this mirror-*negative*, depending on the function of one or another cerebral center." See "An Introduction to the Theory of the Additional Element," in *Malevich III*, p. 159. The translation and the italics are ours.

[11] Malevich originally used the term *dopolnitel'nyi,* supplementary, later amended to *pribavochnyi*, additional; the Russian *pribavochnyi* has the added connotation of surplus, as in *pribavochnaia stoimost'*: surplus value. Malevich himself referred the term to the field of "psychobacteriology," presenting it as a kind of "microbe."

[12] Malevich introduced his theory originally in two talks, the first given on 19 March 1925 in RAKhN, the second, on 16 June 1926 in GINKhUK. Malevich's article on the additional element, written for a GINKhUK anthology, which was not published, later appeared in German as the first chapter of *Die gegenstandslose Welt*. Bauhausbücher 11 (Munich, 1927), in English as "An Introduction to the Theory of the Additional Element," in *Malevich III*, pp. 147–195.

[13] In his analysis of the contradictory development of modern art, Malevich discussed the phenomenon of the blockage, which hinders the development of a young artist (and of painting). Malevich saw himself as a doctor, who strove to raise the blockage, curing the students from "painterly neurasthenia." See Galina Demosfenova's commentary in *SS 2*, pp. 330–331.

[14] Cf. Note 96.

[15] Malevich, "From Cubism to Suprematism in Art: To the New Realism of Painting, to Absolute Creation," in Charlotte Douglas, *Swans of Other Worlds: Kazimir Malevich and the Origins of Abstraction in Russia* (Ann Arbor: UMI Research Press, 1980), p. 107.

[16] A single line in Eisenstein's recollections suggests that *Victory over the Sun* must have figured in their discussions. He attributes the inspiration of the torn screen at the premiere of *The Battleship Potemkin* (7 November 1925, at the Bolshoi Theater) to the tearing of the curtain in *Victory over the Sun*. See Eizenshtein, *Izbrannye proizvedeniia v 6 tomakh*, vol. 3 (Moscow: Iskusstvo, 1971), p. 68.

[17] Eizenshtein, *Memuary*, vol. 2, ed. Naum Kleiman (Moscow: Redaktsiia gazety *Trud* and Muzei kino, 1997), pp. 310–315.

[18] In Berlin, Malevich stayed with the family of Gustav von Riesen, a German diplomat who had served in St. Petersburg before the revolution, and whose son later translated Malevich's book, *The World as Non-Objectivity.* After receiving a letter demanding his return to Russia, and making a hasty departure from Berlin, Malevich left his archive with the von Riesens. A large part of this collection is now in the Stedelijk Museum.

[19] Hans Richter, *Köpfe und Hinterköpfe* (1966), as cited in *Russen in Berlin: Literatur, Malerei, Theater, Film, 1918–1933*, ed. Fritz Mierau (Leipzig: Reclam jr., 1990), pp. 489–490. Hans Richter attempted to realize this script in 1970-1976 together with Arnold Eagle in the United States. His storyboards are now in the collection of the Research Library at the Getty Research Institute, Los Angeles.

[20] Eisenstein, "Statement on Sound," "An Unexpected Juncture," in Eisenstein, *Selected Works: Volume 1, Writings, 1922–1934*, ed. Richard Taylor (London: British Film Institute and Bloomington: Indiana University Press, 1988), pp. 113–114, 115–122.

[21] RGALI (Russian State Archive for Art and Literature), Moscow; depository *(fond)* 1923, inventory *(opis)* 1, administrative unit *(edinitsa khraneniia)* 1943, page *(list)* 1.

[22] Not counting the republication of excerpts from his old texts in 1933 in the collection *Sovetskoe iskusstvo za 15 let: Materialy i dokumentatsiia* (Moscow, Leningrad, 1933), pp. 114–115.

[23] Malevich, *Pis'ma k Shutko* (Eisk: Otdel zhivopisi i grafiki Eiskogo istoriko-kraevedcheskogo muzeia, 1992).

[24] See *FF*, pp. 114, 115–116. These attacks continued even after the release of *The Battleship Potemkin*: in a dispute at ARK (19 March 1926) Vertov commented on the intertitles and the hand-colored banner in the film's finale as a direct borrowing from his films. See *Istoriia stanovleniia sovetskogo kino* (Moscow: Iskusstvo, 1986), pp. 62–63.

[25] Eisenstein, "The Problem of the Materialist Approach to Form," in *Selected Works: Volume 1*, pp. 62–63.

[26] Arvatov, "Agit-Kino i Kino-Glaz," *Kinozhurnal ARK* 8 (1925): 3–4.

²⁷ See note 5.

27 See note 5.

28 See note 74.

29 Walter Benjamin, "The work of art in the age of mechanical reproduction," in *Illuminations,* ed. Hannah Arendt, transl. Harry Zohn (New York: Schocken Books, 1986), p. 237.

30 Cf. Eisenstein, *Selected Works: Volume 1*, p. 191. The translation here is ours.

31 This text was commissioned for the catalog of the exhibition *Film and Photography*, organized in Stuttgart. The exhibition presented the films of the European avant-garde, and Eisenstein was to mount a reel of excerpts from various Russian films, including Vertov's. The catalog text was initially commissioned to Vertov himself, but, too busy with finishing *The Man with the Movie Camera,* he turned the offer down. Eisenstein's essay did not appear in the catalog, as the manuscript had not arrived in Stuttgart on time. It was first published in English in *Close up* 3, vol. VIII (September 1931): 167–181 (transl. Ivor Montagu).

32 Cf. Eisenstein, "The Dramaturgy of Film Form," in *Selected Works: Volume 1*, p. 162. The translation here is ours. Wilhelm von Kaulbach (1805–1874), German painter and graphic artist, known for his neo-classical monumental painting; court painter to King Ludwig I of Bavaria from 1837.

33 Eisenstein, "Imitation as Mastery: Lecture at La Sarraz Conference on Independent Film," in *Inside the Film Factory*, eds. Ian Christie and Richard Taylor (London: Routledge, 1994), pp. 66–71.

34 *FF*, p. 145.

35 Marie Seton, *Sergei M. Eisenstein. A Biography* (London: The Bodley Head, 1952), p. 147.

36 In these experiments, Eisenstein saw a 'liberation' from the mimetic bonds of film. For him, a rupture in the illusion of motion intensified not only a different kind of kinetics but also semantics: the cinematic moments that form the film metaphor. Eisenstein draws on an analogy with verse, where the meaning is enhanced by the rhythm and the rhyme punctuating the break in the line.

37 "Pictorial Laws in Cinematic Problems," p. 82.

[38] Annette Michelson, "Reading Eisenstein Reading *Capital*," *October* 3 (1976): 82. See also Marcadé, "Réflexions de Malévich sur le cinéma," in *Peinture-cinéma-peinture*, ed. Germain Viatte (Marseille: Ed. Hazan—Musée de Marseille, 1989) and François Albera, "Malévich et le cinéma: le chainon manquant," *Revue de la cinémathèque* (Automne 1995): 62–70.

[39] Charlotte Douglas, analyzing the genesis of Malevich's abstractionism, has drawn on Bergson's philosophy of representation: "According to Bergson, if the universe is to be understood, it must be without image because reality is essentially non-pictorial. Images only work in the very limited middle strata of nature." See Douglas, *Swans of Other Worlds*, p. 56.

[40] "Stil' *Nibelungov*," *Sovetskii ekran* 3 (1925); "Arkhitektura i dekoratsii," "Bez uklonov i techenii," *Sovetskii ekran* 5 (1925); "Khoduzhnik v kinoproizvodtsve. Svodka mnenii," *Sovetskii ekran* 10 (1925); Dmitri Kolupaev, "Nuzhen li khudozhnik," "Novyi stil' kinodekoratsii," *Sovetskii ekran* 16 (1925); Lev Kuleshov, "Khudozhnik v kino," *Sovetskii ekran* 29 (1925).

[41] Ernö Metzner, "Arkhitektura, zhivopis', kinodekoratsiia," *Sovetskii ekran* 12 (1925): 8–9.

[42] Juri Ziwjan, "Caligari in Rußland. Der deutsche Expressionismus und die sowjetische Filmkultur," in *Die ungewöhnlichen Abenteuer des Dr. Mabuse im Lande der Bolschewiki. Ein Buch zur Filmreihe Moskau—Berlin*, ed. O. Bulgakowa (Berlin: Freunde der Deutschen Kinemathek, 1995), pp. 169–176.

[43] See the survey of these discussions in François Albera, *Albatros: Les Russes à Paris, 1919–1929* (Paris and Milan: Mazzota, 1995), pp. 31–37.

[44] "The Artist and the Cinema," p. 46.

[45] Ibid., p. 46.

[46] Malevich, "From Cubism to Suprematism in Art," in Douglas, *Swans of Other Worlds*, p. 110.

[47] Malevich, "Suprematism" (1925) in *SS 2*, p. 34.

[48] See V. Rakitin, "The Artisan and the Prophet: Marginal Notes on Two Artistic Careers," in *The Great Utopia: The Russian and the Soviet Avant-Garde, 1915–1932* (New York: Solomon R. Guggenheim Museum, 1992), pp. 25–37.

[49] Florenskii's study of the reverse perspective was written in October 1919 and presented in his talks in the Higher Artistic Technical Workshops (VKhUTEMAS) in 1922; the text was published in Russian for the first time in *Trudy po znakovym sistemam*, issue 3 (Tartu, 1967), pp. 381–416.

[50] Benjamin continued working on this research project from the end of 1927 until March of 1939. Benjamin, *The Arcades Project*, transl. Howard Eiland and Kevin McLaughlin; prepared on the basis of the German volume edited by Rolf Tiedemann (Cambridge, Mass.: Belknap Press, 1999).

[51] El Lissitzky, *Skaz pro dva kvadrata* (Berlin: Skify, 1922; reprint Cambridge: MIT Press, 1991).

[52] Tatiana Goriacheva, "Teatral'naia kontseptsiia UNOVISa na fone sovremennoi stsenografii," in *Malevich, Klassicheskii avangard, Vitebsk—2: Sbornik materialov tret'ei mezhdunarodnoi teoreticheskoi konferentsii*, ed. T. Katovich (Vitebsk: N. A. Pankov, 1998), pp. 45–57. Kogan's drawings for the ballet have been preserved in the Theater Museum in St. Petersburg.

[53] Aleksandra Shatskikh, "Malevich and Film," *Burlington Magazine* 1084 (July 1993): pp. 470–478. Shatskikh has also noted a connection between the script and the seriality of Malevich's work, and the peculiarity of the installation of Suprematist paintings at the exhibitions of 1915 and 1916 (p. 477).

[54] This device recalls Pavel Filonov's staging of *Vladimir Mayakovsky* in 1913, in which the figures of actors were concealed behind the silhouettes drawn on cardboard. It was part of the same Futurist theater project that included a production of *Victory Over the Sun*.

[55] Ludvig Hilberseimer, "Dinamicheskaia zhivopis'," *Kino-Fot* 1 (1922): 7.

[56] *Malevich I*, p. 33.

[57] *SS 2*, p. 323.

[58] *Malevich I*, p. 38.

[59] Transformations of black, white, and red, in a different order, recall the principles of alchemy, wherein creation is a three-stage process: nigredo, albedo, and rubedo. For further mystical and esoteric parallels, see Vasilii Babich, "Fenomenologiia kvadrata," in *Klassicheskii avangard: Vitebsk—2*, pp. 116–130.

60 Malevich, *Suprematism: 34 drawings,* transl. Thomas G. Winner (London: Gordon Fraser Gallery, 1976).

61 *Das weiße Rechteck,* p. 124.

62 See "An Experiment Intelligible to the Millions," in *FF,* pp. 250–254.

63 Kirill Shutko, "Put' kinokov," *Sovetskii ekran* 5 (1929): 4; Nikolai Kaufman, "*Chelovek s kinoapparatom,*" Konstantin Fel'dman, "Kino i Aristotel'"—ibid., pp. 5–6.

64 *FF,* pp. 225–226.

65 *Malevich II,* pp. 88.

66 Benjamin, "Die Erwiderung an Oskar A. H. Schmitz" (1927), as cited in *Russen in Berlin,* p. 522.

67 *Malevich II,* pp. 88.

68 Viktor Shklovskii, "Semantika kino" (1925), in Shklovskii, *Za 60 let* (Moscow: Iskusstvo, 1985), p. 32.

69 Iurii Tynianov, "Ob osnovakh kino" (1927), in Tynianov, *Poetika, Istoriia literatury, Kino* (Moscow: Iskusstvo, 1977), p. 329.

70 "In reality, his visages move only in the imagination of the spectator, and in a picture he manages to convey only a ghostly intention of movement. In this way, it seems to me, the cinema, by its very nature, continues this unbreakable painterly line, organically linked to the painter." See "The Artist and the Cinema," p. 47.

ON EXPOSERS. POSTERS

The article appeared in *Kinozhurnal ARK* 6–7 (1925): 6–8, and was reprinted in *SS 1,* pp. 283–288. A different variant of the text was published in English under the title "About Posters" in *Malevich IV,* pp. 136–143, translated by Xenia Hoffmann. We have followed the original journal version and preserved Malevich's neologism.

[71] The First Exhibition of Film Posters was shown in Moscow on 21 April–2 May 1925 in the State Academy of the Artistic Sciences (GAKhN). The exhibition, organized by the film section of GAKhN, represented sixteen Soviet artists and displayed sixty-four items, which included pre-revolutionary Russian, Soviet, German, French, English, Swedish, Italian, and American posters. (The Russian Archive of Literature and Art has a type-written copy of the exhibition's catalog. See Shatskikh's commentary in *SS 1*, p. 371.) The debate about the exhibition referred to later in the text was organized in May—as the journal *Sovetskii ekran* reported on 12 May 1925, no. 7. *Sovetskii ekran* published two articles, one on the exhibition itself, the other on the debate, which were followed in no. 8 by an article on the psychology of advertising.

[72] The terms 'impenetrable surface' and 'painterly field' are widely used by Malevich in his texts on painting. E.g., "The canvas [...] is a field of vision" on which structure and texture of the painterly body are seen. The structure can be "spotted, fluid, transparent, permeable, and *impermeable.*" See "An Introduction to the Theory of the Additional Element," in *Malevich III*, p. 166.

[73] Malevich uses the term 'pulverization' or 'scattering' in many texts on painting to denote a principal feature of Cubism. Aleksandra Shatskikh refers it to the philosopher Nikolai Berdiaev's article on Picasso. Shatskikh, "Teoreticheskoe i literaturnoe nasledstvo Kazimira Malevicha," in *Kazimir Malevich. Zhivopis' i teoriia,* eds. Dmitrii Sarabianov and Shatskikh (Moscow: Iskusstvo, 1993), p. 180.

Cf.: "Cubism is an art that pulverizes and turns a sum or sums of old conclusions into units of equal strength in order to deduce from them a new economic material conclusion." See "On New Systems in Art" (1919), in *Malevich I*, p. 117. The translation here is ours.

[74] The Itinerants (or Wanderers)—a group of Russian painters of the second half of the 19th century, who rejected the classicism of the Russian Academy to shape a new national artistic idiom, realistic and socially meaningful. Regarding art as a vehicle for humanitarian and social ideas, they formed, in 1870, a Society of Itinerant Exhibitions, and organized traveling shows in an effort to address and edify the people. Their works enjoyed considerable popularity and formed the main body of the collection of S. M. Tret'iakov. The Tret'iakov Gallery (donated by the owner to the city of Moscow in 1892 and nationalized in 1918) played a major role in solidifying the Itinerant oeuvre and in turning a number of Itinerant paintings into popular iconic images—

points of visual reference known to every educated Russian. Malevich's negative appraisal of Russian realist painting is consistent with the spirit and letter of the earlier attacks on the Itinerants, castigated by all vanguard movements in Russia, particularly the Futurists, in the first years of the 20th century—yet it is not, as may seem, outdated. On the one hand, the influential Association of Artists of Revolutionary Russia (AKhRR), founded in 1922, re-actualized the legacy of the Itinerants as a successor to their aesthetic platform. (The Society of Itinerant Exhibitions merged with the AKhRR in 1923.) On the other hand, the medium of film exhibited, from Malevich's point of view, a retrograde tendency, linking it with the "archival" painting of the Itinerants rather than with the latest non-objective developments in visual art. The question of the Itinerant legacy continued to be debated throughout the 1920s. The Formalist scholar and critic Viktor Shklovskii compared the contribution of the Itinerants to art to the way in which "a bullet stuck in the chest partakes in the life of the body." See Shklovskii, "O fakture i kontrrel'efakh" (1920), in Shklovskii, *Gamburgskii schet: Stat'i—vospominaniia—esse, 1914–1933* (Moscow: Sovetskii pisatel', 1990), p. 99.

75 To describe a major artistic practice of Cubism, Malevich initially used the term 'dissonance' or 'discord': "As to the painted planes in Cubism. They were not ends in themselves, but rather their painted forms served for dissonance." Cf. his pamphlet of 1915 "From Cubism to Suprematism in Art," in Douglas, *Swans of Other Worlds*, p. 110.

76 Possibly, the label of the chocolate brand Sarotti.

77 A triangle was the trademark of the Leningrad Factory of Rubber Products.

78 A brand of glue.

79 "Skorokhod"—the name of a Soviet footwear factory (meaning 'a fast walker').

And Visages are Victorious on the Screen

The article appeared in *Kinozhurnal ARK* 10 (1925): 7–9 and was reprinted in *SS 1*, pp. 289–294. Published in *Malevich I*, pp. 226-232, as "And Images Triumph on the Screens," translated by Xenia Glowacki-Prus.

[80] The article was printed with this editorial subtitle as part of a discussion triggered by an intense polemic between Dziga Vertov and Sergei Eisenstein upon the release of Eisenstein's film *The Strike* (see "Malevich in the Movies," p. 15). In the opening sentence, Malevich refers to an article by Boris Arvatov, who also responded to the polemic. See Arvatov, "'Agit-Kino' i 'Kino-Glaz'," *Kinozhurnal ARK* 8 (1925): 3–4.

[81] Production art—a concept developed by Russian Constructivists. Rejecting art for art's sake, the group suggested to transfer "art into production" and to design new artistic forms of life for a new society. The group was led by such theoreticians as Boris Arvatov and the artists El Lissitzky and Aleksandr Rodchenko.

[82] Dziga Vertov declared in his first manifesto "We": "The death of 'film' is necessary for the life of art. We call for the acceleration of its death." *Kino-Fot* 1 (1922): 11–12; for the English translation see *FF*, p. 69. In his second manifesto "The Cine-Eyes. A Revolution," he reiterated: "The death sentence pronounced by the cine-eyes on all films without exception is still valid." See *LEF* 3 (1923): 137; English translation in *FF*, p. 91. Newsreels and issues of *Cine-Pravda* made by Vertov's group in 1918–1923, as well as his film *The Cine-Eye* (1924), were expressly conceived as 'non-art.'

[83] The text in square brackets was excluded from the original publication and restored by Shatskikh from the author's manuscript, currently in the Stedelijk Museum's Archive. See *SS 1*, pp. 372–373.

[84] For Malevich, materialist consciousness is linked with abstract expression and religious consciousness, with the realm of the image (painting). He illustrates the difference between the two by referring to Lenin's cult created after his death. See his treatise *Lenin. From the Book on Non-Objectivity* first published by El Lissitzky in his own translation in the German journal *Kunstblatt* 10 (1924): 289–293. Published in Russian in *SS 2*, pp. 25–29, in English *Malevich III*, pp. 315–341.

[85] Malevich uses the camel metaphor rather frequently in his writings, introducing it in 1915 in his pamphlet *From Cubism to Suprematism in Art: To the New Realism of Painting, to Absolute Creation*: "The art of painting, sculpture, the word, was up until now, a camel loaded with all kinds of rubbish of odalisques, with Egyptian and Persian kings, with Solomons, Salomés, princes, princesses, and their favorite little dogs, with desire, and the fornication of Venuses."

For the English translation see Douglas, *Swans of Other Worlds*, p. 107. The subsequent shift from exoticism to usefulness in Malevich's imagery of 'camel art' ironically responds to the theory of 'production art.' See also "Cinema, Gramophone...," p. 64.

[86] See note 74.

[87] Malevich's term for the main principle of Cubism (see note 75), used here to describe Eisenstein's montage.

[88] Malevich refers to a frame from Czesław Sabinski's film *The Black Heart* reproduced in *Kinozhurnal ARK* 8 (1925): 10. Discussing the frame against the film's "medieval and mystical" title and German painting of the 1860s, Malevich reinvents the implications of the actual film, which he may or may not have seen. *The Black Heart* was devoted to the Donbass miners and their heroic 'fight for coal' during the occupation of Ukraine by the White Army.

[89] Vladimir Gardin's film depicted the schemes of the Catholic clergy, implicated in murders and espionage, in a provincial town in Soviet Western Ukraine. Contemporary Russian critics regarded it as a 'Gothic' picture owing to its gloomy atmosphere of mystery, as well as the dominating presence of a Catholic cathedral—a set built in the studio, lavish and uncommonly expensive for the Soviet film practices of the time. In all likelihood, Malevich had not seen *Cross and Mauser*: his obscure and probably mistaken reference to "Boston and Cleveland" may have been prompted by a stylistic affinity between foreign 'Gothic' films and the frames reproduced in *Kinozhurnal ARK* 8 (1925): 4.

[90] Nikolai Kasatkin and Il'ia Repin were members of the Itinerants. Kasatkin, a secondary painter best known for his works depicting miners, joined AKhRR and was promoted by the authorities as an old realist master. Repin, a nationally revered artist, was celebrated for his critical treatment of contemporary subjects, as well as for his historical paintings and portraits. (After the Revolution he spent the rest of his life in his country house in Finland.) The paintings evoked by Malevich are Kasatkin's *Who is it?* (1898) and Repin's famous *He Returned Unexpected* (1884–1888). The two works rely on a similar narrative motif and compositional devices: a family grouped around a table is disturbed by the intrusion of an unexpected and psychologically estranged relative. In Kasatkin, it is a husband who discovers that during his long military service

his peasant wife gave birth to someone else's child. In Repin, it is a son, whom the artist's contemporaries saw as a political prisoner or exile, awkwardly reentering his middle-class world.

[91] *The Year 1905* was the initial title of Eisenstein's film *The Battleship Potemkin*. The frame referred to by Malevich [*Kinozhurnal ARK* 8 (1925): 7] was not included in the final version of the picture.

[92] The term 'shift' (*sdvig*), often used by the critics in the beginning of the century in connection with the new painting (see, e.g., Jane A. Sharp, "The Critical Reception of the 0.10 Exhibition: Malevich and Benua," in *The Great Utopia*, p. 42), became one of the central concepts of Russian Futurism. It is noteworthy that the Russian Futurist artists had originally introduced it by way of conceptualizing the painterly practices of European Cubism. In his essay on "Cubism" in 1912, the artist and poet David Burliuk observed that a "construction can be dislocated or shifted"; Cubism offers a "canon of shifted construction." 'Shifts' can be exercised in a variety of ways: there are surface and color shifts, as well as linear, general, or particular shifts. Burliuk believed that a "counterpoint to the academic canon" could be found in any epoch: "All barbaric folk arts partly rely on the existence of this second canon of shifted construction (Canon II)." See David Burluik, "Cubism (Surface-Plane)" in *Russian Art of the Avant-Garde: Theory and Criticism, 1902–1934*, ed. and transl. John Bowlt, revised and enlarged edition (London: Thames and Hudson, 1988), pp. 70–77. John Bowlt renders *sdvig* as 'displacement.'

'Shift' was established as a term largely owing to the poet Aleksei Kruchenykh. In the 1910s, Malevich was closely associated with Kruchenykh: they collaborated on the staging of the Futurist opera *Victory over the Sun* (1913) as well as on several Futurist editions: *Igra v adu* (St. Petersburg, 1914); *Tainye poroki akademikov* (Petrograd, 1916). While Kruchenykh applied the concepts of the 'shift' and 'word texture' (*faktura*) to verbal experimentation (cf. Kruchenykh, *Sdvigologiia v russkom stikhe* [Moscow, 1922]), Malevich elaborated the term 'shift' with regard to painterly surface-plane. He analyzed Cubist consciousness as operating in terms of shifts, which reveal on the surface a multiplicity of points of view and various temporal forms. See "On New Systems in Art" (1919), in *Malevich I*, pp. 115–118.

[93] Alongside 'shift' and 'texture,' *faktura* was one of the primary concepts of Russian artistic avant-garde. It was introduced by David Burliuk to enable a strictly painterly analysis of the "nature of the painting's surface" in opposition to the subject-oriented discourse of painting as a

"pile of anecdotes, facts"; cf. Burliuk, "Faktura," in *Poshchechina obshchestvennomu vkusu* (St. Petersburg: izdanie G.L. Kuz'mina, 1912), pp. 102–110. In the 1920s, *faktura* was adopted and adapted by the Constructivists to denote the organic qualities of different materials and, larger, physical objectivity, objectness, of the artifact, with an emphasis on its tactile properties and three-dimensionality. See Hubertus Gassner, "The Constructivists: Modernism on the Way to Modernization," in *The Great Utopia*, pp. 309–311. Russian Formalists expanded the concept to express the non-ideological essence of art's work with its material: in Viktor Shklovskii's words, "*Faktura* is the distinguishing feature of that separate world of specially designed things, which in their integrity we habitually call art." See "O fakture i kontrrel'efakh," in Shklovskii, *Gamburgskii schet*, p. 99. Malevich, who found the Constructivist emphasis on the material exaggerated out of proportion (see his letter to Moholy-Nagy, p. 60), borrowed the term 'texture' for his writings on film. The context suggests that Malevich associates the 'texture of the frame' with peculiarities of lighting and light's interaction with the canvas-screen: it reminds him of the Impressionist painting. Cf. "The Artist and the Cinema," p. 49.

94 Malevich brings together a bucolic Itinerant landscape, *The Cranes are Flying* by Aleksei Stepanov (1891), and a topical painting of the AKhRR school, probably, a work by Efim Cheptsov, *Meeting of a Village Party Cell* (1924). The peasant, the cranes, the agitator, or the kitten mentioned in "Pictorial Laws..." (p. 83) are interchangeable figurative images of different periods. The 'agitator' picked out by Malevich was multiplied in the Soviet painting of the 1920s: cf. *V. I. Lenin's Speech at the Putilovskii Factory in May 1917* by Isaak Brodskii (1926), *Listening to the Agitator* by David Shterenberg (1927), *Communists' Visit to a Village* by Sergei Gerasimov (1927), among others.

95 Arvatov stated: "In addition to Agit-Film and Cine-Eye one more cinematic art is needed—experimental film. In addition to agitation and display we need to develop demonstration reshaping everyday life, a kind of laboratory of new, currently invented forms processed through film montage (clothes, architecture, furniture, gesture, and so on)." See "'Agit-Kino' i 'Kino-Glaz'," p. 4.

96 The name Malevich suggests for the new science of film, *kinology*, refers to his other coinage, *izology*: a science that was to study the "principles of different artistic schools" (from the Russian abbreviation 'izo' for visual arts, *izobrazitel'nye isskustva*). *Izology* would concern itself with

deviations from the 'norm' that occur in the 'organism' of the painter or in the 'body' of a work of art, and the fluid interconnection between the conscious and the subconscious. See Malevich's series of articles for the journal *Nova generaciia in SS 2*, pp. 129–271. *Kinology* is enveloped in similar physiological associations (catarrh, pharmacy). In addition to *biology* (and other sciences that retain their Greek root in Russian) it brings to mind another contemporary coinage, 'pedology': a science studying ways and methods of influencing the child's psyche, which was actively developed by Soviet psychologists in the 1920s under a strong impact of psychoanalysis.

[97] In his manifesto "We," Vertov wrote: "We are *purging* the cine-eye of its hangers-on, of music, literature, and theater... We invite you—away—from the sweet embraces of the romance, from the poison of the psychological novel, from the clutches of the theater of adultery, with your backsides to music, away, into the open, into the four dimensional space." See *FF*, p. 69.

[98] Malevich evokes one of the most popular fables by the Russian poet Ivan Krylov, "The Monkey and the Eyeglasses." The monkey image appears in other texts by Malevich, e.g., "The Secret Vices of Academicians" (1916) in *SS 1*, p. 56.

THE ARTIST AND THE CINEMA

The article was published in *Kinozhurnal ARK* 2 (1926): 15–17, with the following editorial comment: "The editorial board does not agree with a number of opinions expressed by the author, in particular, with opinions regarding the question of abstract art." Reprinted in *SS 1*, pp. 295–299. Translated by Xenia Glowacki-Prus for *Malevich I*, pp. 233–238.

[99] Silent films were colored by non-photographic methods, such as hand-coloring of individual frames. Another technique allowed to make monochrome segments to express a particular mood (the blue color was used for night scenes, red for 'passionate' sequences). Monochrome stock was created by 'tinting' the film base or by 'toning' the emulsion (bathing the film in chemical salts). The problem of color in cinema was widely discussed in Soviet film publications. Cf. *Sovetskii ekran* 21 (1925).

100 In the Soviet release, the film *Dorothy Vernon* with Mary Pickford was entitled *The Reefs of Life*. The action of this costume drama was based on the struggle between Mary Stuart and Queen Elizabeth, with the heroine, Dorothy Vernon, taking the side of the latter.

101 Malevich questions the programmatic concept of Dziga Vertov, the cine-eye (which became his designation of the cameraman, the name of his film group, and the title of his film of 1924). Cine-eye epitomized Vertov's understanding of film as a new means of perception afforded by the camera's mechanical vision. "Our starting point is: the use of the camera as a cine-eye, more perfect than the human eye, for examining the chaos of visual phenomena that fill the space. The cine-eye lives and moves in time and space, it perceives and fixes the impressions in a completely different way from that of the human eye." See "The Cine-Eyes. A Revolution," in *FF*, p. 91. On Malevich's own (negative) view of mechanized vision, see "Malevich in the Movies," p. 19, and note 104 below.

102 Mentioning three Russian artists of the 19th century alongside world-famous masters, Malevich seems to imply that through their paintings, some of which have become fixed in the national visual memory and consciousness as emblems of 'Russianness,' they have exercised an influence on the Russian 'vision of nature' comparable to that exerted by Rubens and Monet on Western visual idiom. Many of Vasilii Perov's popular genre works, such as *Bird catchers* (1870), *Hunters at Rest* (1871), and *Troika* (1866), represent human figures in an outdoor setting, humorously or dramatically. Vasilii Polenov's celebrated lyrical landscapes are *Courtyard in Moscow* (1878) and *Overgrown Pond* (1879). Ivan Shishkin's paintings *Rye* (1878) and *Morning in Pine Forest* (1889) commonly appear in school textbooks as the 'images of the motherland.'

103 Itinerants, see note 74.

104 Malevich describes the lens of the camera—both the film camera and photographic camera—as 'dead' in several texts. Cf. "I have never approved of or supported the *dead* mechanical mirror of the photographic lens" in his letter to Moholy-Nagy (p. 59). More striking is his perception of the eye as a dead lens, based on the assumption that only painting, *zhivopis'*, offers a different, live, system of vision: "The eye-ball of every human being is a *dead lens* projecting circumstances on the mirror-*negative* of the brain..." See note 10.

[105] Malevich's image of artificial kisses is close, in wording and in concept, to Vertov's contemporaneous demand to get away from the "factory of kisses and doves," cf. "Factory of Facts" (1926), in *FF*, pp. 150–151. Film industry of the 1920s was described in similar terms by several authors: as a "rubber" and "pneumatic" world by Malevich; as a world of cheap substitutes imitating expensive 'authentic' materials by Siegfried Kracauer in his essay "Calico-World: The UFA City in Neubabelsberg" (1926). See *The Mass Ornament: Weimar Essays*, transl. and ed. Thomas Y. Levin (Cambridge, Mass.: Harvard University Press, 1995), pp. 281–288. The variety of rubber referred to by Malevich in the Russian original, gutta-percha, valued for its extreme elasticity, was commonly used for fabricating masks, toys, and mannequins: thus, his image also evokes the world of rubber imitating live human body and, ultimately, points to the toy-like quality of silent cinema. Vertov also described film as a world of "toys," "mechanical dolls" (cf. "Film, Fiction, Drama, and the Cine-Eye: A Speech [given at the ARK, 9 June 1924]" in *FF*, p. 115), and Kracauer made the same point: "This [that is film's] world is like a child's toy" (op. cit., p. 281).

[106] In its opening issue in 1922 the journal *Kino-Fot* informed its readers about recent experiments in abstract film by publishing Ludwig Hilberseimer's article entitled "Dynamic Painting." Later, Malevich could have seen some of the works discussed in the article: in January 1926 the writer Ilya Ehrenburg brought back from Paris several experimental films, including *Entre'acte* by René Clair and Francis Picabia, *Le ballet mécanique* by Fernand Léger, and *Cinq minutes du cinéma pur* by Henri Chomette, which were shown in Moscow in the Khudozhestvennyi movie theater.

[107] In 1925, *Sovetskii ekran* initiated a discussion of set design and the artist's work in the cinema, which continued throughout the year. The discussion was centered on several films of German Expressionism and the French picture *L'Inhumaine* by Marcel L'Herbier, considered as examples of the established artists' contribution to the cinematic endeavor. Set designs for *L'Inhumaine* were executed by the modernist architect Robert Mallet-Stevens and the painter Fernand Léger, who also designed the sets for Darius Milhaud's *La creation du monde* staged by the Swedish Ballet in Paris in the same year. Two Russian films made in 1925 were commonly regarded as a response to this artistic tendency in European cinema. One was Iakov Protazanov'a *Aelita* with sets built by the experienced stage designer Isaak Rabinovich, and costumes created by the avant-garde artist Aleksandra Ekster, a collaborator of Aleksandr Tairov's Kamernyi Theater. The

other film was Vladimir Gardin's *Cross and Mauser*, whose celebrated 'Gothic' décor was designed by Dmitrii Kolupaev (see also note 89).

ART AND THE PROBLEM OF ARCHITECTURE. SCRIPT FOR AN ARTISTIC-SCIENTIFIC FILM

The script was drafted in Germany in 1927. The inconsistently numbered manuscript, written on three sheets of paper (32.5 x 20.7 cm), contains drawings in colored and black pencils.
Originally in the von Riesen family archive, it is presently in the Czwiklitzer private collection, Baden-Baden. The text appeared in print for the first time in *Moskau—Berlin, Berlin—Moskau 1900–1950*, p. 306.

[108] Cf. the anthology *Die Kunstismen, Les Isms de l'art, The Isms of Art, 1924–1914*, ed. El Lissitzky and Hans Arp (Erlenbach, München, Leipzig, 1925), which presented Cubism, Futurism, Expressionism, Simultaneism, Dadaism, Purism, Neoplasticism, Constructivism, absolute film, abstract and metaphysical art, and Lissitzky's Proun. Malevich introduced Suprematism.

PAINTING AND PHOTOGRAPHY. A LETTER TO LÁSZLÓ MOHOLY-NAGY

The original is in the von Riesen collection in Stedelijk Museum, Amsterdam. First published in English as "Letter to Moholy-Nagy" in Xenia Hoffmann's translation in *Malevich IV*, pp. 157–159. The letter was written in response to the article by Ernst Kallai "Malerei und Photographie" (Painting and Photography), which appeared in the journal of European Constructivists published in Amsterdam. See *i 10* 4 (1927): 148–157; reprint ed. A. Muller Lehning (Nendeln· Kraus, 1979). Moholy-Nagy initiated a discussion around Kallai's article; his own introduction to it was followed by contributions from Adolf Behne, Max Burchartz, Will Grohmann, Vasily Kandinsky, Ludwig Kassak, Piet Mondrian, and Georg Muche. The discussion closed with Kallai's response in *i 10* 6 (1927): 227–237. Malevich's letter remained unpublished.

[109] Drawing a distinction between photography and painting in terms of different approaches to texture, Kallai remarked: "The painter has an option to make the form of his work justified by a

calculable regularity; to bring its texture down to the smoothness of a polished or enameled surface. Works of this kind are quite numerous (Mondrian, Malevich, Moholy-Nagy, Lissitzky, Buchheister, and so on); despite certain mechanistic inclinations of the artists and their occasional theoretical stings at art, these are works of painting, sometimes magnificent painting." See op. cit., p. 149.

[110] Kallai discussed not exactly 'perception' but rather "tactile experience of reality" ("stoffliche Wirklichkeitsempfindungen," p. 152), associating 'material' with 'matter' in this context. Cf. Malevich's remark in "Suprematism" (1925): "The way Suprematism approaches materials is the exact opposite of the currently swelling propaganda for the culture of the material. This is an aesthetic question, treatment of the material's surface has become an obsession of modern painters." See *SS 2*, p. 34.

CINEMA, GRAMOPHONE, RADIO, AND ARTISTIC CULTURE

The article was written in 1928 and sent to the journal *Kino-Front*, which rejected it with the following comment: "The author's formalist approach to art and the ideas he advocates are not acceptable for publication. Manuscript declined. 16 April 1928. Signature (indistinct)." The manuscript, preserved by Anna Leporskaia (1900–1982), Malevich's collaborator at the GINKhUK, has not appeared in print in Russian. We are indebted to Troels Andersen, who has published the article in English as "The Cinema, Gramophone, Radio and Artistic Culture" (in *Malevich IV*, pp. 63–176, translated by Xenia Hoffmann), for courteously providing the Russian original for the present publication.

[111] A reference to V. I. Lenin's remark in a dialogue with Anatolii Lunacharskii in 1922 as reproduced in Grigorii Boltianskii's collection *Lenin and Film* (Moscow, Leningrad, 1925), p. 19.

[112] The designation of film as the 'great mute' was widely adopted in the early 20th century in Russian, Polish, and French popular criticism but did not take root in the English-speaking countries.

[113]See note 85.

[114] 'Cineresque' is a typical Malevichian coinage with several connotations. It refers, on the one hand, to the French word *pittoresque* (picturesque)—a popular name of movie theaters and cafés in Russia in the beginning of the 20th century. On the other hand, it evokes the 'arabesque' and thus serves as a denotation of a genre: a pretty and empty moving picture.

[115] Robert Lovelace, a character in Samuel Richardson's novel *Clarissa Harlowe* (1747–1748) widely read in Russia in the 19th century, came to denote a philanderer and outlived the popularity of his no-longer-remembered source. The characteristic of film as a "deaf and mute Lovelace" resembles the erotic phraseology in Vertov's critique of cinema (see note 105).

[116] The term 'plastic dances' was broadly applied in Russia to various trends in modern (non-classical) dance—from the 'barefoot dance' of Isadora Duncan, whose school existed in Moscow from 1921 to 1949, to Jacques-Dalcroze's eurhythmics, which prompted the foundation of the Institutes of Rhythm in Moscow and Petrograd in 1919, to the German *Ausdruckstanz*.

[117] Malevich may be referring to Vertov's pronouncements on theater and film (see note 82). The relationship of the stage and the cinema had been consistently debated in the Soviet press between 1924 and 1928, see, e.g., the editorial article "Theater or Cinema?" in the journal *Zhizn' iskusstva* (*FF*, pp. 125–128). The discussion provoked conflicting points of view, for the participants differed in their understanding of 'theatricality.' For the critic Vladimir Blium 'bad theatricality' was exemplified by the *bourgeois* films of German Expressionism, from whose influence the *proletarian* cinema had to be protected. See "Against the Theater of Fools—For Film," in *FF*, pp. 116–120. The film director Abram Room called for purging film from the presence of theater on the grounds of vast differences in acting technique. See "Cinema and Theater," in *FF*, pp. 128–129. The artistic director of the Leningrad Film Studio Adrian Piotrovskii defended the 'cinefication' of contemporary stage (*FF*, pp. 178–180), while Sergei Eisenstein declared film a natural phase in the evolution of modern theater because film was capable of carrying out most completely the project of radical transformation of artistic practice initiated by the stage, namely, montage of short fragments freed from spatial-temporal causality, staging of mass spectacles, manipulation of the audience's psyche, and so on. See "Two Skulls of Alexander the Great," *Novyi Zritel'* 35 (1926): 10.

[118] Coupling the names of Briullov and Benois, Malevich associates two artists of different periods who have little in common, and whose respective contributions to stage design are hardly

commensurate. Karl Briullov's occasional theater projects were few and little-known; Alexandre Benois's consistent work for the stage was acclaimed as important and innovative. Referring his vehement opponent Benois to the first half of the 19th century, Malevich exposes and mocks the antiquated essence of his artistic pseudo-novelty. Yet the humorous verbal gesture, prompted in all likelihood by the sound similarity of the two 'foreign' names of French origin, also reveals a more profound connection between the two artists. In their artistic culture and vision, both Briullov and Benois remain organically linked to the classical heritage of Italy and France, and their academic orientation, further emphasized by the reference to the classicist laurels and un-acceptable for Malevich, denotes the 'foreignness' of this legacy to modern art.

[119] "World of Art" (*Mir iskusstva*)—a group of Petersburg artists who aspired to achieve a synthesis of new modernist West-European trends and stylized elements of traditional Russian folk art. Their journal of the same name, published in 1899–1904 in St. Petersburg by Alexandre Benois, Leon Bakst, and Serge Diaghilev, attacked the realist Itinerant Society and Russian Academy, and exercised particular influence on stage design.

[120] In Russian, the phrase "faces of the acting elements" contains a complex play on words. Using two meanings of the word *litso*, 'face' and 'person,' Malevich 'deconstructs' the Russian expression for *dramatis personae* and reassembles it to produce a quasi-scientific term for the actor: the 'acting element.' Similarly, in the immediately following paragraph Malevich refers to the actor as the 'moving element,' to emphasize both his mobility against the static stage design and his subordination, as part of that design, to the unifying will of the artist.

PICTORIAL LAWS IN CINEMATIC PROBLEMS

Originally published in the journal *Kino i kul'tura* 7–8 (1929): 22–26. The article had remained unnoticed by scholars for many years because the author's name was indicated by a wrong initial: W. Malevich. The following comment was appended to Malevich's text: "The editorial board, while it disagrees with comrade Malevich on several issues, finds that the problem of ap-plying the laws of painting to film raised in his article deserves close attention, as well as time and effort, in order to understand to what extent painting is relevant to cinema." Reprinted in *SS 1*, pp. 301–306.

[121] Malevich's last 'brochure' that came out in Russia in his lifetime was his pamphlet *God is Not Cast Down: Art, Factory, and Church* (Vitebsk: UNOVIS, 1922). See *Malevich I*, pp. 188–223.

[122] See note 117.

[123] See note 74.

[124] The society of the Itinerants included two brothers Makovskii, Konstantin and Vladimir, known primarily for their genre paintings of peasant and urban middle-class life. Eisenstein's film probably brought to Malevich's mind the works of Vladimir Makovskii, which often relied on a juxtaposition of sharply delineated social 'types.' In particular, several frames from *The Battleship Potemkin*, initially entitled *1905*, could have reminded Malevich of VI. Makovskii's painting *9 January 1905 on Vasil'evskii Island* (1905). In the painting, a crowd of demonstrators broken up by a police attack serves as a background for the frontal image of a man stripping his chest bare in a desperate gesture. Calling Eisenstein's frames "Itinerant pictures," Malevich plays on the Russian words for 'itinerant' and 'moving' derived from the same root: from *Itinerant* pictures to *moving* pictures there is but one step.

[125] See note 75.

[126] Vertov was fired from his job at the Sovkino on December 31, 1926. His *Man with the Movie Camera* sparked, in 1929, stormy debates in the press. See "Malevich in the Movies," p. 25.

[127] 'Additional' or 'supplementary' element is Malevich's term central to his analytical system. In 1923–26 Malevich formulated a theory of the additional element in painting, which he understood as a dynamical element deforming the static norms of both representation and perception. See note 12.

[128] The French critic and writer Camille Mauclair was the author of numerous articles and books on French painting, one of which, *L'Impressionisme* (1904), was translated into Russian in 1908. In the journal publication his name was given erroneously as *Meler*. Quoting Mauclair in his article on Cézanne published in *Nova generaciia* in 1929, Malevich called him *Molière* (*SS 2*, p. 151).

[129] The description of Cézanne as a weaver has correspondences in other texts by Malevich and may also be traced back to Mauclair. In *L'Impressionisme*, Mauclair discussed Cézanne as a painter resembling, in his unsophisticated austerity, a medieval artisan (Paris: Librarie de l'art

ancien et moderne, 1904, p. 152) and in his later and more acerbic *L'art indépendant français sous la Troisiéme République* blamed him for the overall degradation of painting from a picture to a rug, *un tapis*, which had substituted all painterly investigation of human life and psychology by a composition of color planes (Paris: La Renaissance du Livre, 1919, pp. 26–27, 33–34). Cf. the polemical structure of Malevich's phrase: "a weaver not of stories but of painting." In his treatise *The World as Non-Objectivity*, Malevich compares different schools of painting in terms of the "structure and texture of the painterly body," the weaving of the color (*Malevich III*, p. 66). The parallel frequently drawn in Malevich's texts between the screen and the canvas not as a surface where the image rests but as a space which it penetrates, also implicitly relies on the analogy with weaving. See, for example, "The Artist and the Cinema" where the future arrival of color in film is discussed as enabling the film artist to "weave painterly planes of textures" (p. 49).

[130] See note 92.

[131] "The man who edited the film" was Vertov's wife and assistant Elizaveta Svilova (1900–1975), who had begun her career in cinema as an editor in the Pathé studio and subsequently worked in the Moscow Film Committee. She edited almost all of Vertov's films. In *The Man with the Movie Camera* she is shown editing the film, while Vertov's brother, the cameraman Mikhail Kaufman, appears on the screen as the 'man with the movie camera.' Malevich, who was perfectly aware of Svilova's role, humorously refers to her as the "*man* who edited the film" to evoke the picture's title and concept.

[132] An allusion to Eisenstein's film *The Old and the New*, released in August 1929 but already shown in March to the 'inner circle.'

[133] Walter Ruttmann's film was released in the USSR in 1928, one year before Vertov's *Man with the Movie Camera*, which was regarded by Soviet critics as an imitation. Upon the release of Vertov's film in Berlin, the German critics also treated the picture as modeled after Ruttmann's, and Vertov sent a letter of protest to *Frankfurter Rundschau*. The newspaper's film critic Siegfried Kracauer compared the two films and preferred Vertov's (*Frankfurter Rundschau*, 12 May 1929). The Soviet director's letter was published, with Kracauer's help, in the evening issue of 12 July 1929.

ANNA MUZA

WEAVING TEXTS: A NOTE ON MALEVICH'S USES OF LANGUAGE

[134] See Christina Lodder, "The Transition to Constructivism," in *The Great Utopia*, pp. 271–272.

[135] Bowlt, "Kazimir Malevich and the Energy of Language," in *Kazimir Malevich, 1878–1935* (Los Angeles: The Armand Hammer Museum of Art and Cultural Center in association with the University of Washington Press, 1990), p. 182.

KAM³

Казимир Малевич

Белый прямоугольник

Статьи о кино

Составитель Оксана Булгакова

ПотемкинПресс
Берлин • Сан-Франциско

Впервые опубликовано в 1997 году в Германии
© «ПотемкинПресс», Берлин · Сан-Франциско, 1997, 2002

Малевич, Казимир
Белый прямоугольник. Статьи о кино
Несимметричное издание на двух языках
Составление и предисловие Оксана Булгакова
Комментарии Оксана Булгакова и Анна Муза
Графическое оформление Грегор Хохмут, impulsio.com

ISBN 3-9804989-7-2

Издательство приносит благодарность
—Трельсу Андерсену, Силькеборг, Дания, любезно предоставившему нам текст
«Кино, граммофон, радио и художественная культура»

—семье Чвиклицер, Баден-Баден/Париж, любезно позволившей нам опубликовать
сценарий «Живопись и проблемы архитектуры»

—Стеделик музеум, Амстердам, за разрешение на публикацию письма Малевича
Ласло Мохой-Надю

PRINTED IN THE UNITED STATES OF AMERICA
www.PotemkinPress.com

Содержание

Оксана Булгакова

Малевич в кино — изология «динамических ощущений» и «пневматических поцелуев»

Что общего между Казимиром Малевичем (1878—1935), пророком беспредметности, освобожденного Ничто, и кино, механическим хранителем «бытовой требухи» и «базарной сутолоки»[1] жизни? Еще в 1924 году Малевич писал о кино, ссылаясь на Ленина, как системе, «фиксирующей действительность вне художественного вымысла»,[2] потому что оно — как наука и религия в его представлении — опирается на конкретность и лишено зрения, то есть бессильно увидеть подлинное, между тем как искусство — абстрактно.[3] Тем не менее, между 1925 и 1929 годами Малевич публикует четыре статьи о кино, которые становятся — как ни парадоксально — *последними* выступлениями художника, взгляды которого объявляются реакционными и мистическими,[4] в русской печати.[5] Эссе «Кино, граммофон, радио и художественная культура» (1928) отклоняется редакцией, как не печатается и короткий текст об отношениях фотографии и живописи, адресованный Ласло Мохой-Надю. Обе рукописи были извлечены из архива и опубликованы Трельсом Андерсеном только в 1978 году.[6] Во французском[7] и начатом в 1995 году русском издании Малевича эти тексты отсутствуют, как и его сценарий «художественно-научного фильма», переживший бомбежки Второй мировой войны в подвале одного берлинского дома. Он был представлен на нескольких выставках, но воспроизводился в каталогах как факсимиле[8] — без расшифровки текста.[9] Возможно, эти семь текстов не исчерпывают всего написанного Малевичем о кино, но поскольку архив его до сих пор не собран, наше небольшое издание на сегодняшний день наиболее полно.

Взгляды Малевича на кино парадоксальны. Он не только отрицает целесообразность миметических способностей кинематографа, что не удивительно как жест родоначальника абстрактного искусства, но и сомневается в том, что кино способно передать динамику и новое зрение, отмежевываясь от представлений футуристов и конструктивистов.

Недоверие Малевича шло не от незнания предмета. Он был не просто близко знаком с режиссерами, радикально реформирующими язык кино — Сергеем Эйзенштейном и Гансом Рихтером, но, судя по его текстам, часто ходил в кино как «обычный» зритель и видел достаточно много — при этом не только фильмы советского левого авангарда, но и развлекательное «зриво» — мелодрамы с Мери Пикфорд, комедии с Монти Бенксом, Игорем Ильинским и датскими комиками Патом и Паташоном. Более того, его тексты свидетельствуют о том, что он был в курсе дебатов о кино, часто служащих импульсом для написания его собственных статей, в которых он использует ходкие идиомы советской прессы. (А в текстах о живописи он часто обращается к метафорам из области кино и фотографии.[10]) Однако проблемы, обсуждаемые им в кино-статьях, связаны с аналитической работой по исследованию изобразительного искусства, которой Малевич занимался экспериментально сначала в Витебске, потом в Петрограде в качестве директора и руководителя одной из пяти секций Института художественной культуры. На новом поле приложения — кино — Малевич проверяет свои гипотезы — теорию прибавочного элемента и эволюционную модель модернизма. Первую концепцию он разрабатывает в 1923—26 годах. Сам термин кажется заимствованным у Маркса,[11] но исследует область Фрейда — взаимодействие сознания и бессознательного в художественной деятельности. Прибавочный элемент, под которым Малевич чаще всего понимает динамику, изменяет установившийся порядок связи «сознания и подсознания», рефлексы движения, он переструктурирует восприятие и художественный мир живописца, разрушая норму репрезентации.[12] Цикл лекций по современному искусству, прочитанный им в 1928—30 годах на педагогическом факультете киевского художественного института,[13] должен был заложить основание новой науки — *изологии*,[14] исследовавшей эволюцию визуальной культуры через историю изобразительных искусств — от импрессионизма до супрематизма. Тексты о кино включают новые формы — плакат, фотографию и

фильм — в поле этой культуры. Преемственность терминов, которые Малевич использует в своих теоретических работах о живописи и в статьях о кино, свидетельствует об этой связи — вплоть до образа верблюда, который на картинах академиков тащит на себе «одалисок, Египетских и Персидских царей Соломонов и Саломей»,[15] в кино же используется для перевозки «барахла быта».

К истории текстов

Первые статьи о кино пишутся в мае—июне 1925 года, как раз в это время Малевич знакомится с Сергеем Эйзенштейном. С начала двадцатых годов Малевич делит дачу в Немчиновке под Москвой со старым другом, профессиональным революционером Кириллом Шутко. С ним он познакомился в 1904—05 году в Москве. Шутко, посещавший позже частную актерскую школу Александра Адашева и студию Мейерхольда, работал в подполье социал-демократической партии. После революции Шутко занимал важные посты в партаппарате, связанные с кино: работал в Агитпропе, руководил издательством «Теакинопечать», входил в редколлегии киножурналов, с 1927 года был референтом по кино и искусству в отделе пропаганды ЦК, а после этого руководил отделом искусства при Госплане.

В начале двадцатых годов Шутко был женат на Нине Агаджановой, тоже профессиональной революционерке, которая писала сценарий фильма «1905 год» — к двадцатилетию первой русской революции. Сценарий должен был ставить молодой режиссер, которому Шутко покровительствовал: Сергей Эйзенштейн (называвший Шутко «серым кардиналом»). Решение о передаче именно ему этого важного госзаказа было принято специальной комиссией, куда входили и Шутко, и Малевич. На их общей даче Эйзенштейн работал с Ниной над планом юбилейного фильма, который станет «Броненосцем Потемкиным», и одновременно писал с Исааком Бабелем другой сценарий по «Одесским рассказам» — «Беня Крик». Как и Малевич, Эйзенштейн был чрезвычайно заинтересован аналитическим исследо-

ванием механизмов воздействия искусства и разрабатывал свою собственную теорию, называемую им в этот период «монтажом аттракционов», которая опиралась на психоанализ, рефлексологию и марксизм. Эйзенштейн пришел в кино после незаконченной учебы на гражданского инженера и с опытом театрального художника, находившегося под явным влиянием кубизма, но учившегося у Любови Поповой, первого конструктивистского сценографа в России.

О знакомстве с создателем «Черного квадрата» Эйзенштейн пишет мемуарный очерк, датированный апрелем 1939 года, в котором, однако, не упоминает ни рассказы Малевича о постановке футуристической оперы «Победа над солнцем»,[16] ни его теории. Вместо этого Эйзенштейн вспоминает физическую силу и — способность к насилию художника, воспроизводя его рассказы о сексуальной мощи ослов и кровавой мести избившим его деревенским парням, которым он раздробил руки и выбил зубы.[17] Возможно, что Эйзенштейн, подписавший декларацию Ассоциации Революционной Кинематографии, устраивавшей еженедельные дебаты по отдельным фильмам и общим вопросам кино, подтолкнул Малевича принять участие в одном из них, касавшемся непосредственно столкновения его самого, Эйзенштейна, с Вертовым. В органе Ассоциации, *Киножурнале АРК*, и печатаются между 1925 и 1926 годами три текста художника, которые всегда снабжаются редакционным примечанием «в порядке дискуссии».

Сценарий и текст о фотографии и живописи пишутся в Германии. После закрытия Гинхука и увольнения в ноябре 1926 года Малевич просит о поездке за границу. Он уезжает 8 марта 1927 в Варшаву, 29 марта отправляется дальше, в Берлин, откуда едет на несколько дней в Дессау, в Баухаус, надеясь найти там работу. В доме Вальтера Гропиуса он знакомится с Ласло Мохой-Надем. Мохой-Надь руководит отделом кино и фотографии в журнале европейских конструктивистов *i 10*, который выходит в Амстердаме. Журнал ведет дискуссию об отношениях между новыми и старыми визуальными искусствами, между живописью и фото-

графией, вызванную статьей Эрнста Калаи, в которой по просьбе редакции участвуют Адольф Бене, Василий Кандинский, Пит Мондриан. Мохой-Надь предлагает Малевичу высказать свое мнение, но — не печатает его. Зато в книжной серии Баухауса, которой руководят Гропиус и Мохой-Надь, выходит книга Малевича «Мир как беспредметность».

В Берлине Малевич видит абстрактные фильмы и знакомится с режиссером Гансом Рихтером, работы которого вдохновляют его на написание сценария беспредметного фильма. «Он считал, что мы должны вместе осуществить эту его мечту», — писал Ганс Рихтер в 1966 году. «Несомненно, мы часто встречались, работая над проектом. Самое странное, что я, несмотря на то, что могу вспомнить многие мелочи давно ушедших лет, напрочь забыл о киноработе с Малевичем. Когда два года тому назад доктор Хафтман, занимавшийся изданием текстов Малевича из собрания фон Ризен,[18] спросил меня, что вышло из кинопроекта, задуманного с этим русским, я сначала вообще не мог вспомнить о подобном факте. Тем большим было мое удивление, когда в изданной книге я увидел цветные иллюстрации кинопартитуры с посвящением «фильм для Ганса Рихтера». Наше сотрудничество, должно быть, относилось к 1926—27 годам. С каким удовольствием я бы хотел в прошедшие сорок лет поработать над этим сценарием!»[19]

После возвращения из Германии Малевич работает в Государственном институте истории искусств, куда смогла спастись часть сотрудников Гинхука. В августе 1928 года Эйзенштейн просит его написать об отношениях между театром, кино и живописью. Эта проблема занимает его самого в связи с приходом в кино звука. Его появление провоцирует дискуссию о превращении обретшего свой язык немого искусства в «сфотографированный говорящий театр», в которой участвует и Эйзенштейн, резко критикуя в июне 1928 года архаизацию визуальной культуры в звуковом кино.[20] В августе того же года, во время гастролей труппы Кабуки в Москве, он пишет эссе, анализирующее принципиально иную работу с

акустическими и визуальными раздражителями в японском театре («Нежданный стык»).[21] Эйзенштейн думает о «захвате» редакции одного киножурнала и предлагает Малевичу сотрудничество в нем, но художник отвергает его предложение. В письме от 13 августа 1928 года, хранящемся в архиве Эйзенштейна, Малевич пишет, что он не согласен с перенятой Эйзенштейном линией «Маяковского левого АХРа» и поэтому в «их» журнал дать ничего не может.[22] Но статья на предложенную тему им уже написана в апреле — «Кино, граммофон, радио и художественная культура». Однако редакция *Кино-фронта*, наследника *Киножурнала АРК*, отвергает ее. Лишь год спустя журнал *Кино и культура*, заменивший *Советское кино* и *Кино-фронт*, печатает новую статью Малевича о кино. Его главным редактором был сценарист Петр Бляхин, в редакционной коллегии значилось имя Кирилла Шутко; журнал занимался, в основном, вопросами не культуры, но техники кино, проблемами пленки, цвета, звука, давая краткое содержание статей на немецком языке. Но именно этот текст Малевича выпал из внимания исследователей почти на шестьдесят лет, потому что был подписан «В. [W.] Малевич», из-за очевидной опечатки. Статья стала последней прижизненной публикацией художника в России.[23] В 1929 году он был уволен из института, осенью 1930 года арестован и подвергнут допросам. Его освобождение в декабре того же года приписывают заступничеству Шутко. Два драматических письма из их переписки 1930 года опубликованы недавно.[24] Малевич умер в 1935 году от рака печени. Шутко был арестован в 1937 и расстрелян годом позже.

Кино-дискуссии и кино-дискурс

Каждый текст Малевича вмешивается в сиюминутную газетно-журнальную полемику, но отсылает к двум полюсам: конкретному (и сегодня забытому) поводу и аспектам современной визуальной культуры, чье динамическое развитие автор пытается соотнести со своей гипотезой о генезисе модернизма, проецируемой им на три проблемы: мимезиса/абстракции, статики/кинетики и визуального восприятия в век оптических аппаратов.

К кино Малевич приближается через рассуждения о киноплакатах, то есть произведениях художника, которые представляют кино в облике современного города. Кстати, Малевич сам не сделал ни одного плаката. Часто приписываемый ему плакат к фильму Фрица Ланга *Доктор Мабузо* (так в оригинале!) — картина маслом, находящаяся в собрании Третьяковской галереи, скорее всего, принадлежит его ученику, Илье Чашнику. Его текст о киноплакатах — реакция специалиста на первую выставку киноплаката и представленный там анахронизм. Новое искусство — реклама и плакат — понимается как старая станковая живопись и развешивается в городе как в музейном зале. Малевич делится собранными в его секции наблюдениями над воздействием шрифта и формы клейма, соединением прямых и кривых, контрастом цветных плоскостей, размещением плакатов в городском пространстве. Но он не услышан. Вторая выставка киноплаката, которая была устроена годом позже в фойе московского Камерного театра, следовала тем же принципам развески и разверстки.

Мимезис, абстракция и кинематограф

Его второе эссе «И ликуют лики на экранах» обсуждает несостоявшуюся встречу между искусством и кино, несостоявшуюся потому, что Малевич понимает кино как этап развития современной живописи, основанной на принципах динамизма и беспредметности, в то время как снимаемые кинокартины возрождают отжившую миметическую традицию. *Конкретно* Малевич вмешивается в полемику между двумя режиссерами, Сергеем Эйзенштейном и Дзигой Вертовым, разгоревшуюся после выхода на экраны дебюта Эйзенштейна *Стачка* и первого полнометражного фильма Вертова *Киноглаз*. Оба режиссера — члены Левого фронта искусств, и их манифесты напечатаны в одном и том же, третьем, номере журнала *Леф* за 1923 год, где, кстати, опубликован и отрывок из текста Малевича «Супрематическое зеркало»!

Теперь Вертов обвиняет Эйзенштейна в плагиате (использовании в финале *Стачки* документальных съемок бойни, которую Вертов сделал своим объектом в *Киноглазе*) и «меньшевизме», в том, что Эйзенштейн, заимствуя все радикальные обновления *Киноглаза*, помогает утверждению суррогатов «искусства».[25] Эйзенштейн же заявляет, что Вертов — оппортунист, импрессионист и эстет, практикующий «искусство для искусства» и не заботящийся о его агитационной действенности.[26] Определения, взятые из риторики борьбы с политической оппозицией, должны помочь утверждению первенства того или другого на арене искусства, но доказательства первенства приходят из-за границы: в 1925 году на выставке декоративных искусств в Париже фильм Эйзенштейна получает золотую медаль, а фильм Вертова — серебряную. Борис Арватов, один из ведущих теоретиков Левого фронта, работавший вместе с Эйзенштейном в Пролеткульте, пытается примирить режиссеров, замечая, что и фильмы, и принципы обоих не так уж далеки друг от друга.[27] Малевич реагирует, собственно, на вмешательство Арватова, резко критиковавшего три года назад позиции Малевича,[28] и отмечает разницу в методах Вертова и Эйзенштейна. В то время, как Вертов работает с фактурой вещи, освобождая ее оптическими деформациями («сдвигами», произведенными камерой) от предметности, Эйзенштейн в композиции кадра достаточно традиционен и близок реалистической эстетике передвижников. Но он чувствует резче, чем Вертов, «закон контрастов». «Сдвиг», определяющий эстетику Вертова, является по Малевичу ядром футуристической поэтики, а закон контрастов — аналитический принцип столкновений плоскостей и направлений — формообразующий для кубизма. Этим термином Малевич описывает монтаж Эйзенштейна, для которого сам режиссер находит понятие «аттракцион», отсылающее к раздражению, рефлексу Павлова (что сродни представлению Вальтера Беньямина о действии потока кадров в кино как «шоке»[29]). Малевича интересует не

невротическое воздействие аттракциона, но закон формального построения, который он вписывает в свою теоретическую рамку.

Вертов не реагирует на статью Малевича. Эйзенштейн отвечает на нее четыре года спустя. «Рассуждать о живописности кадра в кино — наивно», пишет он в «Четвертом измерении в кино». — «Это под стать людям неплохой живописной культуры, но абсолютно неквалифицированным кинематографически. К такому типу рассуждений могут быть отнесены, например, высказывания о кино со стороны Казимира Малевича. Разбирать «кинокадрики» с точки зрения станковой живописи не станет сейчас ни один киномладенец».[30] Малевич не понимает основного принципа кино, считает Эйзенштейн, а именно того, что кадр не существует как единица восприятия, а осуществляется лишь в монтажной динамике. Поэтому Малевич остается — при всей заявленной приверженности к кинетике — в плену у статики, рассуждая о кино. Его понятие динамики — точка зрения живописца, у которого в распоряжении реально нет четвертого измерения. Еще более саркастически Эйзенштейн обращается с Малевичем во втором тексте, написанном в том же 1929 году по-немецки и адресованном не русской публике, а европейскому авангарду: «Драматургия киноформы».[31] Тут Эйзенштейн применяет по отношению к супрематисту его «теорию прибавочного элемента» — в обратном направлении. Прибавочный элемент вносит — по Малевичу — деформацию в статичные формы репрезентации, но стоит вычесть его, и сам Малевич превратится в немецкого нео-классицистического академика: «Гипертрофия целенаправленной инициативы — принципа рациональной логики — заставляет искусство околеть в математическом техницизме (пейзаж становится топографическим планом, «Св. Себастьян» — анатомическим атласом). Гипертрофия органической естественности — органической логики — размывает искусство в бесформенность (Малевич становится Каульбахом[32])...»[33] Однако атака Малевича заставляет Эйзенштейна сформулировать свои мысли о мимезисе в кино. Он не пытается на-

печатать этот текст по-русски и представляет его в сентябре 1929 года как доклад, написанный по-немецки, на конгрессе независимого кино в швейцарском Ла Сарразе! Эйзенштейн берется за тему Малевича и строит доклад как самозащиту: «Подражание как овладевание».[34]

В России Эйзенштейн отзывается об абстрактных фильмах европейского авангарда как о детских игрушках, «enfantillages»;[35] оправдать собственную «миметическую» приверженность он чувствует себя обязанным, лишь оказавшись в кругу создателей этих фильмов — Вальтера Руттмана и Ганса Рихтера, которому он признается, что кино для него слишком примитивное искусство.[36] Эйзенштейновская концепция самооправдания строится на том, что он отказывается от миметической передачи движения в кино, то есть от предлагаемой киноаппаратом иллюзии движения, возникающей из проекции неподвижных фотограмм при определенной скорости, и создает сознательным столкновением неподвижных кадров (часто статуй) «понятие» движения.[37] Но дискуссию по поводу «иллюзионистского кинодвижения» и «понятийного», которые упираются в ключевое для Малевича разделение внешней динамики предмета и внутренней, Малевич и Эйзенштейн не ведут, и Малевич, косвенно реагируя на напечатанный текст «Четвертого измерения в кино», в своей последней статье уничижительно отзывается о «деревенской картине» Эйзенштейна, показывающего, как «откармливают в совхозе свиней или как убирают на «золотой ниве»». Их оборванную полемику Аннет Майклсон, первая исследовательница темы «Малевич и кино», назвала «диалогом глухих».[38]

Текст Малевича, однако, не ограничивается этим узким кругом «домашней грызни» среди людей кино, но соотносится с полемикой вокруг кино в контексте искусств, ведущейся с начала века. Кинематограф был воспринят как развитие фотографии, дополняющее иллюзию воспроизведения природы записью движения. Уже в словесных определениях нового феномена существует этот «приба-

вочный элемент»: *moving* picture или photographie *animée*, хотя сам кинематограф приравнивался к существовавшим формам спектакля: Photo*play*, *théâtre muet* или кинематографическая (=живая) *картина*. Традиционная эстетика поставила фильм в контекст дискуссий о кризисе репрезентации, отсылая его к поэтике натурализма, которой фильм следовал, запечатлевая уродливую и хаотичную, вульгарную и банальную версию природы (в оппозиции к прекрасному, идеальному, *эстетическому*). Статьи Малевича лексически вписываются в этот дискурс. Но это лишь один аспект его размышлений, и слишком просто заключение о «не-встрече» абстракциониста и кино.

Усовершенствование иллюзии было для Малевича не существенно, так как искусство в его (нео-платонической) концепции ни имело ничего общего с фиксированием или дублированием реальности, но было инструментом «сверх-зрения», понимаемого им не как достижение оптических аппаратов, а как продукт культуры и истории. И только в этом смысле кино — кинетическая живопись светом — соотносимо с развитием пластических искусств. Хотя он рассматривает Эйзенштейна и Вертова внутри своей модели эволюции модернизма (от фигуративности к беспредметности, от Сезанна через кубизм и футуризм к супрематизму), важен для него не отказ от имитации природы, а освобождение мышления от уз выработанных категорий и существующих форм, одной из которых является мимезис. Объявляя искусство новой эпохи материалистичным, он имеет в виду, что оно не религиозно, не культово и поэтому не нуждается в образе, картинке. Это искусство и сможет передать метафизическое ощущение супрематического мира.[39]

Малевич далек от наивных представлений об отождествлении киноотпечатка и натуры. Отпечаток сформирован той техникой видения и передачи пространства, над которой работали живописцы, начиная с Ренессанса, и от которой не смогли освободиться киномастера. Современная «металлическая» культура (граммо-

фона, радио, кино) отчуждает от «живого», и мы имеем дело только с отпечатками, превращающими натуру в «абстрактное дело», что еще больше выявляет «модельность» восприятия.

Историчность зрения

Если режиссер, бывший художником, и художник, ставший аналитиком, так не понимают друг друга, то какой может быть роль художника в кино? Для Малевича — это единственный профессионал, который может сознательно оперировать категориями исторического зрения. Скорее всего, текст «Художник и кино», напечатанный в начале 1926 года, является реакцией на ведущуюся в течение года на страницах журнала *Советский экран* дискуссию о роли декораций в кино, в которой европейские фильмы, делающие ставку на декоративную культуру — *Кабинет доктора Калигари, Раскольников, Нибелунги, Бесчеловечная* — противопоставлялись *Стачке*, фильму без декораций![40] Журнал напечатал и эссе немецкого сценографа Эрно Мецнера, работавшего с Эрнстом Любичем и Георгом Вильгельмом Пабстом, «Архитектура, живопись, кинодекорация».[41] Немецкие экспрессионистские фильмы, первые иностранные картины, попавшие в Россию после экономической блокады, были прежде всего фильмами художников. В русском контексте они были восприняты как продолжение «декоративного кубизма» в стиле постановок Камерного театра Александра Таирова, декорации для которого часто делали кубофутуристы — Георгий Якулов и Александра Экстер.[42] В 1924—25 годах дискуссия о «художнике в кино» становится интернациональной. Известные живописцы и архитекторы приглашаются работать на киностудиях, об этом пишут французские, немецкие и русские журналы[43]: Фернан Леже и модернистский архитектор Роберт Малле-Стевенс создают декорации для *Бесчеловечной* Марселя Лербье, а в России Исаак Рабинович, работавший с Евгением Вахтанговым, и Александра Экстер переносят в кинопавильон *Аэлиты* ступенча-

тую сцену Таирова и одевают актеров в «кубофутуристские» костюмы. Русский левый кино-авангард обходился без художника, отдавая предпочтение оригинальным интерьерам фабрики и города, архитектура которого — мосты, вокзалы, лестницы — воспринималась как декорация. Только режиссеры-«староваторы» типа Якова Протазанова, Владимира Гардина или Чеслава Сабинского (на их фильмы и обращает свое внимание Малевич) работали в традиции постановочного фильма, что в визуальном плане означало композиционные принципы живописи и «однофасадной» театральной сцены — без чувства кинематографического пространства и стиля. Режиссеры обучены грубо видеть, замечает Малевич, поэтому воспроизводят в своих картинах смесь разных пространственных систем и превращают время в пространственную категорию: «Один кадр пейзажа принадлежит 1840 году, другой — 80-м годам, третий — 1925 году. Получается, что герой *Закройщика* пробегает во всех формах времени целого столетия».[44]

Именно в этом тексте Малевич демистифицирует подход к кино конструктивистов и идею вертовского киноглаза, который претендует на новое зрение мира при помощи оптических аппаратов (телескопа, микроскопа, объектива). Для Малевича эти взгляды наивны, потому что и способ видения механического глаза камеры сформирован историческим восприятием: «Киноглаз не видит в природе ничего нового, он рассматривает природу через художественный глаз живописца (красочного светописца), всюду видит природу либо по поленовскому глазу, по перовскому, по Моне, по Шишкину, по Рубенсу и т. д. Кино видит пока только ту изобразительность явлений, которую видел художник-живописец».[45]

Новая система зрения не может прийти от аппаратов, являющихся только техникой фиксации, но может быть воспитана визуальной культурой, задача которой состоит в передаче особого видения, не совпадающего с тем, как видит глаз. Искусство играет вспомогательную роль в этой работе. Поэтому все аппараты — граммофон, фотография и радио — не освободились, также как и кинематограф,

от уз старых искусств, внутри которых сложились модели восприятия, — живописи и театра. Зрение сформировано этими стандартами, оно в такой же степени продукт идеологии, как и сама техника репрезентации. «И глаза мои могут быть взяты в паноптикум как атрибуты средневековья для обзора предметности».[46]

Это тема ненапечатанной статьи Малевича 1928 года, реагирующей на недавнее техническое новшество, звук, и предсказывающей будущие изобретения — цвет и стереокино. Но проблема для Малевича не в усовершенствовании техники создания иллюзии. Приглашение Мохой-Надя принять участие в дискуссии по поводу фотографии и живописи уже давало ему возможность высказаться на ту же тему. Для Мохой-Надя раздел четок: живопись занимается цветом, чего фильм и фотография лишены; фотография работает со светом, фильм — со светом и движением; но фотография лишена материальности фактуры — в отличие от живописи. Проведение границ поэтому просто, и фотография, на которую нападает Эрнст Калаи из-за отсутствия фактуры, защищается Мохой-Надем потому, что работа со светом открывает новые возможности. Но взгляды Малевича (фактура лишь психоз современных художников и второстепенная проблема[47]) никак не поддерживают позицию Мохой-Надя в этой полемике, очевидно, поэтому он не печатает отклика русского живописца, для которого живопись, фотография и фильм — феномены одного ряда, подчиняющиеся одним и тем же закономерностям. Такие частные проблемы как фактура или ее отсутствие только прикрывают путь к видению (и пониманию технических средств).

Размышления Малевича об оптическом восприятии как феномене культуры, а не физиологии и телесности, близки взглядам Павла Флоренского, анализирующего перспективу как символическую категорию,[48] и теоретическому проекту Вальтера Беньямина по исследованию исторических моделей восприятия.[49] Новое общество, пытающееся освободиться от стандартов старого, вырабатывая новый

жестовый язык, новые формы одежды и жилья, должно предложить и новые стандарты видения.

Кино как продолжение супрематической живописи другими средствами

Сценарий Малевича — эксперимент с научной тенденцией — должен популяризировать его представления об эволюции визуальной культуры и испробовать возможности фильма. Он работает с тремя основными формами — квадратом, крестом, кругом — и их трансформациями сначала на плоскости, а затем в трехмерном пространстве. Движение геометрических фигур как новый вид развития сюжета было испробовано его сотрудниками сначала в других формах — полиграфических, как в "Сказе о двух квадратах» Лисицкого,[50] или перформативных, как в супрематическом балете, поставленном в Витебске ученицей Малевича Ниной Коган.[51] На эту постановку как на возможный источник сценария Малевича указывает Александра Шатских.[52] В спектакле статисты скрывались за нарисованными на щитах геометрическими фигурами,[53] и их перемещения на сцене выкладывали новые конфигурации (дугу, крест и т. д.). Эта «живая картина» должна была дать наглядное представление о принципах супрематизма и строилась на «интриге» о зарождении фигур из черного квадрата, их движении в пространстве, трансформации и возвращении к квадрату.

Для Малевича фильм не живописен и не миметичен, потому что его пространство не двумерно, как однофасадное «зеркало сцены» театра, а строится по принципам объемности и поэтому сродни пространству живописному — кубистическому или скульптурному, где свет создает пространственное ощущение и объем.[54] Фильм «архитектоничен», как и пространственное искусство супрематизма.

Людвиг Хиршфельд-Мак, Вернер Грефф, Ласло Мохой-Надь экспериментировали в Баухаусе со световыми рефлексами и мобильными, окрашенными цвет-

ными лучами пластинами в разных оптических и кинетических конструкциях. Их «кинетическая светопись» была задумана как преддверие абстрактного фильма. На эти эксперименты Малевич не обращает внимания. Выбор Ганса Рихтера (об экспериментальной работе которого в области абстрактного фильма сообщал в 1922 году первый номер журнала Алексея Гана *Кино-фот*[55]) как режиссера проекта кажется не случайным, потому что Рихтер в своих экспериментах *Ритм 21* и *Ритм 23* работал только с квадратными формами (черной и белой) — в отличие от диагональных «расчесок» Викинга Эггелинга или округлых, «органических» форм Вальтера Руттмана, то есть с базисными для Малевича формами, понимаемыми как выражение «интуитивного разума».[56] Для современного зрителя квадрат стал пустым и непонятным «как непонятен язык китайца, свидетельствующего свою любовь русской девушке»,[57] для Малевича эта живописная плоскость «живее всякого лица, где торчат пара глаз и улыбка»,[58] и превращения форм полны драматизма.[59] «Супрематические три квадрата есть установление определенных мировоззрений и миростроений. Черный как знак экономии, красный как сигнал революции, белый как чистое действие».[60] Малевич считал, что этим трем квадратам соответствуют три стадии развития супрематизма, которые уже были представлены им на выставках 1915—1916 годов и в его издании «Супрематизм. 34 рисунка» (1920).

Фильм Рихтера строится на ритмическом сжимании и исчезновении в глубине квадратных форм. Рихтер не рисует свой фильм, как Вальтер Руттман, а движет вырезанные квадраты разной величины на черной плоскости, которая превращается в белую, когда режиссер использует негатив вместо позитива. Игнорируя свет, он экспериментирует с кинетическими возможностями плоскостей и пространства. Но обращение Малевича к Рихтеру можно рассматривать и как недоразумение. «Фильмы Рихтера похожи на опыты структурной психологии по восприятию геометрических форм, абстрактных квадратов в движении, внутри дан-

ного пространства и времени. Фильм для него — это процесс обнаружения объективных функций перцепции, своего рода мимезис функции органов чувств, в то время как для Малевича кино означает освобождение от этих телесно-конкретных функций», замечает Норберт Шмиц.[61]

Малевич при разработке сценария отдает предпочтение изображению, фотографически наиболее близкому супрематической живописи. Однако его сценарий предполагает выход не только из двумерности в трехмерность, но и в пространство реального города, демонстрируя сначала конструктивистские здания, а потом преобразование этого пространства супрематической архитектурой. Однако сценарий обрывается на шестнадцатом эпизоде первой части, представляющей «плоскостные ощущения»; две другие части, «архитектоника как проблема» и «архитектура в жизни», не расписаны.

Кино и кинетика

Последнее эссе Малевича свидетельствует о том, что он может разглядеть и в кинокартинах «лик» беспредметности. Он может сделать это, потому что видит фильм, осуществивший новую кинетическую светопись — *Человека с киноаппаратом* Дзиги Вертова, оцениваемый самим режиссером как первый опыт «абсолютного киноязыка». Малевич вмешивается опять в сиюминутную газетную полемику.

После 1926 года, после премьеры фильма *Шестая часть света*, заказанного Вертову как рекламный ролик для продуктов советского экспорта (мехов), режиссера увольняют с работы в Совкино, и он может найти «пристанище» только на Украине, где снимает подряд три фильма — *Одиннадцатый, Человек с киноаппаратом* и *Симфония Донбасса*. В это время Вертов резко критикуется и Левым фронтом, примеряющим его фильмы на теорию «фактографичности», и своими начальниками, которые требуют от кино «понятности миллионам», следуя

лозунгу кампании 1929 года, на который должны откликнуться (и откликаются) советские режиссеры.[62] Возможно, текст Малевича принят редакцией потому, что в предыдущем номере (5—6) Константин Фельдман, бывший матрос броненосца «Потемкина», а теперь кинокритик, печатает статью «В спорах о Вертове», поддерживая позицию режиссера, а до этого Кирилл Шутко, член редколлегии журнала, защищает фильм и в *Правде* (в номере от 23 марта 1929 года) и в *Советском экране*,[63] где он требует широкого проката для *Человека с киноаппаратом*. В дискуссии о Вертове Малевич занимает своеобразную позицию. В то время как вертовские фильмы оцениваются по их соответствию или несоответствию принципам документального, производственного, конструктивистского или социально ангажированного искусства, Малевич защищает режиссера как единственного кино-футуриста. Малевич сравнивает два «городских» фильма, которые меряют друг другом с момента их выхода на экраны: *Симфонию большого города* Вальтера Руттмана, пионера абстрактного кино, чей документальный портрет Берлина был воспринят как произведение стиля «новой вещности», и Вертова, движущегося от политических киножурналов к абсолютному фильму.

Теоретик, близкий формальной школе, Осип Брик упрекает Вертова в непонимании языка кино и опоре на слово, при помощи которого Вертов пытается расширить семантику кадра, не учитывая его визуальной информации.[64] Малевич считает, что Вертов впервые показал, как работают в кино принципы современной живописи (и шире — визуальной культуры) — от кубистического «распыления» объекта до футуристической динамики и «сдвига».

В отличие от общепринятого взгляда на кино как высшую стадию живописи в отношении передачи движения — от барокко, импрессионизма, футуризма до кинетических скульптур конструктивистов — Малевич не считал кинематограф *a priori* искусством динамическим и отмечал: «... Футуристы, несмотря на то, что содержанием их произведений является движение, не использовали кино», «но-

вую технику передачи динамических» ощущений», и, наоборот, «кино не использовало идею футуризма для своего обновления и спасения от любовных забот и пылких поцелуев».[65]

Динамика может быть понята по-разному. Для Льва Кулешова, первого русского кино-экспериментатора, динамика и ускорение — это качество машин, предметов модернизма, — автомобиля, самолета, локомотива, моторов, пароходов, заводов. Тело человека может приблизиться к их совершенству, лишь подчинив свое движение искусственному ритму и вписав его в геометрическую схему, став машиной — в рекордах спорта, погонях и кульбитах. Малевич исключает человеческое тело из числа динамических объектов. Все негативные примеры неправильно понятой кино-динамики он берет из слэпстиковых комедий (с Монти Бенксом или русским комиком Игорем Ильинским), то есть из той области, которую другие теоретики (например, Вальтер Беньямин) рассматривали как возможное поле выявления кинодинамики — в столкновении моторики тела и кинетики камеры.[66] Для Малевича эти два типа кинетики — и машины, и человека — слишком предметны и поэтому не отвечают новому динамизму, существующему помимо предметов как «динамическая мощь», как движение, «уловить которое наш *глаз не в состоянии,* но *ощутить* его *возможно*».[67] Его понятие динамики метафизично, абстрактно и строится на различии динамики и движения. Кино определяется им в тексте о киноплакатах как «бегущая» статика, лишь живопись пока смогла передать истинную динамику — ощущение скорости, оторванное от телесности.

Представление о «динамическом динамизме вне движения», динамизме, существующем как энергия помимо тела, не уловимом глазом, сталкивалось с рациональным анализом восприятия и воспроизведения движения техникой кино. В русском кино-дискурсе представления о передаче движения в кино были сформированы Анри Бергсоном, воспринятым через формалистов, чьи новые аналити-

ческие модели в свою очередь были сформированы на основе литературной практики русских футуристов. У Бергсона кино используется как метафора мышления, которое создает не соответствующую реальности модель метафизического ощущения движения и указывает на ограниченность конкретного механизма восприятия. Поэтому формалисты рассуждают о том, что «кинематография искусство смыслового движения».[68] «Фильм далек от материальной репродукции движения — он дает смысловое представление движения».[69] Малевич поддерживает это понимание, для него движение в кино иллюзорно, также как в живописи. Его образ возникает в сознании зрителя.[70]

Русский кино-авангард обращался с движением аналитически — не синтез движения интересовал его, а скорее осознание прерыва, интервала, момент неподвижности между фотограммами. Это проблематизировали Эйзенштейн в своем монтаже статуй и неподвижных предметов, должных создавать «понятие» движения, и Вертов, обративший внимание на интервал как организующий момент киномонтажа.

Малевич, разрабатывающий в теории живописи достаточно метафизическую концепцию движения, не воспринимаемого оптически, заметил эту работу только на примере Вертова и, возможно, только потому, что его кадры были похожи на абстрактные картины футуриста Балла, передающие фантасмагорическое ощущение от скорости, меняющей восприятие. Неслучайно Малевич иллюстрирует свою статью о Вертове сопоставлением кадра из *Человека с киноаппаратом* с картиной Балла «Абстрактная скорость». (Кстати, эта картина была воспроизведена в книге *Измы искусства*, изданной Лисицким и Гансом Арпом в 1924 году в Германии, в которой Малевич представил супрематизм, а Ганс Рихтер абсолютный фильм.) Это и есть та динамика, не уловимая глазом, которая деформирует тело и преодолевает мимезис.

Вертов и Руттман противопоставляются друг другу именно на основе этого принципа. У Руттмана движутся предметы модернизма, вписанные в нарративную схему — от неподвижности к ускорению. У Вертова движение представлено как квинтэссенция модернизма, уравнивающего движение объекта, движение города, движение пленки через камеру и фильма через проекционный аппарат. При этом сама кинотехника становится «прибавочным элементом» в понимании Малевича. Движение разлагается киноаппаратом и воссоздается как кинематографическая величина — сжимается, растягивается, останавливается, дробится, расщепляется, множится в многократных экспозициях, в наложениях друг на друга разнонаправленных движений, и сам распадающийся кинокадр приводит предметы в иной вид движения, чем в природе. Не удивительно, что для описания этого феномена Малевич использует понятие футуристического сдвига.

Взгляды Малевича и сегодня кажутся радикальными. Он противопоставляет кинематограф как феномен «бегущей статики» современной живописи — искусству динамики, которую не увидишь глазом. Художник может передать ощущение скорости, но это ощущение, как и само зрение, оторвано в концепции Малевича от телесности. Зрение определяется не как величина физиологическая или психологическая, а как продукт культуры, и, в первую очередь, живописи. Супрематизм создает новые модели «сверх»-зрения — для абстрактных сущностей. Кино понимается как продолжение супрематической живописи другими средствами. Малевич требует от него подчинения принципам живописи и там, где находит похожесть, принимает это развитие. Поэтому, несмотря на призывы, обращенные к кинорежиссерам и кинохудожникам отказаться от станковой живописи, сам он остается в понимании кино прежде всего — живописцем.

О выявителях. Плакаты

Киносекцией Государственной Академии Художественных Наук была устроена выставка киноплакатов,[71] или — как я назвал бы их — выявителей. Но это были не плакаты. Это — почти декоративно утрированные картины, которые делались по разным принципам станковых искусств, значительно расходящихся с органической сущностью плаката-выявителя. Ведь ни живописное, ни конструктивное искусство не имеют так называемых «непроницаемых планов»,[72] а без последних «выявитель» никогда не достигает своей цели.

Все плакаты, даже сделанные конструктивистами, строятся вне «непроницаемого плана», хотя многие из них и состоят из реального элемента плоскости «как таковой» и фотографии, в чем они и отличаются от так называемого «академического реализма». Но и те и другие плакаты безусловно зависят от станковизма, и поэтому их реальная сущность строится на той же разрыхленной поверхности «картинного живописного поля», или «распыляющей зрение поверхности»,[73] в силу чего «живописное картинное станковое поле» требует от зрителя малого полезного расстояния для восприятия.

По этому техническому признаку различают элементы декоративные как противоположные станковому элементу. Правда, часто непроницаемого плана нет в декоративных плакатах, т. е. нет планов, изолированных от света, линейной и воздушной перспективы, а все это увеличивает в плакате воздушные ямы, разрушающие «упорную поверхность», что в свою очередь лишает возможности установки выявителя в одном плане времени.

Устроенный киносекцией диспут имел, как мне кажется, в виду разрешение вопроса о советском киновыявителе. Но, как и все вообще диспуты, он, конечно, не мог дать того, чего хотелось бы. К вопросу нужно было бы подойти с другой стороны: со стороны лабораторного, научного рассмотрения, подготовив совер-

шенно другую выставку, выставку результатов исследования. При этом только условии можно учесть ту или иную форму выявителя вообще, и в частности — киновыявителя, так как киноплакаты должны, конечно, иметь специфическое отличие от всех вообще картин станковизма, изображающих быт, историю и тому подобное.

В настоящее время работа над «выявителем» находится в области индивидуальных изощрений, вне научной системы. Между тем и этот род искусства также необходимо ввести в план научного исследования. На диспуте на эту тему по существу никто не высказался. Вопрос этот, очевидно, никогда и не ставился в киносекции. В противном случае выставка плакатов не была бы устроена по принципу станковых выставок. Дело Государственной Академии Художественных Наук и ее киносекции устраивать выставки произведений отнюдь не [для] эстетического их восприятия, а для научного исследования экспонатов. И мне казалось, что именно с этого киносекция должна была бы начать организацию нового «киновыявителя». Создание «советского киновыявителя» вне этого подхода немыслимо, ибо только так будет обеспечен правильный путь киноплаката к его форме.

Плаката-выявителя до сих пор нет. В частности — нет «выявителя», специфического для кино. Но, может быть, этого специфического киновыявителя нет по той простой причине, что нет еще и самого кино? А есть только киноаппараты, заменившие собой карандаши, кисти и разноцветную палитру как новый способ передачи тех картинок, над которыми столько сил затрачивали старые живописцы, и кино пока — только новое техническое средство в области наиболее совершенной передачи реального в искусстве, а режиссеры — это новые художники изо, произведения которых напоминают художников-статиков? Отсюда мы имеем не плакаты, а отрывки бегущего на экране содержания в том или другом крошеве статического художественного оформления, причем разновидность этого кро-

шева является отличительной стороной конкурирующих между собой драм, трагедий и их героев.

Сюжетодатель-сценарист берет из жизни те или иные моменты, из которых художник в свою очередь выбирает картину для «выявителя», т. е. для поля, на котором нужно выявить данный момент. Это поле выявителя может быть красным, белым, зеленым, черным. Это та непроницаемая плоскость, на которой нужно выявить картину. И вот здесь часто происходит то, что я имел в виду. Картиной мы аннулируем непроницаемую плоскость — «отличительный элемент поля зрения».

Кому же принадлежит эта область составления выявителей: сценаристу, режиссеру, художнику? Ни тому, ни другому, ни третьему. Все трое всегда конструируют свои произведения по принципу местного значения, т. е. в поле зрения развертывания произведения. Из ряда помножения элементов на элементы получаются фрагменты. Помноженные друг на друга фрагменты дают произведения. По существу это произведения станковые — произведения, не помноженные на время. Декоратор отчасти отличается от станковиста тем, что его элементы всегда помножаются на расстояние, он прежде всего пространственник: ему нужно иметь только в виду так называемые «действующие выявители» на улице. Вне этого он может рассматривать свое «поле выявления» как пространство для форм художественного декорирования рекламируемого явления, которое он возводит всегда в элемент декоративный. Рассчитанные в таком порядке плакаты создают «зыбь афишно-плакатную», в которой лучи зрения не находят себе упора и распыляются по формочкам разного пространственного отношения. Такой «выявитель» гибнет. Другой метод — это приведение к одной целостной конструктивной связи и выявителя, и выявляемого, что создает нужную для художника и правильно организованную целостность в его мастерской, но является совершенно ненужным на улице, так как в последнем случае «выявитель» совпадает с

целым рядом других плакатов, разрешенных в том же плане, и «гибнет». Из этих примеров видно, что нет еще мастера плакатного дела. Эта область, что называется, болтается среди разных течений и направлений в изобразительном искусстве и не может выйти на свой путь. Мастер «выявителей» должен обладать острой чувствительностью к плановой ориентации пространственных отношений, должен уметь учитывать размеры плана, расстояние линий направления выявителей на действующих полях улиц, должен учитывать расстояние выявителей между собой, должен уловить профиль кривой выявителей, так как только при этом учете мы можем установить ближайшую точку к зрителю и поразить безошибочно все поле действия выявителя новым выявителем.

Нужно установить выявитель в ближайшей точке профиля, в то время как выявляемое может быть в каком угодно плане: на выявителе в 100 кв. вершков выявляемое может быть в 1 кв. вершок.

Пространственные отношения в данном случае будут разные, но результат будет лучший, чем в том случае, когда выявляемое будет сделано, например, в размере десятиэтажного дома. (Из опытов Института Художественной Культуры по Отделению фото.) Всякие выявители, как по форме, так и по цвету, должны учитывать характер действующих на улице других выявителей. Без этого учета наилучшие плакаты — в художественном смысле — могут все же погибнуть, утонуть в строе уличного плакатного поля. (Вот почему каждый мастер выявителей должен давать действующие выявители.) Недавно в действующие на улице плакатные поля были вклеены два выявителя кинофильмы *Стачка*. Один — Госкино, другой — «Колизея». Пусть каждый сам судит, какой из них построен на более строгом учете требований плакатного поля. Я полагаю, что первый плакат наиболее удачен, в смысле фиксирования в памяти фильмы *Стачка*, и должен вызвать подражания.

Развеска выявителей также должна быть учтена. Человек, расклеивающий выявители, должен быть грамотен: должен окончить «техникум выявителя», он должен знать — где и по соседству с каким вклеивать новый выявитель.

Конторы продают места под выклейку плакатов, и эти места превращаются в плакатные свалки, где может быть похоронен любой плакат. Конторы, однако, тут мало виновны, так как они продают наиболее видные места, которые становятся «темными», как только вывесят туда десяток-другой выявителей. Дело это достаточно важное для торговых фирм, которым нужно организовать «техникум выявителей».

Многие фирмы, желая выявить свое предложение, воображают, что, если это их предложение будет помещено на первой странице, оно обязательно будет прочтено. На опытах, производимых в Институте Художественной Культуры, было доказано, что, благодаря форме выявителя, крепко запоминаются рекламируемые вещи и на последней странице, хотя реклама по своим размерам значительно уступает выявителю, занимающему целую страницу.

Никакие направления и течения в искусстве не имеют первенства, так как они не возникали на принципах выявителей и могут быть полезны только теми своими элементами, которые тождественны с элементами выявителя.

Брать целиком форму или сочетание элементов из существа самого течения системы будет очередной ошибкой. Выявители не могут быть построены ни по сезанновскому, ни по кубистическому, футуристическому или конструктивистическому принципам. Выявители не могут быть и передвижнического характера.[74] От всех этих направлений могут быть взяты только элементы и принцип.

Можно фиксировать в памяти зрителя форму выявителя, не притемняя соседних выявителей. Наоборот — при организованной вклейке можно взаимно использовать форму всех выявителей, но при сегодняшнем их состоянии больший процент их притемняется, а, следовательно, не достигает цели. На опыте уста-

новлено, что в целом ряде рекламируемых вещей, при строгом размещении их выявителей по открытому закону контрастов кубизма,[75] не пропал ни один из этих выявителей.

Надо признать, что большая часть предприятий вообще и кинопредприятий в частности в рекламном деле ничего не учитывает. Более того — страдает рядом предрассудков, и в силу которых многие плакаты, сделанные художниками с верным учетом действующих уже выявителей, были забракованы. Предприятия рассматривают выявитель как картину, измеряя ее качества по аналогии с картинами станковыми, копаются в аналитических, астрономических и ботанических справках. Одна граммофонная фирма, желая рекламировать пластинку «Stella» («Звезда») проходящей на фоне звездного пространства, заказала художнику плакат, который и нарисовал «Стеллу» среди звезд. Дирекция фирмы задала художнику глубокомысленный вопрос, «правильно ли нарисованы звезды и действительно ли такое количество звезд окружают «Стеллу»»... В другом случае художник показал выявитель, на котором были изображены две пересекающиеся полосы, рассчитанные на контраст по отношению к существующим уже на улице выявителям. Плакат этот вызвал у заказчика ассоциацию креста, тот до смерти перепугался и — в результате удовлетворился выявителем, изображающим Пегаса с седоком, держащим факел; внизу плаката лежали пальмовые листы и разбитое сердце. Некогда был сделан плакат, на котором были нарисованы три горящих свечи. Плакат был сделан так, что его не мог проглядеть ни стар, ни млад. Но фирма от него отказалась в силу предрассудка: «три свечи — это к покойнику!..» Фирма заказала более надежный плакат — из незабудок, на всякий случай отслужив молебен.

Заказчик думает, что его товару должен соответствовать и выявитель, в то время как цель выявителя может быть и другая: дело последнего выявить предложение через какие угодно формы, хотя бы через всех святых.

Не все люди запоминают названия, фамилии, имена, отчества и т. д., но хорошо помнят лица, форму, цвет, число. Для того, чтобы зритель запомнил внешний вид, очень важно, чтобы этот вид стал тем же выявителем. Часто хозяйки, поручая купить товар, предупреждают: «купи с негром» (клеймо[76]) или обращают внимание на «треугольник», т. е. форму.[77]

Я как-то демонстрировал две обложки: все читали — «синдетикон», «синдетикон», тогда как было написано «колдетикон».[78] Когда же обложку перекрасили, оставив те же надписи, зрители обратили внимание, что на первой обложке было не «син», а «кол». Еще пример: на витринах двух магазинов стояли надписи: на одной — «Скороход»[79], на другой — «Обувь». Несмотря на это, выяснилось, что многие заходили в магазин «Обувь», воображая, что заходят в «Скороход». Что было тому причиной? А то, что слово «Обувь» было дано в форме того выявителя, который имел форму знакомого росчерка. Букв зритель не замечал, знакомый росчерк «Скороход» заставлял его заходить в «Обувь». Таким образом, можно дать только один росчерк, и цель будет достигнута.

СВЕТ КИНО

И ЛИКУЮТ ЛИКИ НА ЭКРАНАХ[1]

В ПОРЯДКЕ ДИСКУССИИ [80]

Если по Арватову, Эйзенштейн и Вертов глубокомысленно полагают, что надо в конечном итоге уничтожить всякое искусство, в том числе и производственное, оставив «голое производство — технику», и если Вертов воображает, будто он сейчас делает не искусство,[81] то, значит, и в кинетическое искусство вкралась та же ошибка, что и в живопись. Под словами «долой искусство» нужно разуметь искусство, в котором вместо беспредметности, вместо искусства «как такового», выявляется морда жизни. Идет речь об искусстве, которое из рожи хочет сделать розу. [Розу, но не вообще искусство. Новое искусство и отличается тем от старого, что выявляет свою собственную природу, новые живописцы — беспредметники. [82]]

Если все времена разных человеческих устроительств стремились сесть в экипаж искусства и выявить свое лицо в образе через искусство, то в подражание им наша современная критика направляет современных художников в ту же сторону. Она полагает, что раз буржуазный класс выписывал себя через искусство живописца со всей своей бытовой требухой на холстах, то и современному победоносному рабочему классу почему-то тоже нужно выписать свою требуху, ибо если буржуазный класс утвердил себя в искусстве, то и мы себя должны тоже вымазать на холст и утвердиться в нем по образу и подобию буржуазии.

Очевидно, многим стрелочникам очень интересно направить искусство через художников по тому же предметному пути превращения рож в образы.

[Таковая точка, уже даже с моей точки зрения, является чисто буржуазной.

---

[1] «Ликуют» нужно понимать: делают, пишут (автор).

Искусство для пролетариата должно иметь другое назначение: во-первых, образов с себя не делать, символов тоже, ибо он весь в сути своего существа есть безо́бразен, беспредметный.[83]

Искусство его должно быть как таковое, а художник в его обществе и строе не образомаз, не ликописец его и всей его бытовой требухи.]

Пусть направляющая критика забудет привычку видеть в верблюде специальное животное, созданное природою для того, чтобы возить киргизов,[84] а в художнике видеть мастера, которому дана свыше сила «одухотворять» и перевоплощать безо́бразное в образное.

По словам Арватова — «сколько бы ни болтали отдельные интеллигенты о низвержении всего искусства, кроме производственного, рабочему классу практически надо учитывать, что его достижения не достигли стадии полной организованности и единомышленности общества — и ему приходится убеждать конкретно, т. е. средствами искусства» (агит-живопись и агит-кино).

Следовательно, искусство для него, во-первых, является средством агитационным, как бы специально созданным для этого орудием, как это было в раннем передвижничестве, и как только минует надобность в конкретном убеждении общества, то и искусство агитационное станет ненужным. Искусство перейдет, по его мнению, в производство. Эта точка зрения оставляет еще небольшую надежду на то, что и станковизм изобразительный исчезнет только при условии скорейшего всеобщего достижения единомышленности пролетарского общества. Другая существующая точка зрения говорит, что пролетариат должен себя утверждать в искусстве, как это делали его враги. С этой точки зрения гибель искусства изобразительного, станкового отпадает на неопределенное время, ибо живописная функция искусства исправляется по раз уже пройденному пути. Да и сам тов. Арватов не против искусства агитационного, изобразительного вообще, в том числе и ахровского изобразительного искусства. В то же время Арватов хочет

направить искусство через художника на другой путь, ведущий его к производству, — «искусство в производство». Под этим лозунгом можно разуметь то, что искусство исходит из цели технической. Искусство, таким образом, идет в приклад к целесообразности вещи, дооформляет то, чего не может сделать голая техника, у которой формы вещей являются из чисто физической надобности организма, но не как таковые. Техника нашего организма создала пальцы на руке разной величины, создала не в силу художественно-формовых отношений, а в силу чистой утилитарности. Форма — ради формы не существует, и форма как таковая — тоже, но при этом условии для развития вещей искусство, как и художник, не нужны, а станковизм и подавно. Стоит только сделать перестановку в лозунге «искусство в производство» — «производство в искусстве», — и мы получим совершенно другую точку зрения, которая повлечет ко многим «долой» в голой технике и в целом строе отношений в обществе.

Буржуазия, как и все господствовавшие до нее классы, вымазывали свои лики через художников довольно примитивным способом и, таким образом, тоже зарисовывали всю картину жизни. Пролетариат осуществляет свое господство и будет осуществлять в момент больших технических усовершенствований человеческих органов — ушей, глаз, ног, рук. Одним из таким усовершенствований в области искусства явилось кино. Оно создало новых кинохудожников, постановщиков картин. Всякая постановка так и называется — картиною, а этюд к картине стал называться кадром. Поэтому в большой мере все режиссеры-постановщики это — плоть от плоти древних стариков живописцев, у которых в руках лишь новое орудие производства, которым можно во времени развертывать картину, заснять светом явление и в кинокадрик, как раньше написать светом этюдик.

[Симметрия (композиция) диктуется последними направлениями. Это новые станковисты в динамическом разворачивании жизни во времени, которые раз-

вертывают картину в тысячах кадриках-холстиках; картина получилась в полном объеме представляемой правды или выдумки во времени.]

Каждый постановщик картин имеет свою особенность; это зависит от его родителей-живописцев, от их композиционного воспитания: одни с наклонностями древними, времен Рембрандта, другие барбизонского, третьи импрессионистического, передвижнического воспроизведения явлений, установка которых происходит по законам сказанных направлений искусства.

[В первом случае довлеет идеология производства, во втором искусства, и тогда станковизм живописный становится как таковым, в полной силе.]

В этом их отличие от старой техники, к которой застывшая картина изображения на холсте, воздействуя на зрителя, приводит отразившееся в мозгу изображение в движение. Человек думает о причинах, создавших эпизод, и его последствии. Таким образом, современность имеет новые технические усовершенствования в области изобразительного искусства старого времени, когда оно было эксплуатировано идеедателями и учетчиками общественных взаимоотношений.

Что же касается того, что Эйзенштейн собирается ликвидировать станковизм, подразумевая под станковизмом не агитку, тогда он должен стать на утверждение станковизма агитационного, на котором в данный момент он стоит и углубляет правду агитационного содержания, пользуя контраст для выражения последнего. Его кадры состоят на содержании содержания; в переводе на живописный язык это значит передвижничество, у которого живопись была на том же содержании. Живописцы тогда занимались характеристикой лица, психологическими его состояниями, «настроением», выражали счастье и несчастье, быт, историю, разное горе, надежду и веселье — вместо того, чтобы выявить живопись «как таковую» или в нашем случае «кино как таковое».

Но у Эйзенштейна есть одно преимущество перед другими режиссерами — у него есть некоторое осознание и умение пользоваться законом контрастов,[85] обостренность коих впоследствии должна довести его до полной победы, путем контрастного строения, над содержанием — [до беспредметности, это означает очищение экрана от натурно-агитационной агит-формы, и тогда по-настоящему повалится на его голову все, что только будет под руками у критиков и стрелочников ИЗО].

Итак, каждый режиссер в своей картине стремится передать не форму «как таковую», [не] свет «как таковой», не живопись «как таковую», [не] искусство «как таковое вообще». Он прежде всего свет пользует как техническое орудие для выражения поведения человека, окруженного разными обстоятельствами [взвинченного состояния и расстроенного последними. Геройство, милосердие, справедливость, страдания и т. д. Литература не из букв, а из людей. Как это все похоже на старых живописцев.]

Возьмем хотя бы № 8 *АРКа* и посмотрим кадр *Черное сердце*,[86] недурное, кстати, название, говорящее, что до реализма очень далеко, совсем средневековое мистическое название; сам этюд-кадр построен по типу немецких живописцев 60-х годов. Отношение голов, фигур друг к другу аннулирует действительность пространственно-объемных между ними отношений. Эта композиция никоим образом не может быть современной, в этой установке современных лиц в глубоком прошлом времени, вне пространства, как сознаем его мы сейчас, элемент света использован, как его пользовали передвижники старого времени; или *Крест и маузер*,[87] таинственный знак, обнаруженный в одно прекрасное утро в гор. Бостоне или Кливленде; трактовка этого кадра по времени репинского периода и по психологическому состоянию тождественна картине художника Касаткина «Кто» или Репина «Вернулся» (Третьяковская галерея).[88]

Возьмем *1905 год* — забастовка в похоронном бюро,[89] контраст обостренный, долженствующий противопоставиться по своей неожиданности развертываемой, как сдвиг,[90] картине. По своей фактуре этот кадр целиком импрессионистичен,[91] напоминает времена Ренуара, Эдуарда Мане, Тулуз-Лотрека. На стр. 10 *АРКа* № 8 помещен тип крестьянина, целиком — задание передвижническое или ахровское — раньше «Журавли летят», теперь — «Слушают агитатора».[92]

Таким образом, кино по живописным теориям находится еще в очень далеком прошлом, а сущность искусства по своей природе действительно вышла к новой своей форме, выразившейся в архитектуре, плакате, декорациях. Новое искусство не живописное и не изобразительное. Новое искусство прежде всего архитектурное, и в своем смысле [оно] не было понято и «левыми» художниками, которые вышли к индивидуальной эстетике, интуитивному настроению и создали из хлама фотомонтажного эклектика, чем поставили баррикаду продвижению развивающейся формы нового искусства «как такового». Однако и этот эклектический фотомонтаж — не замена живописного станковизма, как думает Арватов.

Эйзенштейн и Вертов действительно первоклассные художники с устремлением влево, ибо первый опирается на контраст, второй — на «показ вещи» как таковой, но им еще остается большой кусок пути к сезаннизму, кубизму, футуризму и беспредметному супрематизму, и дальнейший ход развития их художественной культуры можно предопределять только от уяснения принципа указанных школ.

Предложение тов. Арватова об экспериментальном кино приветствую, ибо это есть наиглавнейшая задача в киноискусстве;[93] только через этот экспериментальный отдел мы сможем создать «кинологию» и специальную аптеку, без которой организм кино наживет катар.[94]

О «чистом показе» Вертова[95] я скажу, что действительно вещь можно показать «как таковую», изолированной от разных идейных и агитационных содержаний. Не знаю, так ли понимает «чистый показ» вещей Вертов, ибо если так, то это верная установка вопроса в искусстве влево.

Раньше живописцы думали и утверждали, что нет живописи вне идейного содержания или нет содержания, которое бы не содержало живопись. Следовательно, от какой-либо морды аристократа зависела и живопись; вне этого казалось художнику, что живопись была ни на чем не обоснована, размазана, являлась бессмысленной и нецелесообразной. Новые живописцы поняли, что дело не в роже, а дело в живописи, что живопись «как таковая» тоже равноценна другим всем явлениям.

Вертов в «показе вещи» уже наполовину освобождает зрителя от напомаженных идеями вещей, явлений предметов и, показывая вещь «как таковую», заставляет общество видеть вещи не напомаженными, а реальными, подлинными, независимыми от порядка идейного, которые представляют собою картину куда сильнее и интереснее всех ликов и их «содержаний».

Искусство в кубизме освободилось от идейного содержания и стало строить свою форму. Идейной барыне оно служило многие века, чистило ее, пудрило, размалевывало щеки, губы, подводило брови. Сегодня отказалось в пользу своей собственной культуры. То же и кино, пока другая горничная, которой нужно освободиться и понять, как живописцы-кубисты поняли, что живопись может существовать и без образа, и без быта, и без лика идеи. Тогда кино задумается над своей культурой «как таковой».

Эйзенштейн обратил внимание на закон контраста, который делает его кинопостановку интересной, но ему должно обратить внимание на то, что его контрасты

могут создать обстановку, в которой идея может выиграть, но контрасты как таковые в таком случае утеряют свою собственную остроту и контраста как такового при данном условии не выявят. Если закон контрастов будет им осознан, а осознан он может быть только через кубизм как единственную школу о законах контраста, тогда он окажется на высоте, на которой стоит новое искусство будущей культуры.

До сих пор полагали, что новое искусство вообще, и в частности кубизм, есть фальсификат искусства, выдающийся анализ нашей западной критики, аналогичный анализу крыловской обезьяны,[96] которая никак не могла додуматься надеть очки не на хвост, а на глаза, и рассудила разбить их как нецелесообразные.

Также и современная критика решила доказать негодность нового искусства вообще и предупредить пролетариев о появлении непонятного, нецелесообразного явления в искусстве, которое называется кубизм, футуризм, супрематизм.

Эта обезьянья сноровка каждую идею считать единственною целью и сообразностью всего к своему образу заставляла искусство издревле ориентироваться или на попа, или на фараона как на целесообразный лик, как на содержателя великих идей. Художник воспитался на этом методе и думает, что человеческая рожа это и есть та цель, в которой существует художественный образ в идее, что эта рожа и вся его бытовая требуха, базарная сутолока суть его жизни.

Мало того, ему стали доказывать, что он рождается этой сутолокой и все взаимоотношения этих рож составляют общество, членом которого он состоит, а следовательно, должен быть сам похожим на него, а все его искусство должно именно сочиняться из изображений этой сутолоки. Так он понял и стоит потому в передней у замглавов жизни, чтобы запечатлеть их лик, в котором содержится «идея», или разъезжает по земному шару и вымазывает на холсты распластанный священный быт.

Также и кинопостановщики не увернулись от этой хватки традиции, и ликуют лики на экранах.

Художник и кино

В № 10 *Киножурнала АРК* в своей статье «И ликуют лики на экранах» я указывал на тождество трактовки ликов и целых картин на экране, воспроизводимых еще в докинематографической эре, т. е. до того момента, когда техника нашла средство писать живые лики на полотне экрана. Я указывал и на то, что художник-живописец с величайшим трудом пытался щетиной и краской написать природу и лик так, чтобы он был как живой, естественный во всех своих движениях, достижение выразительности которых составляло одно из его наиглавнейших усилий. Но в результате этих усилий художнику в статическом холсте удавалось фиксировать лишь одно впечатление этого движения в одном кадре. В таком безвыходном, обреченном положении художник был до тех пор, пока, с одной стороны, техника изобрела кино и достигла воспроизведения не впечатления, а действительного движения, а с другой — часть живописцев уяснила себе вопрос: «что есть живопись и что есть искусство». С этого момента искусство распалось на два основных разделения: одни стали предметниками (конкретными), станковистами и бытоотражателями, не уяснившими сути искусства; другие — беспредметниками (абстракционерами), уяснившими суть искусства и отказавшимися от портрета и отражения быта.

В той же статье я указывал, что художник-живописец оказал сильное влияние на композиционный характер построения кадров в кино, на работу режиссеров и операторов. Он подчинил кинохудожников своей школе, в силу чего фильма, в которой происходит развитие светописной картины, строится по композиционному закону школ живописных. Я указывал на то, что со временем (которого не так долго осталось ждать) кинотехника достигнет средств оцвечивания кадров, т. е. не только цветной иллюминации форм,[97] но и возможности, при помощи художника-живописца, получения фактуры и особой подкладки на ликах цвет-

ного луча (света) такого качества, которое вызовет у зрителя волнение, подобное получаемому им от живописных картин, скажем, в музеях.

Художник, главным образом живописец, оказал и оказывает огромное влияние на режиссеров и операторов в чисто композиционной и световой трактовке кадров. В *Доротти Вернон*[98] почти половина кадров (моментов) картины построена так, что, в конце концов, не знаешь: снимок ли это с картины Лувра времен Гейнсборо или же это заснято в наше время с живых людей. В *Закройщике из Торжка* есть много мест (кадров), целиком построенных по Перову или Поленову. Смотря на смену кадров этой картины, теряешься во времени, т. к. получается, что фильма по своему временному состоянию проваливается или сдвигается по времени на несколько пространственно-временных расстояний. Один кадр пейзажа принадлежит 1840 году, другой — 80-м годам, третий — 1925 году. Получается, что герой *Закройщика* пробегает во всех формах времени целого столетия; конечно, это не заметно для масс и, может быть, для самого режиссера. У американцев, которые разрабатывают свою постановку в плане одного времени, таких временных сдвигов кадров нет, не говоря уже о классическом подборе всех лиц и предметов, спаянных временем, что очень важно, когда надо добиться хорошего качества и единства всех предметов.

Исследуя все кинопостановки — на предмет выяснения роли художника, — можно собрать огромное количество документов, доказывающих, что художник-живописец оказал огромное воздействие на кинопостановщиков нашего времени, причем до сих пор еще не нашлось ни одного режиссера, который бы увидел киноматериал в другом свете, чем его видел художник-живописец. Киноглаз не видит в природе ничего нового, он рассматривает природу через художественный глаз живописца (красочного светописца), всюду видит природу либо по поленовскому глазу, по перовскому, по Моне, по Шишкину, по Рубенсу и т. д. Кино видит пока только ту изобразительность явлений, которую видел художник-живописец.

Оба — как киносветописатель, так и живописец — идут за правдой, в этом они сходятся.

«Мы, говорят, изображаем только правду, наше искусство только в тождестве этой правды». Последнее убеждение объединяет киносветописателя и живописца и делает все неизменным в кино как таковом.

Ну и будут сидеть на одном месте с правдой, которой не знают ни тот, ни другой, и будут ликовать лики на экранах по образу и подобию живописцев-художников. Ибо киносветописатели — плоть от плоти живописцев-художников, лишь с новым техническим орудием.

Кино, казалось, должно перевернуть всю изобразительную культуру, и, конечно, она будет опрокинута, когда будут в кино абстракционеры, с новой плотью сознания; в противном случае мы будем видеть те же передвижнические картины, которые пишутся пока светописью, т. е. еще не развита чувствительность киноорганизма к цвету. У кино остается сущность живописца-цветописца, развившего свой аппарат до высокого совершенства восприятия и отражения светоцветной природы на экране. Но он не смог дать своим ликам ту движность, которую хотел передать; в действительности, его лики движутся только в воображении зрителя, в картине же ему удается установить только призрак намерения этого движения. Таким образом, мне кажется, что по природе своей кино продолжает неразрывную живописную линию, органически связанную с художником-живописцем.

Но какая получилась чепуха! Живописец-художник приглашается в кино, чтобы играть там роль какого-то захудалого дворника — фонописателя и установщика мебели, вместо того, чтобы руководить этим могучим орудием выражения! Он потерял в нем то право связывать всякую деталь с лицом или фигурой на холсте, которое имел раньше, когда холст его еще не был экраном. Правда, он и сам пока относится к кино очень подозрительно и уверен в том, что этому «мертвому

объективу»[99] никогда не передать того, что, собственно говоря, он передает «мертвой кистью». Но как только он увидит, что через этот мертвый объектив устремляются цветовые лучи, и когда он узнает, что ими можно написать именно живописную картину со всей фактурой, тогда, очевидно, он станет во главе, если кино к этому времени не выйдет на какой-нибудь свой особый путь.

В действительности, киноаппарат нашел себе новых художников-динамиков, новаторов по новым средствам и староваторов по трактовке и обращению со светом и сюжетом. Возможно, динамикам нет надобности в цвете, ибо динамизм больше всего выражается в белом и в холодно-сталевидной окраске, а не в разрумянивании движения; движение динамическое не иллюминируется горячими токами. Кинодинамика в чистом виде должна иметь свою гамму, но эта гамма потребует и своей формы, а как ее принять, когда у Доротти Вернон розовый цвет лица, а у Закройщика рыжие волосы? А ведь Закройщик и Доротти — единственные «конкретные выражения» жизни, без которой кино погибло бы! Следовательно, до тех пор, пока через Доротти Вернон и Закройщика кино вполне связано с жизнью, с действительной кинодинамической постановкой, вытекающей и из сущности кино, придется подождать, ибо это может оказаться не «конкретно» («нужна-де морда жизни, но не безмордие»).

Вот заколдованный конкретный круг, в котором тысячу лет вертятся художники-живописцы, и вслед за ними завертелось и кино, до мозга костей убежденное, что только то конкретно, где существуют гуттаперчевые, пневматические кинопоцелуи.[100] И того, кто осмелился бы дать беспоцелуйный экран, общество назвало бы сумасшедшим утопистом, абстракционно мыслящим выродком конкретно мыслящего общества. Из этого круга конкретных поцелуев путь лежит через новое искусство вообще. Кино только через новые искусства, через чистую абстракцию к новой форме выйдет к своему динамо-кинетическому построению фильма, как, между прочим, уже вышел живописец.

Итак, роль того, по чьему закону сейчас идет кино, является в нем незначительной и даже ставится вопрос о судьбе этой роли. Правда, вопрос о судьбе художника поставлен в кино не самим художником, и это произошло потому, что кинорежиссер, кинооператор, весь производственный коллектив просто стали находить его деятельность с щетинными щетками, палитрами, красками, холстами каким-то подсобным элементом в деле установки кинокартины; художник — лишь деталь во власти режиссера, равно как и полотер, которому нужно натереть зал. В кино выяснилось, что ни художнику, ни полотеру уже не написать картины. На эту арену выступил другой художник — художник-кинописатель, динамик с усвоением всего искусства художника-живописца, который с нетерпением, возможно, ждет палитры цветных лучей, чтобы из них соткать живописные планы фактур по подобию Ренуара, Дега, Милле и пр. Отсюда видно, что и оно находится во власти его со всеми режиссерами, с другой — художник в самом кино во власти режиссера; здесь он прав не имеет, его побивает режиссер, расходясь в композиционном или конструктивном построении места действия. Спор между художником и режиссером в нынешнем кино может быть только по двум причинам: одна кроется в средствах техники и другая — в художественной композиции. Спор по второй причине происходит от запамятования кем-либо из них композиции живописного порядка того или иного крупного художника или течения в живописи (Перова, Поленова, Гейнсборо и др.). Правда, для режиссера, в особенности нашего, это все происходит незаметно, и я уверен, что Протазанов вовсе и не думал, что многие кадры *Торжка* написаны светом и тенью по композиции «Птицеловы» Перова. Но возможно, что в *Доротти Вернон* многие кадры сознательно подгонялись до полного тождества к композиции живописи Гейнсборо.

Итак, если кинорежиссеры сознательно или несознательно находятся на путях художников-живописцев, то тот лучший их них киносветописец и постановщик,

кто осознает все живописные пути и их законы; у такого режиссера и оператора картина будет написана лучше, ибо он, изучив композиции крупного художника-живописца, сможет подобрать классически все элементы для картины, лиц и всей обстановки, до мелочей сумеет все выявить и показать каждую деталь в целом, если она нужна. Это очень важно для создания картины: в этом ее качество и цельность.

На Западе мало-помалу крупные художники-живописцы начинают работать в кино, начиная свою работу с чисто абстрактного элемента, начинают с того, с чего получаем в будущем новые формы.[101] Этот выход современного художника-живописца в кино должен нас и его привести к новой сущности и значению экрана как нового средства показания массам новой жизни искусства.

От ГТК, конечно, безуспешно ждать кинохудожников, потому что ГТК стоит на той же точке зрения, на которой бы художник-живописец мог придти в кино не как декоратор, уборщик, костюмер, а как кинохудожник, кинописец динамических картин, и именовать его режиссером не следует, потому что сегодняшний режиссер есть не тот художник, взявшийся написать на холсте (экране) светотенеписью движущуюся картину. Подобно тому как живописец, устанавливая натурщиков для своей статической картины, присвоил же себе звание режиссера по недоразумению, думая, что он исходит из театра. И само собою ясны все провалы в кино художников-декораторов из театра,[102] которые оформляют в цвете уже созданную картину литературными средствами художника-писателя.

ГТК должно стать новой Академией художеств с новыми техническими средствами выражения и писания динамических картин, но, конечно, в нее должна войти особая система и методы для сцепления исторической спайки искусства живописного и кинетического как конечной технической вершины искусства.

Из всего изложенного роль художника как такового, как нечто целое — очевидна и непонятна как пособника декоратора, как деталь со специальными функциями. Мне кажется, что не менее очевидно положение, что кино должно включать в свою работу крупнейших мастеров-живописцев, деятельность которых могла бы впоследствии принести пользу культуре кино.

Художественно-научный фильм. Живопись и проблемы архитектуры.
Приближение новой пластической архитектурной системы

Девятнадцатый век знаменует собой разнообразие видов искусства. С живописного импрессионизма начинается, собственно говоря, быстрая смена точек зрения на искусство в художественном мире, благодаря чему конец девятнадцатого и начало двадцатого века изобилуют огромным количеством измов,[103] то есть разными течениями и направлениями в живописном искусстве.

Живописное искусство одно из видов искусства, которое наиболее всех стало на путь деформации всех установленных точек зрения. С половины девятнадцатого века до начала двадцатого живописцы проделали глубокие разведки по существу дела, в силу чего возникли течения и направления. Таким образом, мы имеем сейчас около 15 измов, из которых наиглавнейшую роль должен занять кубизм в истории архитектурной проблемы. С кубизма в одной из стадий его развития мы можем считать, что новая архитектурная проблема проступает. Эта стадия мною определяется 4-ой, то есть тот момент, когда художник-живописец переходит к построению своей живописной концепции в пространстве, в котором он устанавливает разнообразные материалы и связывает их конструкцией. Конечно, это были чистые абстрактные наборы материалов в живописном отношении и ощущении, возможно, не имеющие в виду ту возможность, которую выдвинули люди с архитектурным ощущением.

Показать рельеф.

Пикассо.

По этой линии мы видим только зародыши пространственного строения материалов, которые в дальнейшем переносятся художниками на утилитаристический путь и становятся в качестве конструктивным искусством, сначала абстрактным, а потом конкретным, поставившим себе в цель и сообразно этой [цели] утилитар-

ную работу, возникающую из потребностей дня. Показать конструктивистические задания.

Дальше идет новое направление, которое я называю супрематизмом. Сначала это направление стоит на живописной линии (цветопись). Двумерное выражение ощущений потом переходит в трехмерное объемное выражение тех же ощущений. Супрематическое направление является на той же стадии двумерным и трехмерным выражением (плоскость и объем). В последней стадии, объемной, оно создает новый элемент, в силу чего создается и предархитектурное отношение этих элементов, т. е. архитектоника.

1. Показать развитие.

Супремат[ические] плоскости квадрата.

Плоскостные различные ощущения.

2. Архитектонику как проблему.

3. Архитектуру в жизни.

№ 1. Черный суп[рематический] квадрат, второй красный квадрат.

№ 3. Белый квадрат.

№ 2.   красный,   зеленый,   белый.
Движение квадрата дает круг в разных окрасках.

№ 3. Круг занимает свое место в известном пространстве. Черный круг становится сдвинутым с центра, зеленый продвигается к краю границ пространства, а белый вперед с ощущением динамическим.

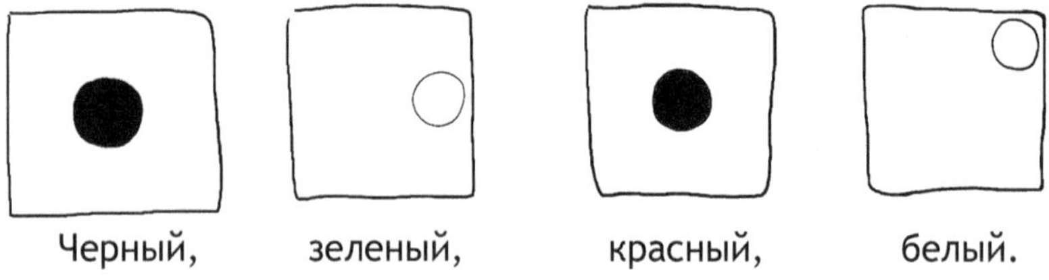

Черный,   зеленый,   красный,   белый.

№ 4. Изменение вида круга с окрашиванием на черный и белый и красный — черный.

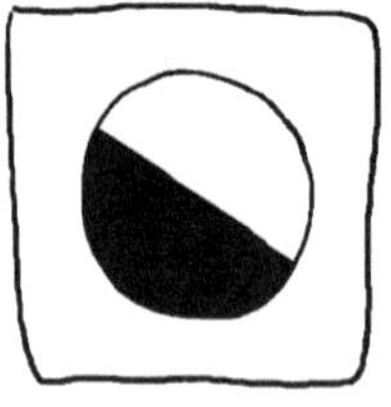

5 Распадение супрем[атического] квадрата на две белые и две черные клетки. В квадрате в двух углах начинается посветление до белого, а черные два угла остаются в неизменности и создают новую форму квадратного отношения.

6. Форма № 5 делает перемещение.

Верхний квадрат, черный, превращается в белый, а белый в черный и образуют новый супрематический элемент, который в следующих изменениях окрашивается в черный и красный цвет и белый и красный.

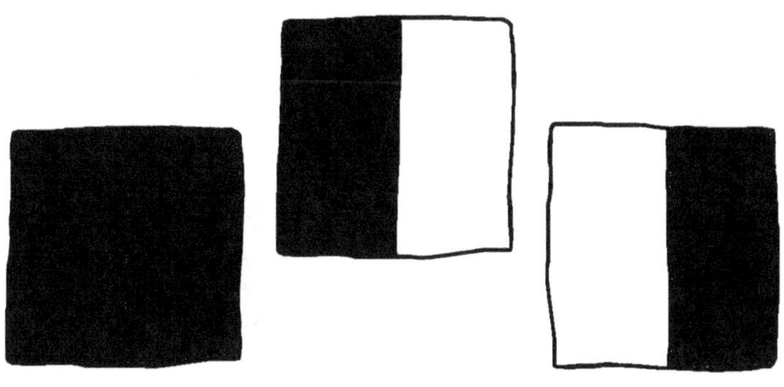

№ 7. Форма № 6 продолжает развиваться и образует новую форму, т. е. опрокидывается из вертикального положения в горизонтальное положение, после чего черная плоскость сдвигается вперед.

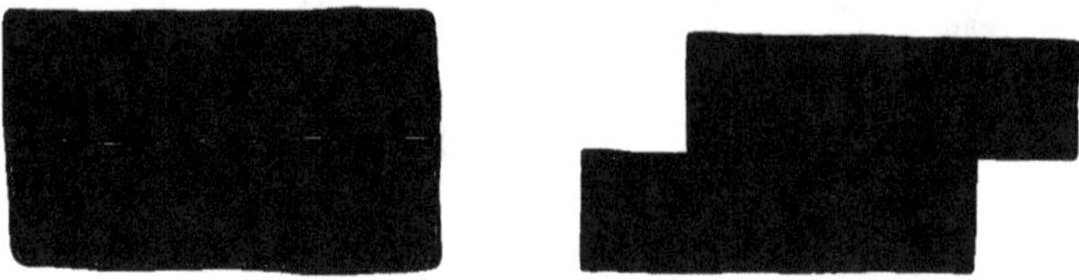

Дальше двигается черная, становится самостоятельным элементом, который и является основным, творящим целую систему отношений.

Формы элементов № 6. Элемент В образует самостоятельный элемент.

Элемент В [и] супр[ематическая] прямая начинают образовывать следующую основную форму крестовиками № 8.

№ 8.

Формы крестовиков начинают развиваться в обстоятельствах динамических.

8 и 9.

Ср. № 9.

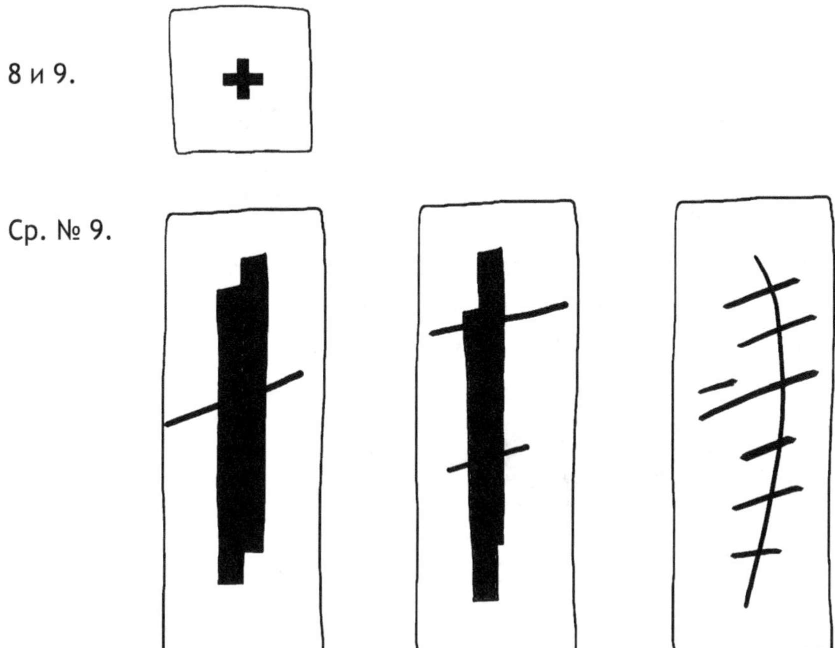

В данном случае развития крестовидного строения происходит развитие удлинения элемента В и элемента А красного к низу. Нижняя конечность обоих, чер[ного] и красного, уже сжата. Верхняя [конечность] элемента А в своей толщине удлиняется и потом распадается на отдельные элементы или же [они] остаются удлиненными и в крестоватых отношениях принимают положение диагонального устремления.

№ 10 форма. Видим, что элемент А собирается в пространства. Два последующих положения образуют крестовину, которая своим вращением образует круг и соответствующую новую фигуру.

№ 11 представляет собой вид колонии супр[ематического] элемента.

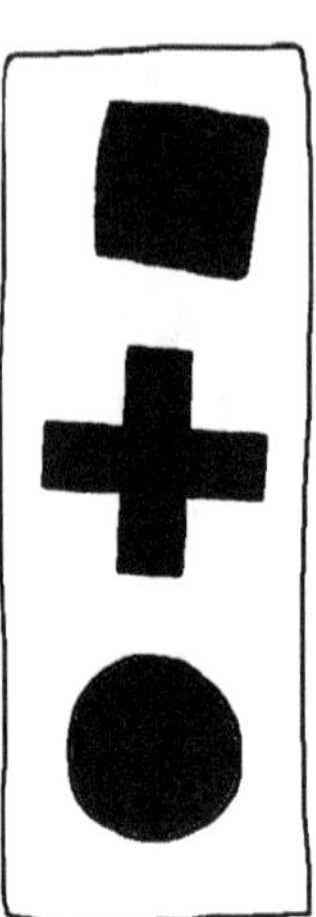

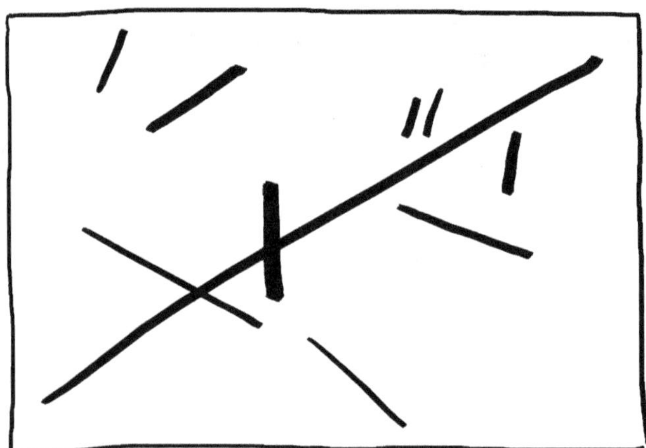

12. Мы видим развитие элемента типа супр[ематического]. Прямая в объемы.

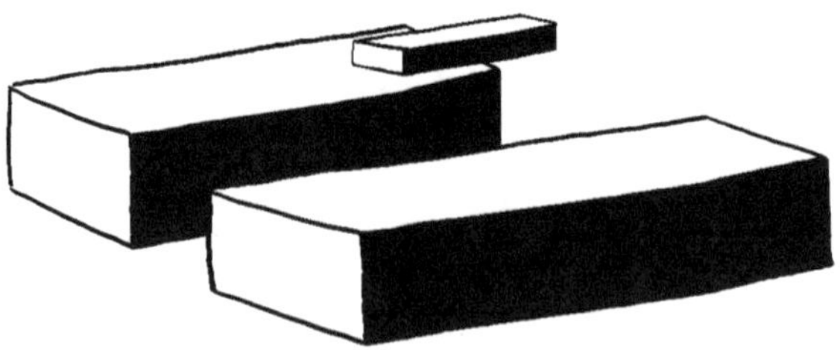

13. Форма 12 развивается по тому [же] принципу, что и плоскость, т. [е.] происходит распадение и спадение элемента. Спадающие движения производят куб, и ближние к нему элементы производят распадение и удлинение с их разномасштабным движением.

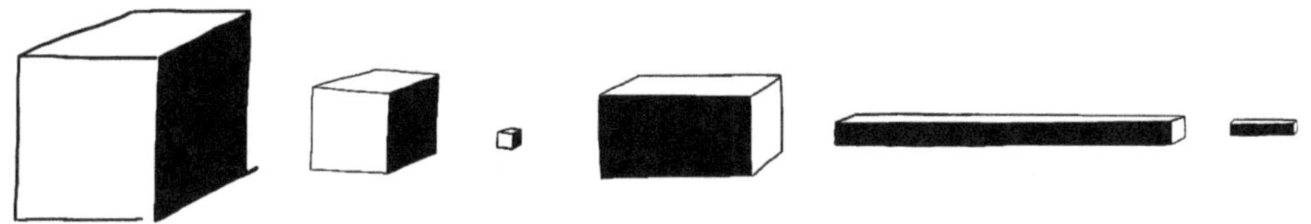

14. Форма № 13 в своем движении образует архитектонический фрагмент.

15. Форма 13 тем же фрагментом образует архитектонический вид (систему).

16. Форма 15 дает проблему новой архитектуры.

[Живопись и фотография]
Письмо Ласло Моголи-Наги[104]

Многоуважаемый Моголи-Наги,
Получив Ваше приглашение принять участие в дискуссии по поводу статьи в *i 10* и ознакомившись с ней, вижу, что дело в ней идет главным образом на защиту живописи, но не противопоставлении фотографии последней. Интересное место есть в этой статье, касающееся и меня, в котором я как бы обвиняюсь в отступничестве от живописи, а, следовательно, от искусства и переходу к механическому роду производства пластических явлений.[105] Поспешу сейчас же опровергнуть вкравшееся недоразумение! Я никогда не стоял, не оправдывал механическую мертвую зеркальность фотографического объектива и никогда не писал в своей теории против живописи, наоборот, всегда отстаиваю живопись как одно из главнейших искусств по целому художническому ощущению живописного мира, конечно, настаиваю на живописи как таковой, беспредметной.

И если автор чувствует, что и в теперешних моих работах чувствуется живопись, другими словами ощущается элемент искусства, то это и есть доказательство того, что ощущения, передаваемые супрематическими элементами, не передаются иначе, как только через плазму искусства, то, что он понимает под живописью. Но тут я должен упомянуть, что живописи в супрематических элементах нет, ибо под живописью я ощущаю нечто другое живописи Сезанна и первой стадии кубизма. Супрематические пластические элементы есть нечто другое, но дело идет не о живописи, но только о методе искусства [как] духовно органической передачи этого или другого ощущения. И если фотографическим способом можно будет передать те же ощущения, то и фотография будет тем же техническим средством, что и кисть, карандаш… не более.

Выдвинутый вопрос автором статьи о фотографии и живописи в другое время не имел бы значения, но очевидно, что сейчас автор заметил движение как бы против живописи, против искусства. Действительно, нет дыма без огня. Механизация, материализация, литографизация, фотографизация, упрощенство начинают выдвигаться преимущественно конструктивистами. Это выдвижение действительно опасно, поскольку машина не может выразить духовных ощущений, не может считаться хорошим средством, тогда кисть и карандаш по техническому средству выше, ибо через кого может протекать то или другое ощущение во всей своей силе.

Для выдвиженцев фотомеханизации печатная квадратная супрематическая плоскость (см. журнал *Мерц*) достаточна, но для меня это мертвый элемент, а дальше какие бы не были монтажи из снятых фотографией элементов, они сами по себе будут мертвы для искусства, содержанием для которого являются те или иные беспредметные ощущения, через них я утверждал полный контакт с миром.

Относительно фактуры, то с моей точки зрения она не играет никакой роли, если ее рассматривать как таковую, ибо фактура вытекает не сама по себе, но только в зависимости от духовного, «душевного возбуждения», как говорит автор статьи, но к этому я бы добавил, что волна, самое духовное возбуждение, возбуждается тем или другим ощущением, в силу этого реализуемое принимает ту или другую фактуру.

Дальше автор пишет, что «благодаря особенности фактуры живописные видения высоко устремленной духовности попадают непосредственно в круг материального сознания действительности». Это положение я бы оспаривал,[106] таковой круг материальной действительности для меня не существует, существуют для меня только ощущения вне осознания их воздейственности.

Таким образом, говорит автор, создается сила напряжения, вдохновения, создается сила, [как и] между отношениями средств живописных и идейной целью существует разноликость в смысле их сущности и реализации.

Эта точка зрения с новыми искусствами отпала, ибо новое искусство безыдейно — беспредметно, сегодня искусство есть только как таковое — этим не исключается напряжение, которое зависит от бывания того или иного ощущения.

Относительно того, что автор думает, что чем богаче поверхность картины фактурными выходами, тем очевиднее созидающий одухотворенный ход процесса живописи, то в этом я сомневаюсь, ибо последнее зависит не от множества фактур, но только от экономического соотношения контрастных элементов последней.

Итак, фотография, как и кино, с моей точки зрения, есть только техническое новое средство, которое живописцам необходимо использовать, как в свое время и сейчас они используют свиную щетину и графит, краску. Они должны стать теми же проводниками ощущений, что карандаш, уголь и кисть.

Если в этом моем письме Вы найдете интерес или ответ по существу, то можете его или отчасти поместить.

Казимир Малевич

12 апреля 1927

Из общей точки зрения на кино можно установить, что кино не является простым обыкновенным техническим средством для передачи той или другой научной мысли, ощущений, переживаний, иллюстраций, идей, мировоззрений и эстетических восприятий. Но что кино есть некое живое существо, талантливое, всемогущее по своему творчеству, необыкновенное по гениальности явление. Компетентность его весьма обширна и охватывает все явления и процессы жизни и, наконец, что его искусство есть самое великое из всех искусств.[107] Дальше идти некуда. Все другие искусства есть только недоразумение некультурного прошлого. Правда, этот гений имеет, однако, недостаток; недостаток этот заключается в том, что кино немой, хотя его немота и глухота не умаляют его гениальности и не лишают его звания великого заслуженного.

Итак, он «Великий Немой».[108] Но есть в нем и еще один недостаток, заключающийся в том, что он, кроме немоты, страдает бесцветностью своего лица и отсутствием рельефности. И еще недостаток в том, что он полон мещанских вкусов и банальщины. Довольно неразборчивое и не разбирающееся в этом существо. Может быть, в этом виновны родители, которые родили глухое и немое существо. А этот недостаток требует исправления введением в его организм цветовосприимчивости и звука.

Это нужно для того, чтобы создать кино как единое целое, совершенное явление. Разрешить этот вопрос думают при помощи научных сил, что эти силы рано или поздно доделают в кино голос и способность цветовосприятия, чем и осчастливят кинослушателей (артиста и артистку).

Этим самым избавят зрителя от ни с чем не связанной, бичующей слух зрителей киномузыки, ибо зритель пришел не слушать, но смотреть.

Но так или иначе, будет ли кино одарено звуковой способностью, будет ли тело его цветовосприимчиво, артисту и артистке все же не удастся войти в его

тело так, чтобы оживить его механическое немое движение живой речью. А так же быть окрашенным в живом цвете.

Но пока что кино будет бесподобное великое механическое мертвое.[109]

Точно также не более счастливый и великий радио, другое рожденное механическое дитя науки, внук граммофона, ограничивающий свой диапазон по преимуществу звуком, тоже бесподобно вопит через громкоговоритель.

В будущем великие подобные достижения техники угрожают нашествием на живую силу человечества (хорошо, что мы к этому времени умрем); великие достижения техники в рождении механического потомства порадуют общество будущего, два бесподобных механических явления, кино и радио, соединят в единое целое, и человечество получит удивительное уже архивеликое мертвое детище, удовлетворяющее зрителя по слуховому и зрительному восприятию творческих проявлений, механическое кино.

Престарелая наука безусловно хотела сделать живое явление, но в силу своего старческого бессилия создала великие механические аппараты.

Итак, из самой гениальности великого немого можно сделать выводы, что из универсальности его никогда не может быть кино как нечто самостоятельное; житейским барахлом до сих пор нагружены как верблюды[110] так называемые свободные [искусства], как это мы видим, в живописи, скульптуре и архитектуре.

Пока будет экран местом, куда будут сваливать обыватели свое бытовое барахло, до тех пор кино не будет самостоятельным искусством, ибо это новый мусорный ящик, изобретенный техническими силами науки, в котором обыватель показывает свою требуху, или верблюд, навьюченный хламом кочующего киргиза.

Искусство живописи и скульптуры по существу должно быть довольно тем, что наконец-то наступило время, в котором появился такой великий гений, который

принял на себя все обывательское барахло для своего показа в разных платьях, и теперь искусство живописи и скульптуры может заниматься своим «как таковым» делом и развиваться самостоятельно.

Итак, чтобы выражать посредством кино все это барахло, нужно ему иметь свой собственный метод, как это было в свое время в живописном и скульптурном искусствах, метод освобождения от «кинореск мещанства».[111] Но кино до сих пор не имеет своих методов освобождения. Кино находится во власти живописи и скульптуры (а главным образом их) — поэтому кино не является чем-то, у которого должно быть свое искусство, своя композиция, своя система и свой материал, как в живописи цвет, форма, законы отношений, а кино по своему существу есть временное явление. Искусство строит элементы и их отношения во времени [и] пространстве, в нем все футуризируется, находится в движении, всесторонне во времени явления развертывается, но это блестяще разрешено футуризмом живописным, кино этого не понял и занялся барахлом; кино практическое, удобное, дешевое распространение знаний, в чем его польза и, может быть, и назначение, и губительное явление в смысле воспитания людей в области художественной культуры. Если кино будет идти по пути «кинореск», тогда кино не может развивать человека и утончать его мироощущение многообразием вероятия элементов в художественно организованном кино. Кино стоит сейчас на самом последнем месте по этой линии, за барахлом и поцелуями не видать художественной формы.[112] А если его сравнить с произведениями живописных искусств, то оно не выдержит никакой критики. Это глухонемой ловелас,[113] вечно шатающийся по будуарам.

Художественный вопрос никогда не может быть разрешен в кино предметно, потому что природа кино — движение, а предметы не есть элементы движения, благодаря чему установить композицию художественного порядка предметов

нельзя. Нельзя, потому что все отношения раз уже скомпонованных элементов не меняются, ибо движущаяся единица общей суммы, передвигаясь среди установленных других элементов, нарушает композицию по форме, а если и пришлось установить композицию по цвету, тогда бы осложнилось все дело до невозможности. Поэтому напрасно будем думать, что если в кино достигнут цветочувствительности, то кино достигнет в цветных репродукциях полного совершенства, что кино станет наряду с живописным искусством.

Итак, каждое художественное произведение в живописи или в скульптуре, даже в архитектуре, не иначе строится или компонуется как в полном сочетании ансамбля одного пятна и формы между собой.

Их отношение устанавливается раз навсегда.

Мы видим разноцветную обстановку комнаты, в комнате находятся две-три фигуры с разными цветными платьями в разных положениях времени.

Эти фигуры, одетые в то или другое платье, имеют цветные нюансы, связанные с бесчисленными рефлексами светоотражения, которые находятся в разных направлениях и которые исходят от всех предметов, в комнате находящихся. Пока фигуры находятся в движении, их отношение ко всему окружающему будет хаотично. Поэтому, чтобы обратить этот хаос в картину художественного произведения, необходимо соотнести все аксессуары и фигуры к той или другой гамме, т. е. к той или другой композиции цветовых или живописных отношений.

В силу этого художественного требования живописец не только копирует формы или цветовые окраски предметов, но и нивелирует силу одного тона к силе другого, т. е. изменяет и подчиняет взаимно интенсивность цветную. Эта нивелировка вызывается тем чувством световой гармонии, которым настроен живописец-художник. Такое же отношение у художника и к форме.

Формовые отношения, т. е. предметы, имеют ту же установку художественной композиции, они также соотносятся и сочетаются в каждом движении фигуры по комнате. Обыватели никогда не замечают этих отношений, как соотносится угол двери или сама дверь, окно рамы, карнизы, столы, стулья, диван и т. д.

Мы заняты рассмотрением одной детали или разговором и не обращаем внимания на художественные соотношения всех форм друг к другу.

Следовательно, эстетически мы не воспринимаем в большинстве случаев ансамбль быта, ибо заняты его содержанием далеко не эстетического порядка.

Художник, наоборот, всегда воспринимает явления через эстетическое восприятие, соотносит предметы и фигуры между собою и часто извиняется, если прослушал содержание разговора. Художник, разговаривая с тем или другим человеком, во многих случаях отвечает моторно, все время фиксируя свое внимание на рассмотрении отношений цветных пятен и формы разговаривающего с ним человека. При этом соотношении он вырабатывает тот тон, в который будут включены все другие цвета или тона.

Таким образом, он устанавливает один основной тон, в силу которого и нивелирует всю силу или часть силы того или другого цвета или, наоборот, выдвигает на передний план тот тон или силу цвета в гораздо сильнейшем напряжении, чем в натуре.

Так написать картину в кино нельзя, ибо пришлось бы людей фотографировать не с живых, а [с] написанных в картине живописцем (может быть, этот опыт и интересен).

Из этого состояния художника и отношения его к явлению мы можем видеть, что художник начисто поглощен работой установления живописной композиции и другого содержания в его работе нет. Пусть даже в таком произведении мы бу-

дем видеть даже фигуры и предметы, то и в том случае мы не можем искать в них другого содержания кроме живописной композиции.

Но есть и другие произведения, в которых мы будем видеть передачу двух содержаний, живописного и бытовой морали. Такое искусство будет компромиссным искусством, сочетающим в себе и приятное, и полезное. Причем в таком случае художник, хотя и поставлен в ежовые рукавицы, но все же пытается это барахло понятного и полезного так или иначе связать в художественную живописную композицию, чего связать в кино до сих пор не удалось, а это будет уже означать, что раз тот или другой вид уже зафиксирован в художественную композицию, то все виды, формы и цвет установлены навсегда статически, такова природа живописи. В этой подлинной художественной установке ничего передвинуться не может. Движения нет.

Таковы законы станковой живописи, и таковы законы будут для всего того, что по этому методу будет воспроизводиться.

Мы можем видеть хороший пример, если обратим свое внимание на культурные парки, т. е. художественное оформление растений, которые формированы по формуле какой-либо художественной живописной эпохи, то мы увидим, что ежегодно садовники стригут деревья, кусты, траву для того, чтобы их формы находились в одном и том же состоянии.

И когда на весну растения собираются к движению, это движение беспощадно нивелируется все тем же законом статики искусства. Нивелировка происходит и равняется на дворец как основную форму архитектурного порядка.

От живописной стороны и формы дворца и будет зависеть форма всего культурного парка.

Если мне скажут, что как же, ведь существуют художественные явления в движениях, что само движение может быть художественным движением, например, марши, пластические танцы[114] и т. д. Тогда я позволю себе ответить, что

все пластические танцы построены на искусстве ритма, но не живописи. А ритм, с моей точки зрения, — искусство сочетания повторности движений, а это будет орнаментальная форма движения. Живопись не может быть орнаментикой, ибо живопись есть в каждом своем моменте воспроизведение того или другого явления, законченный момент. А ритмические движения, рисующие собою орнаментику, есть неоконченное целое (бесконечное).

Таким образом, в пластических движениях или [их] орнаментике мы видим повторность форм. Поэтому само движение в орнаментике отсутствует, хотя и воспроизводится через движение человеческой фигуры, как и через движение живописной картины.

Таким образом, и в этом не живописном ритмическом орнаментальном искусстве, похожем скорее на цветную скульптуру в живом пространстве, мы имеем все тот же закон статики искусства.

Можем ли мы достигнуть художественного фильма в кино?

На этот вопрос я могу сказать, что до сих пор от самого существования кино художественного фильма не было. Фабульные постановки не могут быть поставлены как художественные явления. Это будет только установка голого содержания житейского барахла в известный порядок вытекания логических последствий той или другой функции последнего, которые и должны будут связываться между собою. Художественное их сочетание, собственно говоря, тут не при чем, и потому говорить о «выдающемся по художественной постановке фильме» не следует, ибо это будет означать обман и использование невежественного в этом случае обывателя, который заинтересован таким чревовещательным объявлением только потому, что он хочет увидеть, наконец, содержание своего барахла в художественной форме, забывая о том, что барахло его по своей природе никогда не может быть художественным.

Художественный фильм может быть поставлен в полной своей чистоте только в беспредметной форме, и это только в том случае удастся сделать, когда постановка будет базирована на чистом эстетическом ощущении и восприятии элементов формы и цвета в их беспредметном виде.

Но так как кинотехника не обладает цветной палитрою, то фильм художественный может идти не по живописной линии, но по скульптурной.

Это единственный путь к художественному бесфабульному фильму.

Свет, пространство и форма — вот главные основы этого фильма.

Кстати скажу, что эти основы должны быть применяемы и даже в фильме с предметным содержанием.

Мы привыкли всякую поножовщину, мордобитие и другие шельмования как технику обывателя, через которую он сочно и красочно выражает свое содержание, считать художественной, если ему удастся свое «проявление» «проявить» в кино, в котором он является уже не обывателем, а «обивателем» быта и шельмования.

Но эта привычка такового мышления обывателя дурная, ибо она не дает доступа к проявлению действительно художественного явления.

Итак, обыватели в кино, как и в живопись, и в скульптуру, даже в музыку стремятся всегда привести содержание своего быта для того, чтобы искусство возвеличить, чтобы поднять его качество и ценность, чтобы осмыслить его бессмыслицу. Так себе мыслит всякий обыватель.

Обыватели или содержатели барахла быта по своей наивности и слабоумию всегда видели в искусстве особые усовершенствованные мусорные ящики, совершенство которых заключалось в том, что в [них] приводился в порядок весь хаос житейского барахла. Этими мусорными ящиками, конечно, были художники, которые себя никак не могли представить вне этой функции. Поэтому как обыватель и сам даже художник иначе не мыслили себе искусства, [как] связанного с

похождениями обывателя, и считали, что искусство «исторически» с ним связано и лишь в этой его «исторической истории» поведения искусство художественной культуры может жить и развиваться.

Точно также и «великий немой» существует для того, чтобы в нем проявлять все сто процентов из жизни быта, всевозможных форм проявлений обывателя.

Кино также обмануто и приспособлено к тому же обиходу, к чему раньше приспособляли другие искусства, т. е. живопись и скульптуру, всячески затемняя путь искусства как такового, которого еще никто не видел в кино и видеть не будем, если будет проявляться такая же целесообразная установка шурум-бурума[115] в кино.

Художник, артист театра, режиссер и композитор потрясены таким явлением как кино. Многие перекочевывают из театров в кино вместо того, чтобы развивать художественную культуру в театре во всем ее многообразии, которая не доступна еще для кино ни в одном образе. Но эта перекочевка неизбежна, потому что в театре нет быстрого обновления формы выражения.

Поэтому наши строгие театры должны будут или исчезнуть, либо народить в этом плане новые театры художественной культуры.

Итак, до сих пор метод в кинопостановках двойственный: живописный и декоративно-театральный. Неизвестно почему тот и другой в нем существует. Очевидно потому, что собственного метода в кино еще нет. Нет того формирующего элемента в нем, по которому кино могло формировать свои постановки. Неизвестно, почему театральность в кино изгоняется,[116] но декоративно-театральный метод не изгоняется.

Конечно, причину изгнания театральщины нужно искать в природе самого кино, т. е. в его движении, в котором развертывается в разных планах содержание фильма. А движение театральное всегда развертывает свое содержание в двумерном плане пространства (однофасадность).

Кроме декоративно-театрального метода на первом плане стоит живописный метод выражения содержания фильма, который очень усиленно муссируется.

Мне бы и казалось, что если изгонять театральщину, надо изгонять наравне и живописный метод, ибо то и другое искусство по своему существу двумерное. Существует какое-то недоразумение, которое не выяснено до сих пор. Изгоняется театральное поведение артиста на экране, очевидно, потому, что в его поведении нет новой формы выражения, которую кино как бы нащупывает или хочет выработать в будущем.

Но с другой стороны, весь метод постановки целиком идет по методу живописи станковой, а театр и поведение его артистов воспитано по методу художественной декоративной культуры.

Таким образом, театр стоит исключительно на этой линии. Таковой линии в кино еще нет. Кино в таком состоянии, как оно есть сейчас, не может выдержать никакой критики в сравнении с тем, что завоевал театр, где поведение артиста, художника, композитора представляет собой одну целую, связанную форму художественной культуры.

 Но и театр не может выдержать критики, когда он незыблемо почивает на лаврах форм Брюллова и Бенуа.[117]

О театре существует мнение, что он близок к закату, его сменит кино-театр. И действительно, почив на лаврах заслуженных методов 18 века или начала 19 века, ему ничего не остается делать, как тихо почить.

Кино — новая форма выражения барахла. Вопросы в нем стоят только о новых методах выражения содержания последнего. И это заставляет всякого, работающего в искусстве, идти в кино только потому, чтобы в этой новой форме работать и искать этого усовершенствования методов выражения.

Но это тоже не выход, ибо пока кино обратится из механического мертвого в одушевленное живое, то одушевленный живой человек превратится в великое немоглухое.

Другими словами сказать, от художественной культуры ничего не останется, или художественная культура постепенно будет сведена из своего многообразия к механической тени и механическому звуку и механической музыке.

В результате обыватель имеет от науки удивительные изобретения, которые дают полную стопроцентную нагрузку экономии и дешевки, а также удобства. А впоследствии это все приведет к тому, что наше будущее поколение, будучи воспитанным на кино, радио, граммофоне, потеряет всякое ощущение ко всему живому, ибо всякое живое будет для него каким-то непонятным абстрактным делом.

Таким образом, дешевка и удобства у себя на дому в будущем могут дорого стоить человеку вне дома.

Итак, неправильно понято[е] искусство как вид художественной культуры должно было прийти к кино, снизить свою художественную культуру из всего многообразия до тени, либо совсем уничтожить себя. Ибо вопрос в жизни стоит не об искусстве как таковом, а о содержании бытового барахла.

А для показа последнего действительно не нужно особой роскоши вроде художественной культуры. Оно может быть таким, как видит глаз.

Итак, мы накануне падения театра как учреждения, которое должно стоять на художественной проблеме, и падения вообще всей художественной культуры.

Кино, как я уже сказал, изгоняет из своего экрана театральщину, а следовательно, и план декоративно-живописный, но базируется на живописном плане станкового живописного искусства.

 Но по своей природе оно должно не упускать из виду скульптурный метод выражения. В кинопостановках нужно было бы строго различить эти два метода и

подхода в работе. Для этого светооператорам нужно хорошо ознакомиться со скульптурными методами и живописными, чтобы по-разному освещать то или другое явление в кадре.

Наоборот, артистов для кино создают заново, оскопляя их слух и звук.

После того, когда он станет глухонемым, он становится годным для экрана. В этом деле есть сдвиг. Но нет сдвига в сторону художника-живописца и живописца-декоратора. Но это, может быть, потому, что, собственно говоря, живописец уже давно пишет картины, которые не разговаривают.

Поэтому его метод хотя и сведен к тени, но все же сродни кино.

У меня возникает мысль, не будет ли более подходить по своей природе скульптурный метод отношения к кадру, в котором играет роль в сущности выявления свет, форма, пространство.

Это в том случае, если нельзя найти совершенно своеобразный метод киновыражения.

Еще одно замечание: кино хочет остановиться уже на «исключительно выдающемся по художественной постановке фильме», и поэтому в его организме должны быть художественные начала; для выражения этого начала он формирует свои штаты по театру: писатель, режиссер, композитор, художник.

Может быть, этот должен быть другой, без пианиста, сценариста, режиссера и художника, поскольку не ставится в кино-театре художественной проблемы.

Кинорежиссер и художник играют огромную роль. Кто из них является главным? По анализу любой постановки сказать трудно. В особенности, когда идет речь о художественной постановке.

Ведь вся художественная сторона зависит от художника, но не от режиссера и от того, посколько художник изучил стиль художественной стороны эпохи, если это исторический фильм или фильм быта, постолько ему удается оформить со-

держание в художественной форме. Художник от целого здания до пуговицы должен все знать и по форме, и по цвету.

Кроме того, он должен обладать знанием композиции разных эпох и обладать сам композиционным богатством своей творческой силы.

Второе: каждый художник есть представитель той или другой живописной школы с уклоном в одном случае в сторону декоративного начала, в другом — в сторону станковой живописи, и поэтому каждый кадр художественного фильма ориентируется на то или другое течение в искусстве живописном.

В настоящее время кинопостановки ориентируются на передвижническую композицию. Всякий кадр рассмотрен с точки зрения передвижной композиции, частично на «Мир искусства»,[118] частично на импрессионизм.

Это все относится к тем фильмам, которые ставятся в наше время. Все же фильмы исторического порядка ориентируются на картину живописную того станкового порядка, которое и было в ту эпоху.

Третье положение в кино ориентируется на то, что видит глаз, и стремится снять натуру в упор. Это план натуралистический.

Но и этот план в момент фиксирования того, что видит глаз, обязательно ориентируется на композицию искусства передвижного характера.

Тогда, когда в постановке, что видит глаз, очевидно, нужно подразумевать новый метод, который, очевидно, имеет в виду избежание всякого творческого художественного реализования того или другого вида. В этом плане не нужно уже искать художественной стороны, ибо явление не реализовано в художественную форму. Может быть, это для кино и нужно, ибо художественная форма в живописном плане немыслима.

Кино в сегодняшней его форме переживает банальную форму анекдотического периода передвижничества потому, что его захватили главным образом люди, воспитанные на анекдотизме живописного передвижничества, которое по своему

существу, не в обиду будь сказано, было далеко от художеств, ибо большинство из них воспринимало мир как обывательское барахло, т. е. [жизнь] как таковую, или через призму политической точки зрения, либо через православную (религиозную).

Художественное восприятие было на втором месте, в лучшем случае.

Перенося эту точку в кино, становится сомнительным, чтобы в кино постановки были художественными. У кино нет искусства как художественного выражения восприятия, как в живописи, скульптуре и архитектуре.

Тогда необходимо искать его, как искал живописец, скульптор и архитектор, все время освобождаясь от барахла быта и его точек зрения на искусство. Конечно, искать в передвижничестве ничего нельзя, но пусть кино ищет в тех новых видах искусства, которые сейчас переформировывают и формируют те или другие беспредметные восприятия.

Художник и режиссер в кино это не одно и то же, что режиссер и художник в театре. Художник в театре есть тот мастер, который фабулу связывал в художественную композицию и развернул ее в двумерном плане лицом к воспринимающему зрителю. Режиссер в театре подчинен этой двумерности живописно-декоративного воспроизведения содержания в театре и, в свою очередь, развертывает лица действующих элементов в том же двумерном декоративном плане пространства.

Театр — это то место, в котором художник пишет или строит живописно-декоративную музыкальную картину, сочетая весь аксессуар с формою двигающихся элементов.

Перемещение движущихся элементов предусматривается художником, их сочетания в том или другом месте.

Итак, если кино победит театр, то оно победит или же уничтожит в человеке эстетическое, художественное восприятие мира. Кино, можно сказать, детище

практической и экономической точки зрения на мир, которое не считает его роскошью. Практическая установка на жизнь делает свое дело: художественная культура мало-помалу сводится на нет. Архитектура как искусство уже исчезла, ее заменили экономические коробки, и люди, по мере развития этого, исключительно по своей постановке экономической целесообразности всю художественную культуру сведут на нет. Следовательно, мы накануне замены эстетического восприятия мира практически-экономическим.

ЖИВЬ

ЖИВОПИСНЫЕ ЗАКОНЫ В ПРОБЛЕМАХ КИНО

Для того, чтобы оправдать заглавие статьи, мне, конечно, нужно было бы написать подробный анализ целого ряда кинопостановок с приложением множества иллюстративного материала, свидетельствующего о влиянии живописного изобразительства на строение кинокартины.

Такая работа вылилась бы в брошюру, которую не опубликуешь.[119]

Поэтому я решил ограничиться небольшой статьей, слегка касаясь данного вопроса в связи с работой Дзиги Вертова.

Живописные законы в проблемах кино еще не обнаружены ни режиссерами, ни критикой, ни исследователями кино, хотя пользуются ими все.

Всем кажется, что кино есть самостоятельное искусство, а постановщики убеждены, что они ничего общего не имеют с живописными воздействиями и являются новыми светописателями особенных картин, которых ни одно искусство не могло выразить — кроме киноискусства.

Кинолюди, правда, заметили, что в кинокартины проникает театральщина, с которой нужно вести борьбу.[120] Борьба эта главным образом должна вестись против методов и принципа театра в выявлении той или другой темы в кино.

Конечно, метод театра есть метод художественно-декоративный, имеющий двумерный разворот действия на плоскости. Это его законное поле. От этого выявления темы в театре она не иначе развивается, как в однофасадном плане. А от этого двумерного пространства зависит и вся игра актера. Кроме этого, он не только актер, но и декоративное пятно. Его костюм каждой деталью должен быть тоже связан, как и все его движения, в едином направлении и ритме картины.

Кино разворачивает свою тему также во времени. Вернее, хочет развернуть тему в большем объеме времени, чем театр.

Но эти попытки использовать расширенное время во всех его видах почти недостижимы при данных сюжетных постановках, и картина останется фиксирован-

ной в трехмерном иллюзорном живописном плане. Последнее, т. е. живописный «показ», тоже должно встретить сопротивление, как и театральное искусство, поскольку живописный план вмешивается в кино и воздействует на композицию, на монтаж кадров в целое.

Кинетичность еще не спасает дела и не сводит кино с иллюзорного положения любой живописной картины.

Просмотрев множество кинокартин, я мог только обратить внимание на совершенствование технических возможностей, которыми обладает кино. Но из просмотренных картин я ни одной не увидел, в которой была бы поставлена проблема киноформы как таковой, присущей свойству или особенности кино.

Если же в кино были новшества, то эти новшества целиком лежали в плане живописных проблем. Таким образом, получилось, что проблемы, сделанные в живописи, являются и проблемами киноискусства.

Все кинопостановки развиваются, таким образом, по тем живописным материалам, которые уже лежат в архиве истории живописи. Новейшие бытовые фильмы идут под знаком передвижничества тоже архивно-исторического времени.

Например, Эйзенштейн своими новшествами является старым передвижником, который не только стремится внести новое в кино, но стремится все технические средства кинотехники использовать для выражения картин старого передвижного характера.

Надо признать, что его передвижные картины не являются вульгарными, но их можно поставить наравне с картинами художника Маковского.[121]

Изучение вида живописного изобразительства нужно потому, что все равно влияние живописи на композицию кадра и выражение всей темы продолжают действовать как живописные станковые явления.

Изучив живописные виды изобразительства, мы натолкнемся на массу новейших приемов методов выражения, и тогда вскроются новые горизонты восприятия новейших явлений, скрытых до изучения.

Изучение живописных изобразительных направлений даст возможность правильно, системно организовывать материал и тем самым избегать той путаницы, которая существует сейчас в кинокартинах как по линии композиции кадра, так и по линии контрастов,[122] в особенности в тех формах, которые претендуют на новые открытия.

Изучая живописный материал, в особенности новейший, мы вскроем очень важную линию, линию, на которой тема распадается и растворяется, после чего выступают новые, нам не знакомые раньше явления. Мы увидели бы не образ предмета, а новое содержание последнего.

Передвижничество было китайской стеной, которая преграждала путь всяким проблемам в живописи. Эта стена стоит и до сих пор, и в ней успешно заделываются те пробоины, которые нанесены штормом новейших течений живописи.

Современное кино также имеет свою китайскую стену, охраняющую «проблемы Монти Бенкса» от внедрения новых проблем.

Иначе чем объяснить, что режиссер Дзига Вертов оказался и перед кинокитайской стеной непризнания в то время, когда всякие искания новой кинопроблемы в киноискусстве должны быть широко поощряемы?[123]

Я не знаю, чего хочет и к чему стремится Дзига Вертов, на эту тему я не беседовал с ним, но я ознакомился с его двумя работами: *Одиннадцатый* и *Человек с киноаппаратом*. *Одиннадцатый* меня поразил своей неподкупной искренностью, а также целым рядом моментов, ярко отличающих его от «передвижнического» благополучия.

Но *Одиннадцатый*, все же еще являясь картиной, элементы которой (кадры) связаны одной темой, дает заметить в ней новые «прибавочные» элементы,[124]

которые свидетельствуют о том, что где-то в глубине творческого центра Дзиги Вертова появились новые восприятия, которые требуют нового оформления.

Эти новые ощущения выдвинули некоторые моменты, о которых раньше не приходилось и догадываться ни одному из режиссеров.

В *Одиннадцатом* мы уже имеем значительный процент «абстрактных» моментов, которые и являются результатом новых ощущений, еще не совсем осознанных режиссером. Но и этого уже достаточно.

Рассматривая *Одиннадцатый*, мы присутствуем при появлении новых элементов, которые в конце концов будут организовываться в одно целое сцепление и выразят нам новую форму передачи нового ощущения, дадут нам новую небывалую фильму.

Найти эти признаки и оценить их можно только тогда, когда зритель знает их причину и знает, откуда и из какой области эти явления идут и какой системе эти элементы принадлежат...

И могу сказать, что для того, чтобы разобраться в *Одиннадцатом*, нужно безусловно знать футуризм Боччони, Балла, нужно знать всю систему живописного футуризма. Всякие же изучения с «точки зрения кино» не будут достаточны. На основе их можно сделать огромные ошибки в оценке *Одиннадцатого* или других подобных картин.

Так, например, Поль Сезанн — первоклассный ткач не сюжетов, а живописи — недооценивался импрессионистами; а Моклер — идеолог импрессионизма — прямо отнес П. Сезанна в разряд третьей категории.[125] Это случилось потому, что измерялся или оценивался Сезанн с точки зрения импрессионизма.

Рассматривая Сезанна с этой точки, конечно, в его произведениях мы не сможем найти стопроцентных импрессионистических данных.

Но такое измерение ошибочно, ибо Сезанна нужно было рассматривать с точки зрения еще и живописи, и тогда мы бы оценили его правильно.

То же самое, если бы мы рассматривали *Одиннадцатый* с точки зрения «Монти Бенкса» (и его проблем) то, конечно, оценка была бы другая, а Дзига Вертов был бы насмерть уничтожен. Но если бы мы рассматривали *Одиннадцатый* с точки зрения футуризма, то мы нашли бы много ценного материала для будущей фильмы.

Точка зрения футуризма, с которой я просмотрел *Одиннадцатый*, помогла мне обнаружить целый ряд футуристических элементов. Я не имею всего материала, чтобы более точно установить факты, но те, которые есть, тоже могут дать некоторое представление о футурвоздействии. Я привожу здесь два кадра Дзиги Вертова и футуриста Балла для того, чтобы доказать то, что в данный момент руководили Дзигой Вертовым футуристические восприятия, что в нем были начала динамических напряжений, что от кадров Д. Вертова и Балла мы получаем одинаковое ощущение силы.

Если бы теперь Дзига Вертов был хорошо ознакомлен с футуризмом, то он скоро бы сделал бы выборку из той или другой фильмы футурэлементов и создал бы новую динамическую фильму в чистом виде.

Но и то, чего достиг Дзига Вертов в *Одиннадцатом*, делает его первым открывателем новых возможностей в кинетическом искусстве.

Человек с киноаппаратом является новым шагом вперед.

Этот шаг вперед нужно, конечно, понять. Или, вернее, чтобы его понять, нужно искать аналогичных явлений в области других искусств, например, футуризма и кубизма. Будучи знакомым с этими обоими направлениями, можно обнаружить признаки подобных явлений.

Я обнаружил в *Человеке с киноаппаратом* огромное количество элементов (кадров) именно кубофутуристического порядка. Я не имею под рукой этих элементов, чтобы провести аналогию с элементами кубофутуристическими, но кто видел *Человека с киноаппаратом*, тот запомнил целый ряд моментов сдвига[126]

движения улицы, трамваев со всевозможными сдвигами вещей в разных направлениях движения, где строение движения уже не только идет в глубину к горизонту, но и развивается по вертикали.

Надо сказать, что тот человек, который монтировал кадры,[127] великолепно понял идею или задачу нового монтажа, выражающего сдвиг, которого раньше не было.

Человек с киноаппаратом, как и *Одиннадцатый*, является весьма ценным материалом в кинопроблеме, но эту ценность обязательно нужно выявить и показать в целом уже новом динамическом произведении.

Человек с киноаппаратом в сравнении с *Одиннадцатым* является шагом вперед в том, что представляет собою уже не тему, сохраняющую весь свой образ на протяжении всей фильмы, но представляет собою распадение темы и даже растворение вещей во времени за счет динамического выражения. Правда, как в одной, так и в другой постановке нет еще ясно выраженной единой линии. Обе постановки являются еще смешанными. В них перемеживаются два начала, или два образа. Образ барахла и образ динамики, а потому она не может быть воспринята как нечто целое, законченное. Мало того, она будет вызывать возмущение, благодаря чему может произойти срыв работы Дзиги Вертова, а такой срыв означал бы провал той экспериментальной работы, которая в будущем принесла бы много новостей. Эти новости будут зависеть от скорейшего очищения его фильмы от указанного дуализма. Это — очередная работа Дзиги Вертова.

Конечно, Монти Бенксы, если Дзига Вертов будет идти дальше, не простят ему этого. Но будем надеяться, что Дзига Вертов будет все-таки понят и встретит помощь.

Итак, движение Дзиги Вертова идет непреклонно к новой форме выражения современного содержания, ибо не надо забывать, что содержание нашей эпохи еще не в том, чтобы показать, как откармливают в совхозе свиней или как уби-

рают на «золотой ниве»,[128] а есть еще одно содержание — чисто силовое, динамическое.

Это, пожалуй, сильнейшая зарядка в новой молодой организации, поднимающая энергию всего нашего века.

Поэтому мне думается, что молодым работникам кино для овладения динамикой нашей реконструктивной эпохи скорее следует изучать Балла, Боччони, Руссоло, Брака и др., нежели Монти Бенксов или Пат и Паташонов.

Мои предложения вызовут, конечно, возмущение, ибо мне скажут, что нужно изучать прежде всего достижения кинорежиссеров.

Я тоже соглашусь с этим, но только в том случае, если киномастера дадут вполне самостоятельное киноискусство. Но пока этого нет, то лучшим является все-таки изучение предлагаемых мною живописных мастеров, преимущественно кубофутуристов (все-таки в них больше возможностей, нежели в передвижниках). Больше современности в динамизме Руссоло, нежели в том, как *Монти Бенкс женится*.

Достижения Монти Бенкса равны достижениям в живописи «Кошечка под зонтиком».

Оговорюсь еще раз, что мои предложения не сводятся к тому, чтобы кинорежиссеры стали живописцами. Нет, я предлагаю только материал для изучения, чтобы не идти под слепым воздействием. Второе — выбрать нужные для киноискусства моменты.

Наша архитектура — это была китайская стена, но новейшая живопись и там пробила брешь, много почерпнули архитекторы в новейшей конструктивной живописи для создания последней формы архитектуры, не став, однако, живописцами.

Итак, Дзига Вертов ставит первым эту новую динамическую проблему в кино. Все борцы за честь кино должны рискнуть хотя бы одной постановкой новой ди-

намической фильмы для того, чтобы убедиться, что динамика есть подлинная пища кино. Это его сущность.

Я не спорю, что корову можно заставить возить воду, но чтобы это было присущее ей занятие — то с этим я не соглашусь. Я не спорю, что кино можно заставить показывать достижения Монти Бенксов, но чтобы это было единственным существом и пищею кино, я не согласен.

Итак, давайте дорогу новейшим явлениям, чтобы кино не погибло от хронического катара желудка и достижений Пат и Паташонов и Бенксов.

Еще несколько слов о *Симфонии большого города* и *Человеке с киноаппаратом*. Я мельком услышал шепот на просмотре о том, что в *Человеке с киноаппаратом* имеется наличие элементов *Симфонии большого города*.[129]

Да, отчасти есть, только строить на этом какие-либо выводы не следует. Не следует потому, что между этими картинами есть разница в достижениях.

Возможно, что в *Симфонии Берлина*, по существу, лежала та же задача, что и у Дзиги Вертова в *Человеке с киноаппаратом*, а именно — задача выражения динамической силы. У первого — динамичности города, у второго — динамичности вообще.

Таким образом, «кинодинамист» *Симфонии Берлина* хотел, по существу, показать развитие динамики с момента его статического покоя (город спит) и ее сильнейшим напряжением.

Но оказалось, что Руттман «оказался шурум-бурум». Вместо динамики он показал, как засыпает и просыпается житейское барахло. И он, «кино-шурум-бурум халатник», при помощи кинотехники, показал все свое барахло, собранное им в «городе Берлине» на толкучке зрителей в «симфоническом плане».

Человек с киноаппаратом в своем существе не имеет этой тенденции. Он имеет тенденцию скорее обеспредметить городской центр, не связуя ни один элемент в одну протекающую мысль. Это — сплошные смещения и неожиданно-

сти. Здесь впервые элементы не смогли связаться в одно целое, чтобы выразить сплетню жития.

Дзига Вертов не осмысливает или не оправдывает машину тем, что она вырабатывает папиросы или доит корову, но показывает само движение, самое динамику, силу которой заслонял всегда мундштук папиросы или спина Монти Бенкса. В *Симфонии* же вся ставка на осмысливание даже с очень определенным моральным перчиком.

Таким образом, между этими двумя кинопостановками, по существу, лежит большая разница. Дзига Вертов — отрывает кинообъекты от барахла и переносит в мир динамики, а *Симфония* всегда имеет дело с барахлом, хотя бы и симфоническим.

Установив кинообъектив в сторону еще не изведанной динамики металлической жизни и индустриально-социалистической, мы сможем увидеть новый мир, доселе не разработанный.

РОЖА

Я

Анна Муза
Живь и Явь. Заметки о языке Малевича

В статье «Живописные законы в проблемах кино» Малевич называет Сезанна «первоклассным ткачом не сюжетов, а живописи». *Ткаческую* метафору можно было бы отнести и к словесному мастерству самого Малевича. Его каламбуры и неологизмы, сразу бросающиеся в глаза читателю, образуют первый, поверхностный слой его критической прозы; на более глубоком уровне словесные приемы, менее очевидные, как бы вплетаются в языковую ткань текста. Малевич тщательно выбирает и повторяет в разных формах важные для него корни и перекликающиеся слова, устанавливает взаимодействие внутренних смыслов и ассоциаций, отсылает к образам и понятиям, возникающим из звукового подобия. Эта система соответствий придает циклу статей о кинематографе единство не только тематическое и интеллектуальное, но и фактурное. Отдельные языковые ходы Малевича самоочевидны, другие разобраны нами в комментариях; однако некоторые опорные нити, протянутые им от текста к тексту, заслуживают специального упоминания.

Размышления Малевича о художественном изображении в каком-то смысле заданы самими русскими терминами *живопись* и *живописец*. Важнейшая для него и отчасти парадоксально развитая тема *живого* и *мертвого* в искусстве берет свое начало в ее словесном воплощении.[130] Для Малевича суть *живописи* состоит в рабском вы*писи*вании «морды жизни». *Морда* как лицо животного имеет в этом контексте не столько эпатажно-оскорбительный, сколько буквальный *жизненный* смысл. Настойчивые уподобления искусства то верблюду, то корове направлены против его целесообразности, но также против (ложно понятой) связи с миром *животного, живого*. «Пусть… критика забудет привычку видеть в верблюде специальное животное, созданное природою для того, чтобы возить киргизов…» («И

ликуют лики…») *Лик*, подспудно отсылающий к (ни разу не названной) иконописи, утверждается в языке Малевича в плотски-материальном, *живом* смысле и становится синонимом *рожи*. Эта последняя оказывается особенно частой гостьей в текстах Малевича благодаря звуковой перекличке с *образом* и *выражением*, фольклорным ассоциациям, напоминающим об отражающем рожу зеркале/искусстве, и, наконец, ее семантической привязанности именно к изображению лица, в примитивном или детском рисунке. «Точка, точка, запятая/Вышла рожица кривая…» Живопись в малевичевском понимании напоминает о ее греческом прототипе, зографии, в изначальном смысле этого слова.

Кино следует за живописью прежде всего в сохранении культа жизнеподобия и, несмотря на свои новейшие технические орудия, оказывается еще более устарелым «конкретным» искусством именно в силу доступной ему иллюзии 'живого'. Постановщики кино-картин «пишут *живые* лики на полотне экрана», то есть воспроизводят конкретное обличье жизни. Утверждая, что кинорежиссеры - «плоть от плоти живописцев-художников» («Художник и кино»), Малевич воплощает свою мысль в слово за счет раннего русского калькированного наименования фотографии -- *светописи*. Кинотворчество понятое как свето-пись отсылает к живописи и этимологически и по существу (тем более, что и *живопись* ведет свое происхождение от греческой зо-графии). Мастера кино, наименованные *светописцами* или *киносветописателями*, прямо наследуют своим отцам-живописцам, а не порывают с их традицией, неуместной в ультра-современном кинематографическом деле.

Языковое поведение Малевича вызывает в памяти обращение со словом его соратников-футуристов — Алексея Крученых, Велемира Хлебникова, Давида Бурлюка. Поклонник безумных, «ни умом, ни разумом непостигаемых» слов,[131] Малевич-критик подчиняет свое сочинительство вполне рациональным задачам, но

обнаруживает поэтическую приверженность к обновлению слов и дремлющих в них смыслов. Хлебников предлагал переименовать *планер* в *парило*; Малевич переименовывает кино-плакат в *выявитель*, выговаривая «органическую сущность» этого вида искусства, о которой не дают представления «немые» для русского слуха иноязычные *плакат* и *афиша*. Киноплакаты, которые просто воспроизводят сцены из фильмов, Малевич называет «отрывками бегущего на экране содержания»: от*рыв*ок отсылает к склеенной киноленте и рождает образ физически *вырв*анного из нее и остановленного кадра. На таком же опредмечивании смысла основано сравнение искусства с мусорным ящиком для «*содержания* житейского барахла»: Малевич издевается над понятием *содержания* художественного произведения, переводя его в материальное измерение («Кино, граммофон…») Ненавистное *содержание* изничтожается Малевичем на языковом уровне, всеми возможными способами: кадры у Эйзенштейна «состоят на содержании содержания»; нет «содержания, которое не содержало бы живопись»; «целесообразный лик» мыслится «содержателем великих идей» («И ликуют лики…») *Живопись, отрывок, содержание* у Малевича — слова-выявители, противопоставляющие языковому автоматизму первичное единство имени и явления.

Само по себе «явление», слово и понятие, становится одним из опорных в языке Малевича благодаря его связи с миром видимого, *явного*. Назначение искусства — в вы-*явлении* сути *явлений*, а не в копировании их внешней предметной формы. Обыватель стремится «свое проявление проявить в кино,» и эта привычка «не дает доступа к проявлению действительно художественного явления» («Кино, граммофон…») *Проявление* как акт раскрытия подлинности (напоминающий, конечно, и о фотографическом превращении негатива в изображение) противопоставлено бытовому, стертому смыслу *проявления* как характерной манеры поведения. Изобразительные принципы разных искусств Малевич различает по

тем категориям, которые играют роль в «сущности выявления» (например, свет, форма, пространство в скульптуре). То, что рекламный плакат-*выявитель* должен делать по отношению к фильму или товару, в более широком смысле составляет функцию искусства вообще. С этим связана и повторяющаяся метафора «целесообразного» искусства как грима: «Идейной барыне оно служило многие века, чистило ее, пудрило, размалевывало веки, губы, подводило брови» («И ликуют лики…»). Грим скрывает, искусство «как таковое» раскрывает, *выявляя* свою собственную природу. Даже когда Малевич пользуется «явлением» и родственными словами в привычном, не утрированном смысле, они, как правило, заключают в себе и второе, *малевичевское*, значение — задуманное или возникающее по ассоциации с соседними текстами. В утверждении «Светооператорам нужно хорошо ознакомиться со скульптурными методами и живописными, чтобы по-разному освещать то или другое *явление* в кадре», стандартное *явление* не обратило бы на себя внимания у другого автора. Но в смысловом поле Малевича это *явление* имеет и непосредственную связь с самим процессом бытования, зримости, яви. Нам явлено нечто, что может (и должно) приобрести иной облик в результате творческого освоения. *Явление* в лукавом языке Малевича то оборачивается бюрократической стороной, то напоминает о своем высоком, отчасти религиозном предназначении. Говоря, что «Эйзенштейн своими новшествами *является* старым передвижником…», Малевич обыгрывает оба смысловых оттенка: Эйзенштейна следует признать передвижником, но также, еще более саркастически, Эйзенштейн является нам, являет нам себя в своих новшествах как передвижник.

Среди разнообразных претензий к кинематографическому языку Эйзенштейна обвинение в передвижничестве является, вероятно, уникальным. Парадоксальные ассоциации и сцепление отдаленных имен, чрезвычайно характерные для письма Малевича, свидетельствуют не только о его полемическом пыле, но и о самой языковой «плоти его сознания.» Утверждая, что театр «почиет на лаврах

форм Брюллова и Бенуа» («Кино, граммофон…»), Малевич соединяет двух художников, имеющих между собой мало общего и, более того, несоизмеримых с точки зрения их театральной работы. (С обширной и, по мнению современников, новаторской деятельностью Александра Бенуа-сценографа трудно сравнивать мало известные случайные оформительские заказы Карла Брюллова.) Выпад Малевича, конечно, направлен против замшелого, на его взгляд, псевдо-новаторства его старого противника Бенуа; ассоциация с Брюлловым, рожденная скорее всего звуковым подобием французских имен, выявляет и более глубокую связь между ними. Брюллов и Бенуа — художники, тесно связанные своей живописной культурой с классическим наследием Италии и Франции, и их неприемлемый для Малевича академизм — подчеркнутый и отсылкой к классицистским «лаврам» — обозначает ино-родность этой живописной традиции требованиям современного искусства.

Соединение, сближение несоединимого отличает письмо Малевича: «Ученые» *проблема, элемент, момент* соседствуют с *установкой, выявлением, изобразительством*. Малевич складывает такие фразы, как «… проблемы, сделанные в живописи, являются и проблемами киноискусства» («Живописные законы…»), где мастеровитое (отчасти конструктивистское) *сделать* никак не сочетается с *проблемой* даже в ее своеобразном малевичевском понимании. Он не пренебрегает и лексикой и синтаксисом советской эпохи: «Выход современного художника-живописца в кино должен нас и его привести к новой сущности и значению экрана как нового средства показания массам новой жизни искусства». Язык нового времени привлекателен для Малевича именно своей неуклюжестью, невозделанностью, близостью первобытной словесной свободе. «Красивость» так же неприемлема для него в языке, как и в искусстве. Словесная ткань Малевича грубовата, шершава на ощупь; это не атлас Брюллова и Бенуа, а скорее кожа столь любимого им верблюда.

ЛИК

АРК   Ассоциация Революционной Кинематографии (1924–1935, с 1929 года АРРК — Ассоциация Работников Революционной Кинематографии) — общественная организация, созданная по инициативе публицистов и критиков, заметно влиявшая на политику в области кино. В 1924–1926 гг. издавала собственный *Киножурнал АРК* (главный редактор Николай Лебедев), с 1926–1928 гг. *Кино-фронт* (главный редактор Ипполит Соколов). Именно в этом журнале, который Малевич, судя по его замечаниям, просматривал внимательно, и были помещены три его статьи о кино.

АХРР   Ассоциация художников революционной России (1922–1932 гг., с 1928 г. — Ассоциация художников революции, АХР) была создана на основе Товарищества передвижников и сохранила верность его эстетической платформе.

Гинхук   Государственный институт художественной культуры (Петроград — Ленинград), создан в 1923 году на основе исследовательских отделов при петроградском Музее художественной культуры по инициативе Павла Филонова и Казимира Малевича, с 1925 года Государственный; распущен в ноябре 1926, официальная дата закрытия: 1 января 1927 года.

Госкино Государственная организация по управлению делами кинематографии, создана в 1922 году, в 1924 реорганизована в Совкино.

ГТК   Государственный техникум кинематографии, преобразованный в 1925 году из Госкиношколы и переименованный в 1930 в киноинститут (ГИК, с 1934 года ВГИК).

ИЗО   [Отдел] изобразительных искусств при Народном комиссариате просвещения.

ГАХН   Академия художественных наук, основана в Москве в 1921 году как Российская Академия художественных наук (РАХН) по инициативе Народного комиссариата

просвещения; с лета 1925 года переименована в Государственную Академию художественных наук; оба названия были в употреблении до 1930 года — до объединения с Государственной Академией истории искусств и перевода в Ленинград. Различные секции ГАХН изучали изобразительные искусства, литературу, театр, социологию и философию искусства, фольклор, и объединяли художников и теоретиков разных направлений — Василия Кандинского, Павла Флоренского, Александра Габричевского, Густава Шпета.

СС 1 Казимир Малевич. *Собрание сочинений в пяти томах. Том 1. Статьи, манифесты, теоретические сочинения и другие работы. 1913—1929.* Общая редакция, вступительная статья, составление и подготовка текстов и комментарии Александры Шатских. Москва, Гилея, 1995

СС 2 Казимир Малевич. *Собрание сочинений в пяти томах. Том 2. Статьи, теоретические сочинения, опубликованные в Германии, Польше и на Украине. 1924—1930.* Составление, предисловие, редакция переводов и комментарии Галины Демосфеновой. Москва, Гилея, 1998

Malevich I Kazimir Malevich. *Essays on Art. 1915—1928*, ed. Troels Andersen, vol. I, Copenhagen, Borgen, 1968

Malevich II Kazimir Malevich. *Essays on Art. 1928—1933*, ed. Troels Andersen, vol. II, Copenhagen, Borgen, 1968

Malevich III Kazimir Malevich. *The World as Non—Objectivity. Unpublished Writings. 1922—1925*, ed. Troels Andersen, vol. III, Copenhagen, Borgen, 1976

Malevich IV Kazimir Malevich. *The Artist, Infinity, Suprematism. Unpublished Writings. 1913—1933*, ed. Troels Andersen, vol. IV, Copenhagen, Borgen, 1978

Дега, Эдгар (1834—1917) — французский художник, рисовальщик и скульптор. *49*

Касаткин, Николай Алексеевич (1859—1930) — русский художник, член Товарищества передвижников, с 1922 член АХРР. *41*

Крылов, Иван Алексеевич (1768/69—1844) — русский писатель и баснописец. *44*

Маковский, Владимир Егорович (1846—1915) — русский художник, член Товарищества передвижников, брат Константина Маковского. *80*

Маковский, Константин Егорович (1839—1915) — русский художник-натуралист. *80*

Мане, Эдуард (1832—1883) — французский живописец и график, один из основоположников импрессионизма. *42*

Милле, Жан-Франсуа (1814—1875) — французский художник, известен как автор картин на крестьянские темы. *49*

Мохой-Надь или Моголи-Наги, Ласло (1895—1946) — американский художник венгерского происхождения, экспериментировавший в области полиграфии, фотографии, скульптуры и кино. Работал в Германии, в 1923—1928 гг. преподавал в Баухаусе. С 1937 года руководил Новым Баухаусом в Чикаго. *7, 10, 11, 20, 21, 59*

Моклер, Камиль (1872—1945) — французский искусствовед и писатель, опубликовавший несколько книг об импрессионизме, одна из которых *L'impressionnisme: son histoire, son esthétique, ses maîtres* (1904) была переведена в 1908 году на русский язык. *82*

Моне, Клод (1840—1926) — французский художник- импрессионист. *19, 46*

Пат и Паташон — датские комедийные актеры, работавшие вместе между 1921 и 1937 гг. и известные в России и Германии как Пат (Карл Шенстром, 1881—1942) и Паташон (Хольгер Мадсен, 1890—1949). *8, 85, 86*

Перов, Василий Григорьевич (1833—1882) — русский художник, член Товарищества передвижников. *19, 46, 49*

Пикассо, Пабло (1881—1973) — испанский художник Парижской школы, родоначальник кубизма. *51*

Поленов, Василий Дмитриевич (1844—1927) — русский художник, член Товарищества передвижников. *19, 46, 49*

Протазанов, Яков Александрович (1882—1945) — русский и советский кинорежиссер, поставил около 100 фильмов. *19, 49*

Рембрандт (1606—1669) — голландский художник. *40*

Ренуар, Огюст (1841—1919) — французский художник, близкий импрессионизму. *42, 49*

Репин, Илья Ефимович (1844—1930) — русский художник-реалист. *41*

Рихтер, Ганс (1888—1976) — немецкий художник и создатель экспериментальных фильмов, которые вдохновили Малевича на написание сценария абстрактного фильма.

Рубенс, Петер Пауль (1577—1640) — фламандский живописец. *19, 46*

Комментарии

Оксана Булгакова
Малевич в кино — изология «динамических ощущений» и «пневматических поцелуев»

1 «И ликуют лики на экранах», с. 44.

2 «Ленин», *CC 2*, с. 26.

3 «Мир как беспредметность», *CC 2*, с. 55, с. 60.

4 Борис Арватов охарактеризовал супрематизм как «злейшую реакцию под флагом революции» и советовал Малевичу искать места в «рядах догнивающего индивидуалистического, доведенного до полного солипсизма эстетства». — *Печать и революция*, Москва, 1922, № 7, с. 343—344, цит. по *CC 1*, с. 362. Разгромная статья об исследованиях Гинхука называлась «Монастырь на госснабжении» — Г. Серый, *Ленинградская правда*, 10 июня 1926.

5 Если в 1918—24 гг. Малевич публикует 39 статей и несколько брошюр, то между 1925 и 1935 гг. в русских журналах печатаются только четыре статьи о кино и одна статья, сопровождаемая открытым письмом, в журнале *Современная архитектура* (1928, № 5, с. 157—159). Цикл его лекций по эволюции изобразительных искусств мог быть напечатан только на украинском языке в Харьковском журнале *Нова генерація* (1928—30 гг.).

6 *Malevich IV*, pp. 157—159, pp. 163–176.

7 Ср. K. Malévich. *De Cézanne au suprématisme; Le miroir suprématiste; La lumière et la couleur; Les Arts de la représentation*. Lausanne, L'Age d'homme, 1974, 1977, 1981, 1994, eds. Jean-Claude and Valentine Marcadé; K. Malévich. *Ecrits*, ed. Andrei Nakov, Paris, Champ libre, 1975; Paris, Lebovici, 1986.

⁸ См. каталог выставки «Москва — Берлин, Берлин — Москва», *Moskau — Berlin, Berlin — Moskau. 1900—1950*, eds. Irina Antonova, Jörn Merkert, München, New York, Prestel, 1995, p. 306.

⁹ Впервые опубликован на немецком языке в издании *Das weiße Rechteck. Schriften zum Film*, ed. Oksana Bulgakowa, Berlin, PotemkinPress, 1997, pp. 58—66.

¹⁰ Ср.: «Глазное яблоко у каждого индивида является мертвым *объективом*, проектирующим обстоятельства на зеркальном *негативе* мозга, который способен производить в зависимости от того или другого центра те или иные изменения отраженных в зеркальном *негативе* явлений». Курсив — мой, *СС 2*, с. 69.

¹¹ Первоначально Малевич употреблял термин «дополнительный», который позже был заменен на «прибавочный» (ср. «прибавочная стоимость»). Разумеется, семантическое поле термина шире; сам Малевич отсылал термин к области «психобактериологии» и представлял в виде «микроба».

¹² Малевич впервые представляет эту теорию в докладах, сделанных 19 марта 1925 года в РАХН и 16 июня 1926 на своей секции Гинхука. Его статья о прибавочном элементе для сборника Гинхука, набор которого был рассыпан, была напечатана как первая глава в немецком издании *Die gegenstandslose Welt*. Bauhausbücher 11, München, 1927, pp. 8—63, см. *СС 2*, с. 55—104.

¹³ При анализе противоречивого современного развития Малевич обнаружил феномен блокады, который мешает молодому художнику. Малевич видит себя врачом, который стремится эту блокаду снять, вылечив студентов от «живописной неврастении» — см. комментарии Галины Демосфеновой в *СС 2*, с. 330—331.

¹⁴ Ср. сноску 94.

¹⁵ *СС 1*, с. 27.

[16] О том, что постановка «Победы над солнцем» была предметом их разговоров Эйзенштейн упоминает в одной строчке (см. Сергей Эйзенштейн. *Избранные произведения в шести томах*, Москва, «Искусство», 1964—1971, в дальнейшем *ИП*, том 3, с. 68), замечая, что его идея разорвать экран на премьерном показе *Броненосца Потемкина* 7 ноября 1925 года в Большом театре была вдохновлена разрыванием занавеса в представлении «Победы над солнцем».

[17] Сергей Эйзенштейн. *Мемуары*, составление, предисловие и комментарии Наума Клеймана, Москва, Редакция газеты Труд, Музей кино, 1997, том 2, с. 310—315.

[18] Малевич гостил в Берлине в семье Густава фон Ризена, немецкого дипломата, который служил до революции в Санкт Петербурге. Его сын был переводчиком книги Малевича *Мир как беспредметность*. Семье фон Ризен Малевич оставил свой архив, покинув в спешке Берлин после получения письма, требующего его возвращения в Россию. Сейчас большая часть этой коллекции находится в Стеделик музеум.

[19] Hans Richter. *Köpfe und Hinterköpfe*, 1966, цит. по Fritz Mierau. *Russen in Berlin. Literatur. Malerei. Theater. Film. 1918—1933*, Leipzig, Reclam jr., 1990, pp. 489—490. Ганс Рихтер пытался осуществить этот сценарий в 1970-1976 гг. вместе с Арнольдом Иглом в США. Его рисунки находятся сегодня в специальной коллекции института Гетти в Лос-Анджелесе.

[20] См. «Будущее звуковой фильмы», *ИП*, том 2, с. 315—316.

[21] См. *ИП*, том 5, с. 303—310.

[22] Российский государственный архив литературы и искусства, фонд 1923, опись 1, единица хранения 1943, лист 1.

[23] Не считая перепечатки отрывков из его старых текстов в 1933 году в сборнике *Советское искусство за 15 лет. Материалы и документация*, Москва-Ленинград, 1933, с. 114—115.

²⁴ К. Малевич. *Письма к Шутко*, Ейск, Отдел живописи и графики Ейского историко-краеведческого музея, 1992.

²⁵ Дзига Вертов. «О *Киноправде*». — Д. Вертов. *Статьи. Дневники. Замыслы*, ред. Семен Дробашенко, Москва, «Искусство», 1966, с. 79. Эти атаки продолжались и после выхода *Броненосца Потемкина*: титры и раскрашенное от руки знамя в финале фильма Вертов отмечал на диспуте в АРК 19 марта 1926 года как прямое заимствование из своих картин — ср. *История становления советского кино*, Москва, «Искусство», 1986, с. 62—63.

²⁶ *ИП*, том 1, с. 114.

²⁷ Борис Арватов. ««Агит-Кино» и «Кино-Глаз»», *Киножурнал АРК*, Москва,1925, № 8, с. 3—4.

²⁸ Ср. прим. 4.

²⁹ Walter Benjamin. «Das Kunstwerk im Zeitalter seiner technischen Reproduzierbarkeit», (1935/36), 2. Fassung, *Gesammelte Schriften*, Bd. I. 2, Frankfurt am Main, Suhrkamp, 1989, XIV.

³⁰ Статья была опубликована в августе 1929 г. Цит. по *ИП*, том 2, с. 57.

³¹ Этот текст был заказан для каталога выставки «Фильм и фотография» в Штутгарте. Поначалу текст для каталога выставки, представляющей фильмы европейского авангарда, для которой Эйзенштейн смонтировал ролик из отрывков разных русских фильмов (в том числе и работ Дзиги Вертова), был заказан Вертову, но тот, занятый окончанием работы над *Человеком с киноаппаратом*, отказался. Эссе Эйзенштейна не было напечатано в каталоге, поскольку его текст не дошел вовремя. Впервые опубликовано по-английски: *Close up*, volume VIII, no. 3, September 1931, pp. 167—181.

³² Вильгельм фон Каульбах (1805—1874) — немецкий художник и график, известный своими нео-классицистическими монументальными полотнами, с 1837 года придворный художник баварского короля Людвига I.

[33] С. Эйзенштейн. «Драматургия киноформы», публикация и комментарий Наума Клеймана. *Киноведческие записки*, Москва, 1991, № 11, с. 181.

[34] Напечатан по-русски под названием «Мысли к киноконгрессу в Сарразе», перевод Наума Клеймана. *Киноведческие записки*, Москва, 1997/98, № 36/37, с. 49—54.

[35] *ИП*, том 2, с. 274.

[36] Marie Seton. *Sergei M. Eisenstein. A Biography*, London, The Bodley Head, 1952, p. 147.

[37] Эйзенштейн видел в этих экспериментах «освобождение» от миметических уз кино и связывал именно с прерывом иллюзии движения усиление семантических процессов (создание кинометафоры). Он объяснял этот феномен путем аналогии со стихом, в котором ритм и рифма, подчеркивая обрыв строки, ставят семантические акценты.

[38] Annette Michelson. «Reading Eisenstein Reading *Capital*». Part 2, *October*, 1976, № 3, p. 82. Ср. также Jean-Claude Marcadé. «Réflexions de Malévich sur le cinéma» (*Peinture — cinéma — peinture*, ed. Germain Viatte. Marseille, Ed. Hazan— Musée de Marseille, 1989) и François Albera. «Malévich et le cinéma: le chainon manquant», *Revue de la cinémathèque*, Paris, Automne, 1995, pp. 62—70.

[39] Шарлотта Дуглас, анализируя генезис абстрактного искусства Малевича, обращает внимание на философию репрезентации Анри Бергсона: «По Бергсону, если вселенная может быть познана, то это возможно вне рамок репрезентации, так как реальность в своей сущности внеобразна. Образы (картины) существуют лишь в ограниченной области природы.» — Charlotte Douglas. *Swans of Other Worlds. Kazimir Malevich and the Origins of Abstraction in Russia*, Ann Arbor, Michigan, UMI Research Press, 1980, p. 56.

[40] *Советский экран*, Москва, 1925, № 3 («Стиль *Нибелунгов*»); № 5 («Архитектура и декорации»; «Без уклонов и течений»); № 10 («Художник в кинопроизводстве. Сводка мнений»); № 16

(Д. Колупаев, «Нужен ли художник»; «Новый стиль кинодекорации»); № 29 («Декорации в кино»; Лев Кулешов, «Художник в кино») и др.

⁴¹ *Советский экран*, Москва, 1925, № 12 (22), с. 8—9.

⁴² См. Juri Ziwjan. «Caligari in Rußland. Der deutsche Expressionismus und die sowjetische Filmkultur», *Die ungewöhnlichen Abenteuer des Dr. Mabuse im Lande der Bolschewiki. Ein Buch zur Filmreihe Moskau — Berlin*, ed. O. Bulgakowa, Berlin, Freunde der Deutschen Kinemathek,1995, pp. 169—176.

⁴³ См. обзор этих дискуссий в книге François Albera. *Albatros. Les Russes à Paris 1919—1929*, Paris, Milan, Mazzota, 1995, pp. 31—37.

⁴⁴ «Художник и кино», с. 46.

⁴⁵ «Художник и кино», с. 46.

⁴⁶ *CC 1*, с. 33.

⁴⁷ *CC 2*, с. 34.

⁴⁸ Исследование Флоренского об обратной перспективе было написано в октябре 1919 года и представлено в серии докладов в 1922 году во ВХУТЕМАСе; текст был впервые напечатан по-русски в 1967 году в *Трудах по знаковым системам*, выпуск 3, Тарту, с. 381—416.

⁴⁹ Над начатым в конце 1927 года исследованием Беньямин работал до марта 1939 года. Walter Benjamin. *Das Passagen-Werk*, ed. Rolf Tiedemann. Frankfurt am Main, Suhrkamp, 1983.

⁵⁰ Эль Лисицкий. *Сказ про два квадрата*, Берлин, Скифы,1922 (репринт Cambridge, MIT Press, 1991).

51 Татьяна Горячева. «Театральная концепция УНОВИСа на фоне современной сценографии». — *Малевич. Классический авангард. Витебск — 2. Сборник материалов третьей международной теоретической конференции*, под ред. Т. Котович, Витебск, Н.А. Панков, 1998, с. 45—57.

52 Alexandra Shatskikh. «Malevich and Film», *Burlington Magazine*, July 1993, № 1084, pp. 470—478. Рисунки Н. Коган к балету хранятся в Театральном музее Санкт Петербурга. Шатских также отмечает связь сценария с сериальностью работы Малевича и особенностью развески супрематических картин на выставках 1915 и 1916 гг. — p. 477.

53 Это решение близко оформлению Павлом Филоновым спектакля «Владимир Маяковский» (из программы футуристического театра, в рамках которой ставилась и «Победа над солнцем») — фигуры актеров скрывались за нарисованными на картоне силуэтами.

54 «Кино, граммофон…», с. 73.

55 Людвиг Гильберсеймер. «Динамическая живопись», *Кино—фот*, Москва, 1922, № 1, с. 7.

56 *СС 1*, с. 53.

57 *СС 2*, с. 323.

58 *СС 1*, с. 53.

59 Трансформации черного, белого и красного (хотя и в другой последовательности) напоминают алхимические концепции, в которых процесс творчества представлен тремя этапами nigredo, albedo и rubedo. О мистических и эзотерических параллелях — см. Василий Бабич. «Феноменология Квадрата». — *Малевич. Классический авангард. Витебск — 2*, с. 116—130.

60 *СС 1*, с. 188.

61 *Das weiße Rechteck*, p. 124

[62] Ср. Леонид Трауберг. «Эксперимент, понятный миллионам», *Жизнь искусства*, 1 января 1929; Сергей Эйзенштейн. «Эксперимент, понятный миллионам», *Советский экран*, 5 февраля 1929, № 6, с. 6—7.

[63] К. Шутко. «Путь киноков», *Советский экран*, 25 января 1929, № 5, с. 4. Журнал печатает несколько статей в защиту Вертова — Николай Кауфман. «Человек с киноаппаратом»; Константин Фельдман. «Кино и Аристотель» — там же, с. 5—6.

[64] Осип Брик. «*Одиннадцатый*», *Новый Леф*, 1928, № 4, с. 27.

[65] *СС 2*, с. 222.

[66] Walter Benjamin. «Die Erwiderung an Oskar A. H. Schmitz» (1927). — W. Benjamin. *Gesammelte Schriften* II, 3. Frankfurt, Suhrkamp, 1980, pp. 1486—89.

[67] *СС 2*, с. 215—216. Курсив мой.

[68] Виктор Шкловский. «Семантика кино» (1925). — В. Шкловский. *За 60 лет*, Москва, «Искусство», 1985, с. 32.

[69] Юрий Тынянов. «Об основах кино» (1927). — Ю. Тынянов. *Поэтика. История литературы. Кино*, Москва, «Искусство», 1977, с. 329.

[70] «В действительности, его лики движутся только в воображении зрителя, в картине же ему удается установить только призрак намерения этого движения. Таким образом, мне кажется, что по природе своей кино продолжает неразрывную живописную линию, органически связанную с художником-живописцем.» — «Художник и кино», с. 47.

О выявителях. Плакаты

Статья была опубликована в *Киножурнале АРК*, Москва, 1925, № 6—7, с. 6—8 и переиздана в СС 1, с. 283—288. Иная версия этого текста была опубликована на английском языке Трельсом Андерсеном в переводе Ксении Гофман под названием «About Posters» в издании *Malevich IV*, pp. 136—143. Мы следуем русской журнальной версии.

[71] Речь идет о «Первой выставке киноплаката», проходившей в Москве в помещении Государственной Академии художественных наук (ГАХН) с 21 апреля по 2 мая 1925 года, на которой было представлено 64 экспоната. Выставка, организованная кинокабинетом ГАХН, демонстрировала киноплакаты дореволюционные, советские, а также немецкие, французские, английские, шведские, итальянские и американские. В выставке участвовали 16 советских художников. Машинописный каталог выставки хранится в Российском Архиве литературы и искусства, фонд 2057, опись 1, единица хранения 99, листы 1—17 — см. комментарии Александры Шатских, *СС 1*, с. 371. Дискуссия о выставке в ГАХН проходила в мае — см. отчет об этом в *Советском экране*, 12 мая 1925, № 7, где были помещены две статьи: о самой выставке и о дискуссии в ГАХН, продолженные в № 8 статьей о психологии рекламы.

[72] Термин «непроницаемый план», также как «картинное поле», широко используется в работах Малевича о живописи. «Холст [...] есть поле зрения», на котором выявляется структура и фактура «живописного тела», оно может быть пятнообразным, расплывчатым, проницаемым и *непроницаемым* (*СС 2*, с. 78). Непроницаемым планом обладает, согласно Малевичу, только супрематическая живопись.

[73] Александра Шатских отсылает термин Малевича «распыление», при помощи которого он во многих текстах о живописи описывает основную черту кубизма, к статье Николая Бердяева о Пикассо («Пикассо», *София*, 1914, № 3) — см. А. Шатских. «Теоретическое и литературное наследие Казимира Малевича». — Д. Сарабьянов, А. Шатских. *Казимир Малевич. Живопись и теория*. Москва, «Искусство», 1993, с. 180. Ср. «Кубизм — искусство распыляющее, превращающее сумму или суммы старых заключений в равносильные единицы, чтобы из них вывести

новый экономический материальный вывод». — «О новых системах в искусстве» (1919), *СС 1*, с. 168, с. 182—183.

[74] Передвижники — объединение русских живописцев и скульпторов, создавших в 1870 году Товарищество передвижных выставок в противовес Академии художеств. В объединение входили Исаак Левитан, Иван Крамской, Николай Касаткин, Илья Репин, Владимир Маковский, Василий Перов, Василий Поленов и другие. В начале XX века передвижники и их реалистическое и общедоступное (в прямом и переносном смысле) искусство стали излюбленными мишенями русского авангарда; в этом отношении многочисленные ссылки Малевича на передвижников, рассыпанные в его статьях о кино, полностью созвучны уничижительно-саркастическому тону ранней авангардистской критики. В 20-е годы передвижничество не теряет актуальности для Малевича не только благодаря его реанимации в «кино-изобразительстве» и кинематографических «передвижных картинках», но и в связи с деятельностью АХРР, Ассоциации художников революционной России, в которую Товарищество влилось в 1923 году. Ср. замечание В. Шкловского того же времени: «Бывают минуты если не падения искусства, то растворения в нем ряда чужих ему элементов. Таково, например, творчество наших передвижников. Тогда искусство живет помимо этих элементов, которые участвуют в жизни, как пуля, сидящая в груди, участвует в жизни тела», созвучное Малевичу и своей биологической фразеологией — «О фактуре и контррельефах» (1920). — Виктор Шкловский. *Гамбургский счет. Статьи—воспоминания—эссе (1914—1933)*, Москва, «Советский писатель», 1990, с. 98.

[75] Понятие Малевича, впервые введенное им в брошюре *От кубизма к супрематизму. Новый живописный реализм* (Петроград, 1916), где он употребляет термин «диссонанс» вместо контраста, описывая основной художественный принцип кубизма (*СС 1*, с. 27). В работах Витебского периода, *О новых системах» в искусстве* (1919), он уже пользуется термином «схема контрастов» — *СС 1*, с. 165.

[76] Возможно, имеется в виду клеймо фирмы Саротти, производящей шоколадные конфеты.

[77] Треугольник был клеймом Ленинградской фабрики резиновых изделий.

[78] Марка клея.

[79] Марка обуви.

И ЛИКУЮТ ЛИКИ НА ЭКРАНАХ

Статья была опубликована в *Киножурнале АРК*, Москва, 1925, № 10, с. 7—9 и переиздана в *СС 1*, с. 289—294.

[80] Статья была напечатана с этим редакционным подзаголовком в рамках дискуссии, вызванной резкой полемикой между Вертовым и Эйзенштейном после премьеры эйзенштейновского фильма *Стачка* (см. «Малевич в кино», с. 13). Малевич ссылается в своем тексте на статью Бориса Арватова, отзывающегося на эту полемику, «"Агит-Кино" и "Кино-Глаз"», *Киножурнал АРК*, Москва, 1925, № 8, с. 3—4.

[81] Дзига Вертов заявил в своем первом манифесте «Мы», опубликованном в журнале Алексея Гана *Кино-фот*, 1922, № 1, с. 11—12: «Смерть "кинематографии" необходима для жизни искусства. Мы призываем ускорить ее смерть»; во втором манифесте «Киноки. Переворот» (*Леф*, 1923, № 3, с. 137) он подтвердил: «Смертельный приговор, вынесенный киноками в 1919 году всем без исключения кинокартинам, действителен и по сей день». Кинохроника и выпуски *Киноправды*, снимаемые группой Вертова в 1918—1923 гг., также как его фильм *Киноглаз* (1924), понимались принципиально как «не искусство».

[82] Текст в квадратных скобках был исключен из журнальной публикации и восстановлен Александрой Шатских по рукописи Малевича, хранящейся в архиве Стеделик музеум — *СС 1*, с. 372—373.

[83] Материалистическое сознание связано в концепции Малевича с абстрактным выражением, религиозное — с миром образа (картины); эту разницу он анализирует на примере создания культа Ленина после его смерти, см. трактат «Ленин. Из книги о Беспредметности», переве-

денный Лисицким на немецкий язык и опубликованный в журнале *Kunstblatt*, Potsdam, 1924, № 10, с. 289–193. Русская публикация — *СС 2*, с. 25–29.

[84] Образ верблюда встречается в статьях Малевича много раз, появляясь впервые в брошюре *От кубизма к супрематизму. Новый живописный реализм* (Петроград, 1916): «Искусство живописи, скульптуры, слова — было до сей поры верблюдом, навьюченным разным хламом одалиск, Египетскими и Персидскими царями Соломонами, Саломеями, принцами, принцессами с их любимыми собачками, охотами и блудом Венер.» — *СС 1*, с. 27. Восприятие Малевичем хлама, которым навьючен верблюд-искусство, сдвигается от экзотизма ориенталистской живописи до бытового жанризма. Ср. «Кино, граммофон…», с. 64.

[85] Термин Малевича, которым он определял основной принцип кубизма (см. сноску 75); здесь он описывает этим термином монтаж Эйзенштейна.

[86] Сопоставляя воспроизведенный в журнале кадр из *Черного сердца* Чеслава Сабинского (№ 10, с.10), «средневековое мистическое» название кинокартины и немецкую живопись 1860-х гг., Малевич переводит в другой план содержание, возможно, неизвестного ему фильма, посвященного борьбе донбасских шахтеров за уголь во время белогвардейской оккупации.

[87] Фильм Владимира Гардина был посвящен интригам католического духовенства, замешанного в убийствах и шпионаже, в одном из провинциальных городов советской Западной Украины; он рассматривался русской критикой как фильм «готический» благодаря сумрачной атмосфере тайны и редким для советского кино этого времени дорогим декорациям выстроенного в павильоне католического собора. Не вполне понятная ассоциация с Бостоном и Кливлендом могла возникнуть у Малевича, скорее всего видевшего лишь помещенный в журнале (№ 8, с. 4) кадр, которым иллюстрировалась статья Бориса Арватова ««Агит-Кино» и «Кино-Глаз»», благодаря стилистической связи фильма с иностранными «готическими» картинами.

[88] Имеются в виду картины Николая Касаткина «Кто?» (1898) и Ильи Репина «Не ждали» (1884–1888). Обе упомянутые Малевичем картины, и мало известное сегодня полотно Касаткина, и широко известная работа Репина, строятся на схожей ситуации и близких композиционных

принципах: в круг семьи, сгруппированной около стола, неожиданно вторгается ставший чужим родственник. На картине Касаткина это муж, вернувшийся после многих лет солдатской службы и обнаруживший, что его жена прижила на стороне ребенка; на картине Репина это сын, воспринимавшийся современниками как политический заключенный, который возвращается с каторги или из тюрьмы.

[89] Первоначальное название фильма Эйзенштейна *Броненосец Потемкин*. Кадр, воспроизведенный в № 8, с. 7 журнала, на который ссылается Малевич, не вошел в картину.

[90] Термин «сдвиг», часто употребляемый критиками (например, Александром Бенуа, ср. «Дневник художника», *Речь*, 21 октября 1913) в начале века при описании новой живописи, стал одним из центральных понятий русского футуризма. При этом русские художники-футуристы впервые ввели это понятие, осваивая практику кубизма. Рассматривая элементы кубистического построения, Давид Бурлюк отмечает, что «конструкция может быть смещенной или же *сдвинутой*»; кубизм предлагает «канон *сдвинутой* конструкции». Сами же «сдвиги» могут иметь различную природу: сдвиг линейный, плоскостной, красочный, частный и общий. Бурлюк отмечает, что «противовес академическому канону» был во все времена: «Все варварские народные искусства построены отчасти на существовании этого II канона (сдвинутой конструкции).» — Д. Бурлюк. «Кубизм», *Пощечина общественному вкусу*, Санкт Петербург, изд. Г.Л. Кузьмина, 1912. (В издании 1912 года эта статья появилась под подписью Н. [Николай] Бурлюк, впоследствии ее авторство было уточнено).
В значительной мере утверждение понятия «сдвиг» произошло благодаря поэту Алексею Крученых. Малевич тесно сотрудничал с Крученых с 1913 года — как над постановкой футуристической оперы «Победа над солнцем», так и в создании футуристических книг (*Игра в аду*, Санкт Петербург, 1914; *Тайные пороки академиков*, Петроград, 1916). В то время как Крученых развил понятие сдвига и фактуры слова для языковых экспериментов (А. Крученых. *Сдвигология в русском стихе*, Москва, 1922), Малевич разработал понятие сдвига для живописной плоскости, анализируя кубистическое сознание как осваивающее явления в системе сдвигов, выявляющих на плоскости множественность точек зрения и разнообразные формы времени («О новых системах» в искусстве», *СС 1*, с. 167—168).

[91] Фактура — одно из опорных понятий русского художественного авангарда, введенное Давидом Бурлюком для сугубо живописного анализа «характера поверхности картины» в противоположность «предметному» рассмотрению живописи как «нагромождения анекдотов, фактов» («Фактура». — *Пощечина общественному вкусу*, с. 102—103). В 20-е годы, в связи с теорией и практикой конструктивизма фактура стала обозначать природные свойства материала и — шире — вещность, материальную само-бытность «сделанного предмета», в том числе в фотографии и фотомонтаже. (См. Hubertus Gassner. «The Constructivists: Modernism on the Way to Modernization». — *The Great Utopia. The Russian and the Soviet Avant-Garde 1915-1932.* Solomon R. Guggenheim Museum, 1992, pp. 309—311). Понимание фактуры как вне-идеологической сущности работы искусства со своим материалом закрепилось в теории русских формалистов (ср. «Фактура — главное отличие того особого мира специально построенных вещей, совокупность которых мы привыкли называть искусством.» В. Шкловский. «О фактуре и контррельефах» (1920). — Виктор Шкловский. *Гамбургский счет*, с. 99.) Малевич, отрицательно относившийся к повышенному, на его взгляд, интересу конструктивистов к материалу (см. статью «Живопись и фотография»), нередко пользуется этим термином применительно к кино. Как правило, говоря о фактуре кадра, он подразумевает особенности освещения и взаимодействия света с полотном/поверхностью экрана, и вспоминает в этом контексте живопись импрессионистов. Ср. «...художник—кинописатель [...] с нетерпением, возможно, ждет палитры цветных лучей, чтобы из них соткать живописные планы фактур по подобию Ренуара, Дега, Милле, и др.» — «Художник и кино», с. 49.

[92] Скорее всего, имеются в виду картины Алексея Степанова «Журавли летят» (1891) и Ефима Чепцова «Заседание сельской ячейки» (1924) из собрания Третьяковской галереи. «Журавли», «Агитатор» или «Кошечка под зонтиком», упоминаемая в статье «Живописные законы в проблемах кино», с. 85, — заменимые сюжеты «предметного» искусства в разные времена. Агитатор, выделенный Малевичем как определяющий сюжет советской живописи, был размножен во второй половине 20-х годов картинами «Выступление Ленина на Путиловском заводе в мае 1917 года» И. Бродского (1926), «Слушают агитатора» Д. Штеренберга (1927), «Приезд коммунистов в деревню» С. Герасимова (1927) и др.

⁹³ Арватов писал: «…кроме Агит-Кино и Кино-Глаза необходимо еще одно киноискусство — экспериментальное кино. К воздействию и показу надо присоединить быто-пересоздающее демонстрирование, своего рода пропущенную через кино-монтаж лабораторию новых, сейчас изобретаемых форм (костюм, архитектура, мебель, жест и т. п.)» — ««Агит-Кино» и «Кино-Глаз»», с. 4.

⁹⁴ Название новой науки о кино Малевич согласует со своим термином «изология», обозначающим дисциплину, изучающую принципы разных художественных школ. «Изология» должна была исследовать норму и ее нарушение в «организме» художника или «теле» искусства, анализируя изменение связи «сознания» и «подсознания», см. цикл статей в Харьковском журнале *Нова генерація* в *СС 2*, с. 129—273. «Кинологию» Малевич тоже окружает медицинскими ассоциациями (аптека, катар); этот термин напоминает не только «биологию», но и современный неологизм «педологию» — разрабатываемую советскими психологами науку о методах трансформации детской психики, возникшую под сильным влиянием психоаналитических идей.

⁹⁵ В своем первом манифесте «Мы» Вертов утверждал: «Мы *очищаем* киночество от примазавшихся к нему, от музыки, литературы и театра, ищем своего, нигде не краденого ритма и находим его в движениях вещей. Мы приглашаем: вон — из сладких объятий романса, из отравы психологического романа, из лап театра любовника, задом к музыке, вон, в *чистое* поле, в пространство с четырьмя измерениями, в поиски своего материала» — Вертов. «Мы. Вариант манифеста» (*Кино-фот*, 1922, № 1, с. 11), перепечатано в кн. Дзига Вертов. *Статьи. Дневники. Замыслы*, с. 46.

⁹⁶ Образ, заимствованный из басни И. А. Крылова «Мартышка и очки», используется Малевичем и в других текстах, ср. «Тайные пороки академиков» (1916) в *СС 1*, с. 56.

Художник и кино

Статья была опубликована в *Киножурнале АРК*, Москва, 1926, № 2, с. 15—17, с редакционным замечанием «С рядом положений автора — в частности, вопросом об «абстрактном искусстве» — редакция не согласна». Переиздана в *СС 1*, с. 295—299.

[97] Немое кино использовало нефотографические методы создания цвета — либо кадрики колорировались от руки, либо целые куски фильма были окрашены в монохромный тон для придания особого настроения (синий для ночных сцен, красный — для пожара); при этом окрашивалась либо сама пленка (вираж), либо эмульсия, в которую она погружалась (тонирование). Проблема цветного кино широко обсуждалась в советской кинопечати (см. *Советский экран*, 18 августа 1925, № 21).

[98] Фильм *Доротти Вернон* шел в советском прокате под названием *Рифы жизни*. Действие этого костюмного фильма было построено на конфликте между Марией Стюарт и королевой Елизаветой, чью сторону принимала героиня, Доротти (Мери Пикфорд).

[99] Описание камеры как *мертвого* объектива часто встречается и в других текстах Малевича — ср. его письмо к Мохой-Надю: «Я никогда не стоял, не оправдывал механическую *мертвую зеркальность* фотографического *объектива*». Но более удивительно его уподобление глаза мертвому объективу, предполагающее, что только *живопись* дает другую (живую) систему зрения: «Глазное яблоко у каждого индивида является *мертвым объективом*, проектирующим обстоятельства на зеркальном *негативе* мозга, который способен производить в зависимости от того или другого центра те или иные изменения отраженных в зеркальном *негативе* явлений». Курсив — наш, *СС 2*, с. 69.

[100] Это высказывание Малевича близко вертовскому требованию «Прочь от фабрики поцелуев и голубей!» — Д. Вертов. «Фабрика фактов», *Правда*, 26 июля 1926 (цит. по Д. Вертов. *Статьи. Дневники. Замыслы*, с. 88). Коммерческая кинопродукция 20-х годов часто отождествлялась с миром «гуттаперчевым» и «пневматическим» (Малевич), миром резины, имитирующей живое тело, и миром дешевых заменителей, имитирующих дорогие материалы (ср. аналогию с ка-

лико, дешевым хлопком, использовавшимся для имитации кожи, в эссе Зигфрида Кракауэра «Мир калико», 1926 (Siegfried Kracauer. «Calico-World. The UFA-City in Neubabelsberg». — *The mass ornament*: Weimar essays. Translated, edited, and with an introduction by Thomas Y. Levin. Cambridge, Mass., Harvard University Press, 1995, pp. 281—288). Из гуттаперчи изготавливали маски, детские куклы и манекены, поэтому возможный смысл этого прилагательного — «кукольный» мир (о мире кино как мире «игрушек», «механических кукол» говорит и Вертов — «О Кинопровде», выступление в АРК 9 июня 1924, цит. по Д. Вертов. *Статьи. Дневники. Замыслы*, с. 79). Те же ассоциации с миром детской игрушки развивает и Кракауэр: «Этот мир подобен детской игрушке» (p. 281). Ср. также противопоставление «живых артиста и артистки» мертвому телу кино в «Кино, граммофон, радио и художественная культура», с. 63.

[101] Малевич, возможно, был знаком с опытами в области абстрактного кино, о которых сообщал журнал *Кино-фот*, публикуя в первом номере статью Людвига Гильберсеймера «Динамическая живопись», *Кино-фот*, Москва, 1922, № 1, с. 7. В январе 1926 года Илья Эренбург привез из Парижа несколько экспериментальных фильмов, в том числе *Антракт* Рене Клера и Франсиса Пикабиа, *Механический балет* Фернана Леже, *Пять минут чистого кино* Анри Шометта, которые демонстрировались в кинотеатре «Художественный».

[102] Журнал *Советский экран* в течение всего 1925 года вел дискуссию о декорациях и работе художника в кино (см. «Малевич в кино», с. 18). Примерами, к которым обращались участники дискуссии, было кино немецкого экспрессионизма и французский фильм *Бесчеловечная* (1923) Марселя Лербье. Декорации к этому фильму были созданы модернистским архитектором Робером Малле-Стевенсом и художником Фернаном Леже, который в том же году оформил одну из постановок Шведского Балета в Париже («Сотворение мира» Д. Мийо, хореограф Ж. Борлин). Как реакция на эту европейскую тенденцию в русском кино рассматривались постановка Яковом Протазановым в 1925 году *Аэлиты*, костюмы для которой были сделаны Александрой Экстер, оформившей три спектакля в театре Александра Таирова, а декорации театральным художником Исааком Рабиновичем, и «готический» фильм В. Гардина *Крест и маузер* (1925), художник Д. Колупаев (см. сноску 87).

Художественно-научный фильм
«Живопись и проблемы архитектуры»

Набросок сценария написан в Германии в 1927 году. Несистематически пронумерованная рукопись состоит из трех листов (32,5 х 20,7 см) и снабжена карандашными цветными и черно-белыми рисунками. Она находилась в коллекции семьи фон Ризен, сейчас — в частном собрании Чвиклицер, Баден-Баден. Впервые опубликована как факсимиле в каталоге *Moskau — Berlin, Berlin — Moskau 1900—1950*, p. 306.

[103] Ср. издание *Die Kunstismen. Les Ismes de l'art. The Isms of Art. 1924—1914* (Измы искусства), составители Эль Лисицкий и Ганс Арп. Эрленбах—Цюрих, Мюнхен, Лейпциг, 1925, в котором были представлены кубизм, футуризм, экспрессионизм, симультанизм, дадаизм, пуризм, неопластицизм, конструктивизм, абсолютный фильм, абстрактное и метафизическое искусство, а также проун Лисицкого. Малевич представил в этом сборнике супрематизм.

[Живопись и фотография]

Оригинал хранится в коллекции фон Ризен в Стеделик музеум. Впервые опубликовано по-английски под названием «Letter to Moholy-Nagy» в переводе Ксении Гофман в издании *Malevich IV*, pp. 157—159.
Написано в ответ на статью Эрнста Калаи «Живопись и фотография», опубликованную в журнале европейских конструктивистов, издававшемся в Амстердаме, *i 10*, 1927, № 4, с. 148—157 (репринт 1979). Мохой-Надь инициировал дискуссию вокруг этой статьи, в которой приняли участие Адольф Бене, Макс Буххарц, Вил Громан, Василий Кандинский, Людвиг Кассак, Пит Мондриан, Георг Муха и сам Мохой-Надь, и которая закончилась ответом Калаи (*i 10*, 1927, № 6, с. 227—237). Письмо Малевича опубликовано не было.

[104] Так в оригинале. Современная транслитерация имени «Мохой-Надь», но в двадцатые годы эта транслитерация была более принятой.

[105] Эрнст Калаи, проводя различие между фотографией и живописью на основе разной работы с фактурой, замечал: «Художнику дана возможность сблизить закономерность формы своего произведения с исчисляемой закономерностью, приравнять его фактуру гладкости отполированной поверхности или эмали. Есть достаточно много произведений такого плана (Мондриан, Малевич, Мохой-Надь, Лисицкий, Бухгейстер и т. д.); несмотря на механистические замашки и теоретические выпады их создателей против искусства эти произведения являются живописью, подчас великолепной живописью» — *i 10*, 1927, № 4, с. 149.

[106] Эрнст Калаи говорит скорее не об осознании, но о «тактильном ощущении действительности» (stoffliche Wirklichkeitsempfindungen — p. 152), понимая материал в этом контексте как «материю». Ср. также высказывание Малевича «Отношение супрематизма к материалам прямо противоположно ныне нарастающей агитации в пользу культуры материала. Это эстетический вопрос, обработка поверхностей материалов является психозом современных художников». — «Супрематизм», *Europa Almanach*, Potsdam, 1925, русская публикация в *CC 2*, с. 34.

КИНО, ГРАММОФОН, РАДИО И ХУДОЖЕСТВЕННАЯ КУЛЬТУРА

Текст был написан в 1928 году и отправлен в редакцию *Кино-фронта*, которая отказалась его печатать, снабдив следующим примечанием: «Формалистический подход к искусству и развитые автором идеи для публикации неприемлемы. Рукопись отклонить. 16 апреля 1928», подпись неразборчива. Рукопись хранилась в собрании Анны Александровны Лепорской (1900—1982), сотрудницы Гинхука, по-русски не публиковалась. Любезно передана нам для данного издания Трельсем Андерсеном. Текст был опубликован им на английском языке в переводе Ксении Гофман под названием «The Cinema, Gramophone, Radio and Artistic Culture» в издании *Malevich IV*, pp. 163–176.

[107] Отсылка к высказыванию Ленина в беседе с Луначарским в 1922 году, опубликованному в сборнике Григория Болтянского *Ленин и кино* (Москва-Ленинград, 1925, с. 19).

[108] Принятое с начала века описание кино как «великого немого», le grand muet, было характерно для русской, польской, и французской публицистики.

[109] Малевич повторно использует определение «мертвый» по отношению к фотографическому объективу в отличии от *живописи*, ср. *СС 2*, с. 69.

[110] См. сноску 84.

[111] «Кинореска» — типичный для Малевича сложносоставный каламбур, с одной стороны отсылающий к распространенному в начале века названию кинотеатров или кафе, «Питореск» (фр. (le) pittoresque, живописный и живописность, красочность), с другой стороны, служащий названием жанра по аналогии с арабеской: красочная и пустая кино-картинка.

[112] Ср. сноску 100.

[113] Отсылка к герою романа Самюэля Ричардсона (1689–1761) *Кларисса Гарлоу*, ставшему синонимом соблазнителя. Характеристика кино как «глухонемого ловеласа» созвучна любовной фразеологии в критике кинематографа Вертовым (см. сноску 100).

[114] Пластические танцы — этим термином в русскоязычном пространстве описывались разные направления современного танца — и «босоножки» Айседоры Дункан, чья школа существовала в Советском Союзе с 1921 года, и евритмия Жака-Далькроза, на чьих принципах в Москве и Петрограде были созданы в 1919 году Институты ритма, и немецкий Ausdruckstanz.

[115] Шурум-бурум — крик старьевщика, оповещавший о его появлении. Забавное словосочетание, возможно возникшее из «старье берем», должно было нравиться Малевичу своей звуковой формой и поэтической «без-умностью», напоминавшей футуристическое словотворчество. Шурум-бурум может означать у Малевича и старье, и старьевщика: ср. : «Мне ненавистны авторитеты прошлого, как «шурум-бурумы» бродят они в новом мире и ищут старья…» — «Мир мяса и кости ушел» (1918) в *СС 1*, с. 113; «Руттман оказался шурум-бурум», — «Живописные законы в проблемах кино», с. 86.

[116] Малевич имеет в виду, скорее всего, высказывания Вертова (ср. примечание 95 к статье «И ликуют лики на экранах»). Дискуссия о театре и кино велась в советской печати в 1924–1928

гг. (см. «Театр или кино». От редакции. *Жизнь искусства*, 3 марта 1925, с. 3—4) и сталкивала разные точки зрения, потому что понимание «театральщины» не было единым. Для Владимира Блюма («Против театра дураков — за кино», *Жизнь искусства*, 28 октября 1924, № 44, с. 10—11; 18 ноября 1924, № 47, с. 3—4) примером плохой театральщины было немецкое *буржуазное* кино экспрессионизма, от влияния которого надо уберечь *пролетарское* кино; режиссер Абрам Роом призывал изгнать театр из кино из соображений разной специфики актерской игры («Кино и театр», *Советский экран*, 19 мая 1925); Адриан Пиотровский отстаивал идею «кинофикации» современного театра (ср. «Кинофикация театра», *Жизнь искусства*, 22 ноября 1927), а Сергей Эйзенштейн заявлял, что кино является закономерным этапом современного театра, так как оно способно наиболее совершенно выполнить предложенную театром программу радикализации художественной практики: монтаж коротких фрагментов вне пространственно-временной обусловленности, инсценировка массовых действий, психотерапия зрителя и т. п. («Два черепа Александра Македонского», *Новый зритель*, 1926, № 35, с. 10).

[117] См. «Живь и Явь. Заметки о языке Малевича», с. 93.

[118] «Мир искусства» — объединение петербургских художников-модернистов, в которое входили Александр Бенуа, Леон Бакст, Мстислав Добужинский, издававшее одноименный журнал (1899—1904).

ЖИВОПИСНЫЕ ЗАКОНЫ В ПРОБЛЕМАХ КИНО

Текст был впервые напечатан в журнале *Кино и культура*, 1929, № 7—8, с. 22—26, и долгое время не привлекал внимания исследователей, так как инициал имени в журнальной публикации был указан ошибочно: В. Малевич. В конце статьи было помещено примечание: «Редакция, не разделяя взглядов т. Малевича по отдельным вопросам, находит, что поднимаемая автором проблема использования законов живописи в кино заслуживает пристального внимания, и ей следует посвятить время и силы, чтобы знать, в какой мере живопись применима в кино». Перепечатана в *СС 1*, с. 301—306.

[119] Последней прижизненной книжной публикацией Малевича в России была брошюра *Бог не скинут. Искусство. Церковь. Фабрика*, Витебск, Уновис, 1922. — *СС 1*, с. 236–265.

[120] См. сноску 116.

[121] Скорее всего, Малевич имеет в виду Владимира Маковского, члена Товарищества передвижников. (Но и картины его брата, Константина, были близки той же натуралистической эстетике.) К числу картин Вл. Маковского принадлежит «9-ое января 1905 года на Васильевском острове» (1905), массовая композиция с «крупным планом» мужика, раздирающего на груди рубаху, который мог вызвать в памяти кадр из фильма Эйзенштейна *Броненосец Потемкин* (первоначальное название *1905 год*). Во фразе Малевича следует отметить ехидный каламбур: *передвижные* (вместо обычного *передвижнические*) картины Эйзенштейна ассоциируются и с передвижниками, и с *движущимися* картинами — кино.

[122] Ср. сноску 85.

[123] Вертов был уволен с работы в Совкино 31 декабря 1926 года и работал после этого на украинской студии. Вокруг *Человека с киноаппаратом* велась бурная газетная дискуссия (см. «Малевич в кино», с. 23).

[124] Термин «прибавочный элемент» один из центральных в аналитической системе Малевича; над разработкой теории прибавочного элемента в живописи (понятого как динамический элемент, деформирующий статическую норму репрезентации и восприятия) Малевич работал в 1923—26 гг. Трактат «Введение в теорию прибавочного элемента» был впервые напечатан как первая часть книги *Die gegenstadslose Welt* («Мир как беспредметность») в 1927 году, см. *СС 2*, с. 55–105.

[125] В публикации имя французского критика и писателя Камилла Моклера, автора статей и книг об импрессионизме, одна из которых была переведена на русский язык, было указано неправильно: Мелер. Малевич цитирует его в своей статье о Сезанне (*Нова Генерація*, Харьков, 1929, № 6 — *СС 2*, с. 151), называя его там «Мольером». Описание Сезанна как ткача ассоциа-

тивно связано с другими текстами Малевича, а также, возможно, с работами Моклера. В книге *Импрессионизм* Моклер назвал Сезанна художником, напоминающим своей неизощренной простотой средневекового мастера (Camille Mauclair. *L'Impressionisme, Paris, Librairie de l'art ancien et moderne*, 1904, p. 152), а в более позднем и резком «Независимом искусстве Франции» признал его виновным в общей деградации живописи от картины к ковру (tapis), который игрой цветовых планов заменил все живописные исследования жизни и психологии человека. (*L'Art Indépendant Français sous la Troisième République*, Paris, La Renaissance du Livre, 1919, pp. 26—27, 33—34). Ср. с этим полемическое строение формулы Малевича, «ткач не сюжетов, а живописи». С другой стороны, часто встречающиеся в текстах Малевича параллели между холстом и экраном не как поверхностью, на которой изображение располагается, но как пространством, в которое оно проникает, также внутренне близки «ткаческой» метафоре. В своем труде *Мир как беспредметность* Малевич сравнивает разные школы живописи «по строению живописного тела, по характеру *ткани* цветов» (*СС 2*, с. 79). В статье «Художник и кино» Малевич использует аналогию кинорежиссера, живописца, и ткача («соткать живописные планы фактур»).

126 См. сноску 90.

127 Елизавета Свилова (1900—1975), ассистент и жена Дзиги Вертова, начала работу в кино как монтажница в фирме Пате, работала потом в Московском кинокомитете, монтировала почти все работы Вертова, включая *Человека с киноаппаратом*. В этом фильме мы видим ее за работой над монтажом, брата же Вертова, Михаила Кауфмана, оператора фильма, мы видим на экране как «человека с киноаппаратом».

128 Отсылка к фильму Эйзенштейна *Старое и новое*, вышедшему в прокат в августе 1929 года, но показанному в марте друзьям и знакомым.

129 Фильм Вальтера Руттмана *Берлин. Симфония большого города* вышел в советский прокат под названием *Симфония большого города* на год раньше фильма Вертова, в 1928 году, и *Человек с киноаппаратом* рассматривался критиками как вторичный по отношению к нему (Г. Ленобле, *Кино*, № 17, 1929). Когда и немецкие критики после выхода вертовского фильма в

прокат в Берлине стали писать о подражании Руттману, Вертов послал 7 августа 1929 года протестующее письмо в *Франкфуртер Рундшау*; критик газеты, Зигфрид Кракауэр, сравнивая оба фильма, отдавал предпочтение вертовскому (*Frankfurter Rundschau*, 19 мая 1929, № 369). Письмо было опубликовано при посредстве Кракауэра в вечернем выпуске 12 июля 1929 года.

Анна Муза

Живь и Явь. Заметки о языке Малевича

[130] О «живом» и «мертвом» у Малевича см. «Малевич в кино», с. 17 и сноску 99.

[131] «О поэзии» (1919), *СС 1*, с. 149.

KA^ZAM